MW00997742

First Edition, first printing

Library of Congress Cataloging-in-Publication Data

Names: Rasbach, Dennis A., author.
Title: Joshua Lawrence Chamberlain and the Petersburg Campaign: His Supposed Charge from Fort Hell, his Near-Mortal Wounding, and a Civil War Myth Reconsidered / by Dennis A. Rasbach.
Description: California: Savas Beatie, 2016. | Includes bibliographical references and index.
Identifiers: LCCN 2016030719| ISBN 9781611213065 (hardcover: alk. paper) | ISBN 9781611213072 (ebk.)
Subjects: LCSH: Chamberlain, Joshua Lawrence, 1828-1914. | Petersburg (Va.)--History--Siege, 1864-1865. | Virginia--History--Civil War, 1861-1865--Campaigns. | Generals--United States--Biography. | United States. Army. Maine Infantry Regiment, 20th (1862-1865) | United States--History--Civil War, 1861-1865--Campaigns. | United States. Army--Biography.
Classification: LCC E476.93 .R37 2016 | DDC 355.0092 [B] --dc23
LC record available at https://lccn.loc.gov/2016030719

SB

Published by
Savas Beatie LLC
989 Governor Drive, Suite 102
El Dorado Hills, CA 95762

Phone: 916-941-6896
(web) www.savasbeatie.com
(E-mail) sales@savasbeatie.com

Savas Beatie titles are available at special discounts for bulk purchases in the United States by corporations, institutions, and other organizations. For more details, please contact Savas Beatie, P.O. Box 4527, El Dorado Hills, CA 95762, or you may e-mail us at sales@savasbeatie.com, or visit our website at www.savasbeatie.com for additional information.

Proudly published, printed, and warehoused in the United States of America.

Dramatis Personae Photo Credits: Chamberlain (LOC), Warren (LOC), Griffin (LOC), Tilton (LOC), Sweitzer (LOC), Knowles (USAHEC), Hofmann (USAHEC), Crawford (LOC), Cutler (LOC), Ayres (LOC), Bartlett (LOC), Willcox (LOC), Beauregard (NA)

To Corporal Samuel Jewett Smith,
whose selfless service helped preserve our Union.

Corporal Samuel Jewett Smith, saddler and artificer,
Company F, 21st Pennsylvania Cavalry (dismounted),
the great-great grandfather of the author. He served
with Sweitzer's brigade at Petersburg. *Author*

Table of Contents

Table of Contents (continued)

List of Maps

List of Maps (continued)

THERE is no dispute Joshua L. Chamberlain led his brigade in an attack at Petersburg on June 18, 1864. There is also no doubt that he suffered a severe wound during that assault that nearly killed him. Indeed, Chamberlain himself wrote about both. Many historians and other writers have published books and articles about this assault, and all of them claim the Maine officer led his men that day against Rives' Salient near the Jerusalem Plank Road from a location upon which would later be erected "Fort Hell."

A lone medical doctor begs to differ. The result of his deep research through the primary sources and a firm understanding of the terrain is Dennis Rasbach's *Joshua Lawrence Chamberlain and the Petersburg Campaign*. According to this new study, Chamberlain's actual attack was nearly one mile north of where nearly everyone else believed it took place. In support, Dr. Rasbach offers a small mountain of documentary and geographical proof to support his revisionist theory. How can this be so?

The answer is relatively simple—and unfortunately not at all uncommon in Civil War studies. Previous writers uncritically accepted Chamberlain's account of the event, written decades after the attack, that he led his men against Rives' Salient. Others erred because they simply parroted the narrative penned by earlier authors. The result, repeated multiple times, became historical "fact." All of these writers committed a serious misstep: They did not bother to conduct their own research in the primary sources, hold them in hand, and walk the field to see if they made sense. They ignored the readily available documents that prove without reasonable doubt that Chamberlain's attack was well to the north in the vicinity of the Baxter Road.

The author of this book avoided these common gaffes because he came to the subject of Chamberlain's attack from outside the field. Being a surgeon, and not a professional historian, he approached the subject unburdened with preconceptions. As a result, he did not blindly accept the historical consensus because he had no vested interest in perpetuating it. His interest was in accuracy.

Instead of copying those who came before him, he dirtied his hands in the primary accounts. He methodically studied them, compared them, and thought deeply about them. Once he mastered the primary textual source material, he pored over historical maps, and then he walked the ground on the battlefield. Finally, he turned to the people most knowledgeable on the subject of the terrain along the eastern front of the Petersburg battlefield to help him confirm his impressions and conclusions that he had formed after weighing all the evidence. In other words, he relied upon research, logic, reason, and the topography to piece together the events of June 18, 1864. He brought his personal strengths to bear: discipline, mastery of factual data, and critical analysis—all of which he had relied upon to become and remain a successful surgeon.

Dr. Rasbach's findings have caused no little furor in the Civil War community—a mini-battle of its own raging below the radar of most students of the conflict. Throughout he has patiently refuted their objections. Indeed, his work is so thorough and convincing that he was successful in petitioning the state of Virginia to relocate the marker commemorating Chamberlain's attack to a more suitable location.

Joshua Lawrence Chamberlain and the Petersburg Campaign is a textbook case of how a Civil War book (or any non-fiction book) should be researched and written. Indeed, it is an outstanding example of scholarship. It is my hope aspiring and established historians alike will read it and appreciate how better to pursue their craft.

Bryce A. Suderow

author (with Edwin C. Bearss) of
The Petersburg Campaign: The Eastern Front Battles, June-August 1864, Vol. 1, and
The Petersburg Campaign: The Western Front Battles, September 1864-April 1865, Vol. 2

I am a physician and amateur genealogist, not a Chamberlain scholar or writer. Given that, you might be wondering how this book came to be.

It all started in the 1960s, with a teenage boy rummaging through a dusty attic. There I discovered the name of my great-great grandfather, Samuel Jewett Smith, inscribed on a roster of Company F, 21st Pennsylvania Cavalry, along with a picture of my relative in his Civil War uniform with a musket at his side. This, along with other interesting curiosities, remained in the dust and darkness of the attic (and in the recesses of my consciousness) as I pursued my education, married, raised a family, and built my career as a surgeon.

Somewhere along the line I developed an interest in genealogy. Months stretched into years as I researched my family tree. In the process, I came across Samuel Jewett Smith's obituary in the archives of the local newspaper, and obtained his Civil War enlistment and pension records. These found their way into a filing cabinet, where they remained for many more years.

One of my wife's best college friends resides in Gettysburg, Pennsylvania. We visit there at least once a year, and I have toured the battlefield many times. Through my interest in Gettysburg, I became familiar with Colonel Joshua Lawrence Chamberlain—"Saint Joshua," as he is called by some in that town. When the movie "Gettysburg" was released in 1993, I was inspired by Chamberlain's charge (not to mention the music of the soundtrack). It quickly became one of my favorites.

In 2013, about 50 years after my encounter with the roster in the attic, my wife and I joined the Civil War Round Table of Southwest Michigan. One of our assignments was to read Bruce Catton's *A Stillness at Appomattox*. As I began to follow the march of the Army of the Potomac through the Wilderness and southward to Cold Harbor and Petersburg, eventually climaxing in the events at Appomattox, I noticed that many of the place names corresponded with engagements listed on the Civil War roster of Samuel Jewett Smith's Company F, 21st Pennsylvania Cavalry. This piqued my interest and led to an intensive study of the movements and actions of the 21st Pennsylvania Cavalry (which was dismounted and serving with the V Corps in Colonel Jacob Sweitzer's brigade of General Charles Griffin's division between June and October 1864). I visited the various battlefields at Petersburg three times in 2014-15.

During this investigation, I collected pertinent excerpts from *The Official Records of the Union and Confederate Armies* and immersed myself in several books, including *The Petersburg Campaign: The Eastern Front Battles*, by Edwin C. Bearss and Bryce Suderow. In this latter work I came across the following colorful and inspiring description of Griffin's attack at Petersburg:

> Griffin's division struck with more élan than Crawford's. When Griffin's command moved to the attack, Col. Jacob B. Sweitzer's (91st Pennsylvania) brigade[1] was deployed to the right, Col. Joshua L. Chamberlain's to the left, and Brig. Gen. Joseph J. Bartlett's in reserve. Supported by Crawford's left flank brigade (Col. James Carle's), Sweitzer's and Chamberlain's blue clads stormed across the ridge separating the two branches of Poor Creek. Although hammered by the rebel artillery and ripped up by well-aimed infantry volleys, the Yanks fought their way through the pines and into the ravine beyond. Here the advance was checked. These gains, which had carried the battle flags of Griffin's division and Carle's brigade to within 150 yards of the Reb's main line of resistance, had been made at a heavy cost. Among the desperately wounded was Colonel Chamberlain.[2]

1   On June 18, 1864, Colonel Sweitzer was in command of the 2nd Brigade of Griffin's division. The parenthetical reference in the quote is apparently intended to refer to the regiment within the brigade that he was commanding before he was elevated to brigade command. If so, it is erroneous. Sweitzer was attached to the 62nd Pennsylvania, and was mustered out with that command on July 13, 1864. Sweitzer's battle line to the right of the Baxter Road was led by Col. E. M. Gregory of the 91st Pennsylvania, and this is probably the source of the confusion.

2   Edwin C. Bearss and Bryce A. Suderow, *The Petersburg Campaign: The Eastern Front Battles, June-August, 1864* (El Dorado Hills, CA, 2012), 125-6.

During my first visit to the battlefield, I trudged through the woods on the ridge between the two ravines of Poor Creek (also known as Taylor's Creek, or Taylor's Branch) near the railroad cut on the Baxter Road section of Siege Road. There, I had the thrilling sense that I was likely standing on the ground where my ancestor had fought.

I intensified my search for additional information about the engagement at the front of Petersburg. I was specifically interested in the action that took place on the terrain near the Baxter Road between the two branches of Taylor's Creek.

The initial focus of my attention was Col. Jacob Sweitzer's brigade. Colonel William S. Tilton's report for June 18, 1864, which covered the action of both Colonel Sweitzer's brigade and Colonel Chamberlain's brigade, portrayed the two units fighting side by side. Armed with this knowledge, I obtained a copy of Diane Smith's book *Chamberlain at Petersburg: The Charge at Fort Hell*, and contacted the author by telephone and email, hoping to learn more about Sweitzer's brigade and the 21st Pennsylvania Cavalry through their association with Chamberlain. I also queried Savas Beatie, publisher of *The Petersburg Campaign*, seeking a way to contact the authors of that work, in the hope they might be able to supply additional details. Savas Beatie's Administrative Director, Yvette Lewis, put me in touch with Bryce Suderow, who turned out to be a veritable fountain of information regarding the Civil War in general, and the Petersburg Campaign in particular. Bryce is a prodigious researcher with an enormous network of contacts within the Civil War community. He has become a good friend and mentor, guiding me through this entire process.

Unfortunately, Diane Smith's account of Chamberlain's charge, which I hoped would be filled with details of the engagement of the 21st Pennsylvania Cavalry and Sweitzer's brigade, did not complement and supplement the information contained in Colonel Tilton's report. In fact, in many respects it seemed to contradict it. The result was confusion rather than clarity, which prompted me to intensify my efforts to uncover the truth.

On my return trip to the Petersburg National Battlefield, I had the pleasure of meeting Julia Steele, the Cultural Resource Manager at the park. She was genuinely interested in helping me and went out of her way to provide maps, sketches, photographs, and other primary source materials to facilitate my research. Julia and Bryce quickly became my two most helpful and reliable sources of information.

Ted Chamberlain, one of the organizers of our local Civil War Round Table is a distant relative of Joshua Lawrence Chamberlain, and an avid Chamberlain scholar. He and his wife Faye are enthusiastic living history interpreters of Joshua and Fanny Chamberlain. Ted is also a retired university professor. He kindly read and reread the manuscript in its various early iterations, making corrections and suggestions for further research. It has been a pleasure to watch our friendship grow through our shared interest in this topic.

I met Dr. Philip Shiman and David Lowe, both members of the Civil War Fortifications Study Group, on a third trip to Petersburg in April 2015. We spent a beautiful sunny spring day studying maps and photographs and walking the battlefield together to evaluate the terrain. Through these two veteran battlefield scholars, I gained perspective on what high-resolution photographic enhancement and GIS (Geographic Information Systems) data can contribute to modern historical research.

The entire enterprise has been personally rewarding on many levels, but the most gratifying outcome of writing this book has been the clearing of many clouds, the dissipation of confusion, and the development of new insights that have become seeds for inquiry in a variety of different directions.

My hope is that readers will sense the same excitement and adventure my collaborators and I experienced through discovering and carefully considering what the historical documents actually tell us. If nothing else, our experience should encourage others, professionals and amateurs alike, to view established dogmas with a critical eye. Who knows what other myths are out there, waiting to be explored.

Colonel Joshua Lawrence Chamberlain

He was serving as the Chairman of the Department of Modern Languages at Bowdoin College in Brunswick, Maine, when he took a leave of absence to study languages in Europe. With the arrival of war, Chamberlain instead enlisted in the 20th Maine Infantry. He performed extraordinary service at Gettysburg on the army's far left flank, and is known also for his courageous participation in the skirmish at the Quaker Road on March 29, 1865. Chamberlain commanded the 1st Brigade (Griffin's division, V Corps) and was honored with a field promotion to the rank of brigadier general after being wounded at Petersburg. He would later be elevated to the rank of brevet major general. His superiors bestowed upon him the honor of presiding over the parade of the Confederate infantry and the stacking of arms at Appomattox Court House on April 12, 1864.

After the war, Chamberlain was elected governor of Maine for four consecutive one-year terms, served as president of Bowdoin College from 1871-1883, and as Surveyor of the Port of Portland, Maine. He was awarded the Medal of Honor in 1893 and died in 1914 (partially as a result of his horrific June 18, 1864 wound).

Major General Gouverneur Kemble Warren

A civil engineer from New York, Warren is best known for having recognized the importance of defending the exposed left flank of the Union line on Little Round Top at Gettysburg on July 2, 1863. He was elevated to command the V Corps during the spring 1864 reorganization of the Army of the Potomac. Warren handled the corps with varying levels of success from the Wilderness through the Petersburg Campaign. Often at odds with his superiors, Warren was summarily relieved of command by Maj. Gen. Philip Sheridan in the aftermath of Five Forks on April 1, 1865. Warren would spend the remaining years of his life trying to clear his name.

Major General Charles Griffin

An 1847 graduate of the United States Military Academy and career artillery officer, Griffin commanded the 1st Division of the V Corps through the 1864-65 campaigns. Chamberlain's 1st Brigade was in Griffin's division on June 18, 1864. Griffin replaced Gouverneur Warren at the head of the V Corps during the final days of the war, and was present at Appomattox Court House for the surrender ceremony.

Major Washington Augustus Roebling

General Warren's aide-de-camp was a graduate of Rensselaer Polytechnic Institute in upstate New York and a civil engineer before and after the Civil War. Roebling's "Report of the Operations of the 5th Corps, A. P., in Genl. Grant's Campaign from Culpeper to Petersburg" provides an insightful look at V Corps activities from May 4 - August 21, 1864. Roebling is best known for designing and overseeing the construction of the Brooklyn Bridge in New York City after the war. He developed caisson disease from working in the underwater pneumatic chambers used to erect the foundations of the bridge's twin towers and was forced to do much of his work from home. His wife Emily Warren Roebling, the sister of his former commander, took over many of the onsite responsibilities of the chief engineer.

Lieutenant Colonel Theodore Lyman III

This Harvard-trained natural scientist and aide-de-camp to Maj. Gen. George Gordon Meade was an astute observer and a precise recorder of the activities at the Army of the Potomac's high command level. He chronicled his experiences in a series of private notebooks, which have been compiled and published as *Meade's Army: The Private Notebooks of Lt. Col. Theodore Lyman.*

Colonel William Stowell Tilton

The commanding officer of the 22nd Massachusetts Infantry and 2nd Massachusetts Sharpshooters (Col. Jacob Sweitzer's 2nd Brigade, Griffin's 1st Division, V Corps), a prewar Massachusetts manufacturer and merchant, spent his war service alternating between regimental and brigade command. Tilton was wounded and captured during the Seven Days' Battles in June 1862 as a major in the 22nd, and while leading a brigade at Gettysburg, mired himself in a controversial decision on July 2, 1863. He was in command of the regiment on June 18, 1864, but was elevated as acting commander of the 1st Brigade after Col. Joshua Chamberlain was struck down. Tilton served in that capacity until August 22, 1864. He mustered out of service with his volunteer regiment on October 17 of that year, and was later awarded the rank of brevet brigadier general.

Colonel Jacob Bowman Sweitzer

A lawyer by training, he served as a brigade commander in Griffin's 1st Division, V Corps, from Chancellorsville until he mustered out with his regiment, the 62nd Pennsylvania Infantry, in July 1864. Sweitzer's brigade was engaged at Petersburg alongside Chamberlain's command on June 18, 1864. A promotion to the rank of brevet brigadier general dated March 13, 1865, was his final military award.

Major Oliver Blachly Knowles

He was born in 1842 in Philadelphia, Pennsylvania, the son of a merchant. During his youth he developed a fondness for horses. When full grown, Knowles stood two inches taller than six feet. While still a teenager, he enlisted as a private in Capt. William Boyd's Company C, 1st New York (Lincoln) Cavalry in 1861. Knowles proved both gallant and fearless, and rapidly rose through the ranks. He accompanied Colonel Boyd when the latter was placed in command of the 21st Pennsylvania Cavalry in August 1863. When Boyd was wounded at Cold Harbor in early June 1864, Major Knowles rose to command the regiment, which at the time was dismounted and serving in Colonel Sweitzer's brigade. The young Knowles was honored with a promotion to brevet brigadier general of volunteers in March 1865, and appeared to have a bright future ahead of him when he died of cholera just one year later at the age of 24.

Major Charles Shiels Wainwright

The chief of artillery of the V Corps from 1864 to the end of the war was a good soldier and astute observer. His detailed journal, published posthumously as *A Diary of Battle: the Personal Journals of Colonel Charles S. Wainwright, 1864-1865*, provides us with insight into the day-to-day operation of the V Corps, along with acerbic critiques of his commanders and their wartime decisions.

Colonel John William Hofmann

A prewar merchant and member of the militia, the ranking officer of the 56th Pennsylvania led the 2nd Brigade, 4th Division, V Corps at Petersburg. Hofmann was honored with a promotion to brevet brigadier general of volunteers at the end of the war. Although history spells his name with one f, the name on his gravestone is spelled "Hoffmann—which may or may not be correct. According to the person who ordered up his marker, the former colonel, in his own hand on an application to the GAR, spelled it that way.

Brigadier General Samuel Wylie Crawford

The native Pennsylvanian graduated from medical school in 1851 and began his military career as an assistant army surgeon. After Fort Sumter, Crawford accepted a major's commission in the infantry and rose steadily though the ranks. He personally seized the colors of the regiment he led at Gettysburg on a charge down the slope of Little Round Top on July 2, a dangerous practice he repeated rhetorically as a division commander at Petersburg on June 17, 1864, when he became entangled in a quarrel with General Ledlie of the IX Corps over a captured Confederate flag.

Brigadier General
Lysander Cutler

The Massachusetts (and later, Wisconsin) businessman, school teacher, and Indian fighter began his military career as colonel of the 6th Wisconsin—part of the Iron Brigade of the West. His superior recommended he be given command of the famous outfit, but Solomon Meredith, who had better political connections, won out. Promoted to brigadier general after Fredericksburg and given a different brigade in 1863. His infantry were the first on the field at Gettysburg, where they suffered heavily slowing down the Rebel advance. He was tapped to command the 4th Division, Warren's V Corps, in May 1864 and fought through the Overland Campaign and at Petersburg. On August 21, 1864, a shell fragment ended his career when it ripped up his face and left him disfigured. He was promoted to brevet major general, but barely survived the war, dying in 1866 of a stroke.

Brigadier General
Romeyn Beck Ayres

The native New Yorker graduated West Point in 1847, a classmate of Charles Griffin. To his undying regret, he participated in the Mexican War but missed active combat. He was at Fort Monroe when the Civil War arrived. He served as Gen. William "Baldy" Smith's division chief of artillery in 1861, and led large artillery formations in all the army's battles through Fredericksburg. Frustrated by the slow rate of advancement in the "long

arm," he transferred to the infantry and commanded the 2nd Division, V Corps at Chancellorsville and Gettysburg. The army's reorganization reduced him to brigade command (4th Brigade, 1st Division, V Corps), which he led through the Overland Campaign before assuming command of the division once more in time for Petersburg.

Ayres continued serving in the Regular Army after the war. He is buried in Arlington along side his mother-in-law, who played a prominent role establishing Confederate hospitals in Richmond during the war.

Brigadier General
Joseph Jackson Bartlett

A prewar New York attorney, he enlisted in the 27th New York in 1861 and rose through the ranks to eventually command a brigade in Charles Griffin's division at Petersburg. When Griffin was tapped to replace Warren as V Corps commander after Five Forks in early April 1865, Bartlett assumed command of the 1st Division. He received a promotion to brevet major general at the end of the war, and served as ambassador to Sweden and Norway under President Andrew Johnson.

Major General
Orlando Bolivar Willcox

Unlike Ayres, this 1847 graduate of West Point gained combat experience in the Mexican War and as an Indian fighter on the frontier. Willcox resigned from the service in 1857 and was serving as an attorney in Michigan when the Civil War began. He entered as colonel of the 1st Michigan Infantry and had the unfortunate luck of being wounded and captured at First Bull Run while leading a brigade. He was released a year later, appointed brigadier general of volunteers in 1863, and led his division throughout the Overland Campaign and at Petersburg. He eventually rose to brevet major general in a career that spanned four decades of professional service. He led the first Union troops to enter Petersburg following its capture. Willcox received the Medal of Honor in 1895 for gallantry at Bull Run.

Captain John Bigelow

The 20-year-old Harvard senior from Brighton, Massachusetts, enlisted in 1861 with the 2nd Massachusetts battery. He served with the 1st Maryland Artillery at Malvern Hill, the last of the Seven Days' Battles, where he was seriously wounded. His war career was further sidetracked by a long bout of malaria, but he finally returned to action as the captain of the 9th Massachusetts in June 1863. Bigelow was wounded once more performing valiant service at Gettysburg on July 2 along the Wheatfield Road close to where Longstreet's assault crushed the Peach Orchard Salient. Bigelow returned to his battery three months later and was assigned to serve in Warren's V Corps for General Grant's 1864 campaign. Bigelow was promoted to brevet major for gallant action at Petersburg on June 18, 1864, where his guns supported Chamberlain's charge.

Captain Adelbert B. Twitchell

A graduate of Maine's Bowdoin College in 1860, where he became acquainted with Joshua Chamberlain, Twitchell taught in a public high school in Newark, New Jersey, for a year before enlisting in the 5th Maine Infantry in 1861. He saw action at First Bull Run and received a commission as 2nd lieutenant in the light artillery battery of the 5th Maine. In the summer of 1863, he was commissioned captain of the 7th Maine Light Artillery, in which role, and as a result of his Bowdoin College connection with Joshua Chamberlain, he entered the narrative of Chamberlain's experience at Petersburg. Twitchell received a commission as brevet major of artillery in recognition of his service during the Siege of Petersburg.

Major General Pierre Gustav Toutant Beauregard

The Louisiana native born to French Creole parents trained as a civil engineer at the United States Military Academy, served in the Mexican War, and was serving as superintendent at West Point in 1861 when he resigned to accept a commission as brigadier general in the Confederate Army. He commanded the defenses of Charleston, where firing upon Fort Sumter triggered the beginning of armed conflict. He was in command of the army that produced the first large-scale victory of the war at First Bull Run. Transferred west, he helped organize the Army of Mississippi and planned the attack at Shiloh, where he assumed army command when Gen. A. S. Johnston fell. Beauregard's most important service was the successful defense of Petersburg from June 15-18, 1864, a brief span that overlapped by two days Chamberlain's presence at the front. After the war Beauregard was active as a railroad executive and civil engineer.

Brigadier General Bushrod Rust Johnson

The Ohio Quaker broke ranks with his family and attended West Point, where he graduated in 1840. He fought Seminoles in Florida and waged war south of the border in Mexico. Johnson left the service under a cloud in October 1847 when it was suspected he was selling contraband goods. He found work as a college professor of natural philosophy, chemistry, mathematics, and engineering, and took part in state militia activities.

Johnson began his Civil War service as a colonel of engineers in the Tennessee militia, and was injured at Shiloh just after assuming command of a division. He capably led a division in the Department of North Carolina and Southern Virginia under General Beauregard in 1864 and served well during the Bermuda Hundred Campaign and in front of Petersburg. After the war, he worked once more as a professor and served as the chancellor of the University of Nashville.

Major General Charles William Field

The Kentucky native was an 1849 graduate of the United States Military Academy and was serving there as an assistant instructor of Cavalry Tactics at West Point when he resigned his commission in 1861 to fight for the Confederacy. Field was severely wounded in the leg at Second Manassas. Promoted to major general in 1864, he assumed command of the division formerly led by John Bell Hood and fought with varying degrees of success throughout Petersburg before surrendering at Appomattox. Field served as a businessman, inspector general, and doorkeeper of the U. S. House of Representatives after the war.

Major General Joseph Brevard Kershaw

The prewar lawyer and politician from South Carolina commanded the 2nd South Carolina Volunteers at the First Battle of Bull Run. He was commissioned brigadier general in early 1862, and performed well at Gettysburg, Chickamauga, and during the fighting from the Wilderness to Cold Harbor and Petersburg, before moving to the Shenandoah Valley and serving with General Early's army. After the war, Kershaw worked as a judge, postmaster and president of the State Senate of South Carolina.

Colonel J. L. Chamberlain, of the Twentieth Maine Regiment, commanding the First Brigade of the First Division, was mortally wounded, it is thought, in the assaults on the enemy yesterday, the ball having passed through the pelvis and bladder. He has been recommended for promotion for gallant and efficient conduct on previous occasions, and yesterday led his brigade against the enemy under a most destructive fire. He expresses the wish that he may receive the recognition of his service by promotion before he dies for the gratification of his family and friends, and I beg that if possible it may be done. He has been sent to City Point.[1]

—Maj. Gen. G. K. Warren, June 19, 1864

The above telegram is transmitted to the lieutenant general commanding, with the earnest recommendation that Colonel Chamberlain's wish be gratified.[2]

—Maj. Gen. G. G. Meade, June 19, 1864

1 *The War of the Rebellion: A Compilation of the Official Records of the Union and Confederate Armies,*128 vols. (Washington, DC, 1880-1901), Series 1, vol. 40, pt. 2, 216-17, hereafter cited as *OR.* All references are to Series 1 unless otherwise noted.

2 *OR* 40, pt. 2, 217.

Brigadier General Joshua Lawrence Chamberlain

Library of Congress

The following day, this telegram was transmitted:

> Colonel Joshua L. Chamberlain, Twentieth Regiment Maine Infantry Volunteers, is, for meritorious and efficient services on the field of battle, and especially for gallant conduct in leading his brigade against the enemy at Petersburg, Va., on the 18th instant, in which he was dangerously wounded, hereby, in pursuance of authority from the Secretary of War, appointed brigadier-general of U. S. Volunteers, to rank as such from the 18th day of June, 1864, subject to the approval of the President of the United States.[3]

— By command of Lieutenant-General Grant,
Special Orders No. 39, June 20, 1864

The Nearly Mortal Wound

Joshua Lawrence Chamberlain of the 20th Maine was a Medal of Honor recipient and one of the best-known figures of the American Civil War. His tenacious defense of the refused extreme left flank of the Union line at Little Round Top, and his courageous bayonet charge, immortalized in the 1993 epic movie "Gettysburg," launched him into the pantheon of Civil War heroes.

Chamberlain served in twenty-one battles and numerous skirmishes. He was cited for bravery four times, had five horses shot from under him, and was wounded six times.[4] His most serious and life-threatening injury was sustained at Petersburg, on June 18, 1864, while he was in command of the 1st Brigade of General Charles Griffin's 1st Division, General Gouverneur K. Warren's V Corps, Army of the Potomac. In that engagement, he was shot through the pelvis with a Minié ball while leading a charge of his brigade. In a brief 1899 account entitled "The Charge at Fort Hell," Chamberlain recalled his evacuation to the field hospital of the 1st Division, V Corps, where staff surgeons operated to remove the bullet that brought him down:

> After a while, an ambulance came galloping up to the foot of the hill, and I was put into it and galloped through rough stumpy fields to a cluster of pines where our division had a rude field hospital. Most of the surgeons there had been or were

3 OR 40, pt. 2, 236-37.

4 L. C. Bateman, "The Hero of Gettysburg," in *Lewiston Evening Journal* (September 1-6, 1900), 4-6.

attached by my headquarters, and I knew and loved them, for they were noble men. The first thing done was to lay me upon a table improvised from a barn-window or door, and examine the wound. I remember somebody taking a ramrod of a musket and running it through my body—it was too wide [long] for any surgeon's probe—to discover the bullet, which they did not at first observe sticking up with a puff of skin just behind my left hip joint. This they soon cut out, and closed the cut with a bandage. Some slight dressing was put upon the round hole on the right side, and I was gently laid on a pile of pine boughs.[5]

Unfortunately, the removal of the slug does nothing to undo the damage it caused during its passage to its final resting place. In this case, the bullet had severed Chamberlain's urethra, which led to the pooling of urine in the soft tissues of the pelvis, rather than its complete elimination from the body. The surgical objective is to restore continuity of the drainage tract. Unfortunately for Chamberlain, the initial effort to accomplish urethral-bladder catheterization was not successful. However, Joshua's brother Tom soon arrived on the scene with Dr. Abner O. Shaw of the 20th Maine, and Dr. Morris Townsend of the 44th New York, both surgeons from Chamberlain's former 3rd Brigade. Both men were determined to do everything possible to save the life of their friend.

"The pain wore into a stupor," was how Chamberlain later recalled his suffering. "Then through the mists I looked up and saw dear, faithful Doctor Shaw, Surgeon of my own regiment, [which was] lying a mile away. My brother Tom had brought him. He and good Dr. Townsend sat down by me and tried to use some instrument to stop the terrible extravasations that would end my life. All others had given it up, and me too," added the wounded officer. The doctors labored in what appeared a vain effort, continued Chamberlain,

> to find the entrance to torn and clogged and distorted passages of vital currents. Toiling and returning to the ever impossible task, the able surgeon undertaking to aid Dr. Shaw said, sadly, "It is of no use, Doctor; he cannot be saved. I have done all possible for man. Let us go, and not torture him longer." "Just once more, Doctor; let me try just this once more and I will give it up." Bending to his task, by a sudden miracle, he touched the exact lost thread; the thing was done. There was a possibility, only that even now, that I might be there to know in the morning. Tom

---

5   Joshua Lawrence Chamberlain, "The Charge at Fort Hell" (1899), in William Henry Noble Papers, Special Collections Library, Duke University, 13-14. Retrieved from joshualawrence chamberlain.com/chargeatfort hell.php.

stood over me like a brother and such a one as he was. Truehearted [Maj. Ellis] Spear with him, watching there like guardians over a cradle amidst the wolves of the wilderness.[6]

The Depot Field Hospital had been hurriedly set up at City Point on June 18, just as a train of ambulances was beginning to arrive loaded with wounded from the initial assaults against Petersburg. Less than twenty-four hours later, General Meade dispatched a stretcher and eight men under the direction of Surgeon Morris Townsend to carry the wounded "Lion of the Union" sixteen miles to City Point. Surgeon E. B. Dalton, Chief Medical Officer of the Depot Field Hospital, directed that Chamberlain be placed on the 400-bed hospital steamer *Connecticut* (one of two boats with a sufficiently light draft to be able to come alongside the pontoon wharves hastily constructed on the Appomattox River). The steamer conveyed the colonel to the U. S. General Hospital at the Naval School in Annapolis, Maryland, where he arrived on June 20.

Chamberlain would survive, spending much of his life in tremendous pain, and finally die in 1914 from an infection in the same old wound.[7]

Promotion "On the Spot"

Desiring to recognize Chamberlain's gallant and meritorious service to the Army of the Potomac prior to his death, General Grant honored the colonel with a rare "on the spot" battlefield promotion to the rank of brigadier general:

Colonel J. L. Chamberlain, of the 20th Maine, was wounded on the 18th [of June]. He was gallantly leading his brigade at the time, as he had been in the habit of doing in all the engagements in which he had previously been engaged. He had several times been recommended for a brigadier-generalcy. On this occasion, however, I promoted him on the spot, and forwarded a copy of my order to the War Department, asking that my act might be confirmed without delay. This was

---

6 Chamberlain, "The Charge at Fort Hell," 15-16.

7 *OR* 42, pt. 1, 196, and ibid., *OR* 40, 40, pt. 1, 269-70; Barnes, *Medical and Surgical History of the War the Rebellion*, vol. 2, pt. 2, 363. Neither Chamberlain nor his medical attendants believed he would survive. It is interesting to note that a review of medical records from the Civil War reveals that some 79% of victims of similar urethral injuries *did not* succumb to them. Herr and McAninch, "Urethral Injuries in the Civil War," *Journal of Urology*, vol. 173, no. 4, 1090-93. For more information on Chamberlain's wound, see Appendix 2: Chamberlain's Wound, Treatment, and Civil War Medicine, 184-187.

done, and at last a gallant and meritorious officer received partial justice at the hands of his Government, which he had served so faithfully and so well.[8]

There are two important points to consider regarding this promotion. First, the "on the spot" designation is not technically accurate because the elevation of rank was ordered on the second day following the battle, and Chamberlain was officially informed of it by telegram after his arrival at the U. S. General Hospital in Annapolis.[9] Second, although some sources suggested this was the only instance of a battlefield promotion of this kind in the history of the Civil War,[10] such is not the case. One month earlier General Grant had exercised his authority to confer a similar honor on Col. Emory Upton, who fell injured while leading twelve regiments in an assault at Spotsylvania:

> Before leaving Washington, I had been authorized to promote officers on the field for special acts of gallantry. By this authority, I conferred the rank of brigadier-general upon Upton on the spot, and this act was confirmed by the President. Upton had been badly wounded in this fight.[11]

Chamberlain's battlefield promotion from colonel to general was the last time Grant used his authority in this manner.

Competing Views

Chamberlain's gallantry and worthiness of honor are undisputed. There are, however, competing views on the location of his June 18, 1864 attack. One view holds the action occurred near the Baxter Road and Pegram's (or Elliott's) Salient. The other view, claimed by Chamberlain himself and supported by most historians since then, places the action near the future Fort Sedgwick and Rives' Salient farther to the south. The significance of this matter is not limited solely to the clarification of Chamberlain's personal whereabouts at Petersburg, important and interesting as that may be. The actual position of the 1st Brigade

---

8 Ulysses S. Grant, *Personal Memoirs of U. S. Grant,* 2 vols. (New York, 1885), vol. 2, 381-82.

9 H. C. Henries, "At Annapolis," in *The Bangor Daily Whig and Courier,* June 28, 1864.

10 United States Army, Maine Infantry Regiment, *Reunions of the Twentieth Maine Regiment Association at Portland* (Waldoboro, ME, 1881), 25.

11 Grant, *Personal Memoirs of U. S. Grant,* vol. 2, 350.

of the 1st Division has implications for the entire tactical strategy of the V Corps on June 18.

If the divisions of Brigadier Generals Romeyn B. Ayres and Lysander Cutler occupied positions at the left flank of the Army of the Potomac, and if Chamberlain was with the rest of Griffin's 1st Division to its right, but attacking from the vicinity of future Fort Sedgwick and the Jerusalem Plank Road, then two V Corps divisions were already occupying ground left of the Jerusalem Plank Road on June 18. This would have significant implications with respect to later Federal troop movements and the attacks of June 21-24. If, however, Chamberlain was detached from his division and operating alone, separated from Sweitzer's brigade by two V Corps divisions, that would have seriously compromised General Griffin's command and control of his 1st Division.

The Baxter Road Scenario

The consensus position of the National Park Service into the mid-twentieth century seems to have been that Chamberlain's advance occurred along with that of the rest of Griffin's division near the Baxter Road, alternately known as the Norfolk Stage Road, the Suffolk Road, and the Sussex Road. This plank road took quite a few twists and turns as it navigated the terrain, coursing toward the southeast from Petersburg.

Petersburg National Battlefield Historian Joseph M. Hanson prepared a map of troop movements in the Petersburg Campaign for the 1942 edition of the Master Plan of the National Battlefield. A portion of this map, revised by historians of the National Park Service in 1952, appears on the next page. It depicts Warren's V Corps on the left flank of the Union attack on June 18. The assault moves across the Taylor property, sweeping to the northwest toward Elliott's Salient (also known as Pegram's Salient). To the west of the Norfolk Railroad, the thrust occurs almost exclusively north of the Baxter Road.

Until the recent release of Sean Chick's *The Battle of Petersburg, June 15-18, 1864*, Thomas J. Howe's *Wasted Valor: the Petersburg Campaign, June 15-18, 1864* was the only detailed account of Grant's first offensive at Petersburg. Howe described Griffin's two attacking brigades, Chamberlain on the left and Sweitzer on the right, together taking the first crest south of Brigadier General Samuel Crawford's 3rd Division, positioned near the Taylor property north of the Baxter Road. He noted that Chamberlain's right was anchored on the railroad cut (which is nowhere near Rives' Salient). Howe also commented on the strength of the newly constructed Rebel works near the Baxter Road: One

Hanson Map of Troop Movements in the Petersburg Campaign, 1952. LC

Federal soldier dreadfully viewed "a fort with five embrasures on the face that fronted us."[12]

This is significant because it contradicts the views of the Rives' Salient proponents, who minimize the strength of the "hastily thrown up earthworks of the Rebel's new line" and doubt Chamberlain could have confused them for Fort Mahone and other original works of the Dimmock Line covering Petersburg on its east and south sides. Howe's map "Federal Assaults 3 p.m. – 6 p.m., June 18, 1864" (page 126 of *Wasted Valor*) in harmony with the old master plan map, depicts Chamberlain attacking to the south of the Baxter Road, but well to the north of Rives' Salient. Thus, a traditional view held by many historians up to the end of the twentieth century, was that Chamberlain's brigade moved with Griffin's division, maintaining proximity to the Baxter Road, and that Chamberlain was never near Rives' Salient.

12 Sean M. Chick, *The Battle of Petersburg, June 15-18, 1864* (Lincoln, NE, 2015); Thomas J. Howe, *Wasted Valor: The Petersburg Campaign, June 15-18, 1864* (Lynchburg, VA,1988), 128.

The Rives' Salient Scenario: "The Charge at Fort Hell"

Based upon Chamberlain's own recollections, recorded during the later years of his life, and on the writings of numerous Chamberlain biographers and historians of recent decades, there is an alternate interpretation. This view holds that Chamberlain's brigade charged and carried the position that subsequently became Fort Sedgwick (also known as "Fort Hell"), after which the brigade advanced from the south along the Jerusalem Plank Road against the permanent Confederate works at Rives' Salient, under murderous enfilading fire from Fort Mahone to the west.

"Rives' Salient" refers to a redoubt at Battery 25, where the new Harris Line joined the "permanent" Dimmock Line of Confederate fortifications. "Rives' Salient" may also designate the general area surrounding Batteries 25-27. The name of the salient derived from its location on land belonging to one Mr. Timothy Rives.[13]

The first, and probably only, charge against Rives' Salient (at least during 1864) occurred on horseback nine days before Colonel Chamberlain's arrival on the Petersburg battlefield. On June 9, Maj. Gen. August V. Kautz's Union cavalry division rode up the Jerusalem Plank Road to engage a small and poorly armed contingent of Virginia reserve troops led by Maj. Fletcher Archer in what would later come to be known as "The battle of old men and young boys." In this confrontation, the ragtag band of Confederate defenders at Rives' Salient found themselves outnumbered and nearly surrounded, receiving fire from the front, flank, and rear. A Confederate veteran recalled:

> We very shortly noticed the enemy running out to overlap us on our left. It is well known, and has been well described, what the results of this movement were; how our men at the Rives' Salient had to stand a murderous fire upon them on their flank and rear, while facing the enemy in front. It proved a "bloody angle" for those devoted men who held that position. Mr. John E. Friend was among the first

---

13 See discussion of Confederate forts below, and the Col. W. H. Stevens "Sketch of the Confederate and Federal Lines around Petersburg." Rives was an honest and respected citizen of Petersburg, but a vocal and polarizing political figure with less-than-stellar Confederate credentials, having delivered a famous speech against secession as a delegate to the Virginia State Convention in 1861.Timothy Rives, *Speech of Mr. Timothy Rives of Prince George and Surry on the 29th March, 1861, Report of the Committee on Federal Relations, being under consideration in committee of the whole,* (Richmond, VA, 1861), 1-30.

to fall. He had behaved with great coolness and bravery; he was shot dead by a man stationed behind a tree in Rives' yard.[14]

Having breached the Confederate lines, Yankees "clustered like bees on Mr. Rives' front porch." Timothy Rives arrived on the scene in his buggy soon after the fight ended and was promptly taken prisoner by the Union soldiers, his buggy commandeered to carry away the body of a fallen Federal officer.[15]

Although he won the fight, General Kautz had second thoughts about the wisdom of trying to hold a position behind the Confederate line. With obvious signs of growing enemy strength and no sign of friendly infantry support forthcoming, he promptly withdrew his cavalry. Rives' Salient reverted to Rebel control. Had it not been for the subsequent evolution of the myth of an association of the position with the wounding and promotion of the "Hero of Gettysburg" in a charge from "Fort Hell," the name Rives' Salient may have been nothing more than an obscure reference in a history book.[16]

Hell and Damnation

Even though Chamberlain titled a 1899 memoir "The Charge at Fort Hell," we must remember that "Fort Hell" did not even exist when he was leading his brigade at Petersburg. Several weeks would pass before Union forces erected a fort at the place where their entrenchments crossed the Jerusalem Plank Road. By virtue of its proximity to the enemy line, Fort Sedgwick became one of the most dangerous places along the entire Union front. Only a few hundred yards separated Fort Sedgwick and the Confederate entrenchments directly opposite it. Opposing picket details in the gap between the lines were within easy shouting distance of one another. Firing between the two sides continued

---

14 Glenn, "Brave Defense of the Cockade City," 10.

15 Ibid., 14.

16 A. M. Keiley, *In Vinculis; or, The Prisoner of War, being the Experience of a Rebel in the Federal Pens, interspersed with Reminiscences of the Late War, Anecdotes of Southern Generals, Etc.* (New York, 1866), 26. There was no special leniency for a southern man of uncompromising Union sympathies at the hands of Yankee captors. A fellow Virginia prisoner wrote that, although Timothy Rives was old, and "a man so deaf that he had heard no voice that was not a shout for a dozen years," his plea for permission to return to his house to ascertain the safety of his motherless daughters was rudely refused with threats and oaths. He was whisked off to prison, where he later died of disease, only to be returned to Petersburg for burial by his friends in the fall of 1865, "in the midst of the desolation with which war had scourged his happy home."

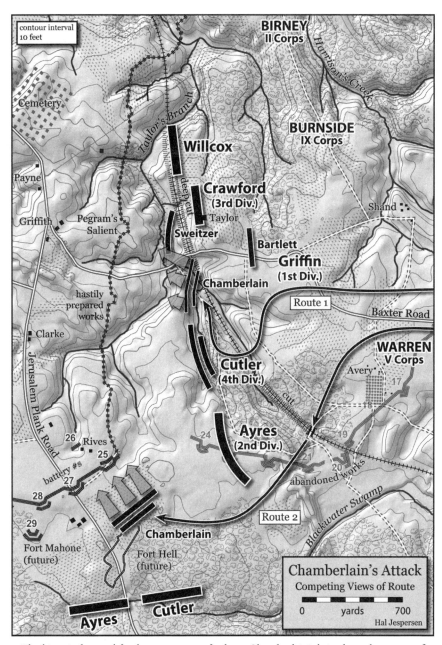

The historical record (and common sense) places Chamberlain's brigade at the center of the V Corps line to the left of Sweitzer's brigade near the Baxter Road (Route 1). The competing Charge at Fort Hell scenario has Chamberlain moving left while skirmishing across a mile of open field, isolated from the rest of the army at least a mile to the north while advancing toward Rives' Salient along the Jerusalem Plank Road (Route 2).

almost incessantly. As early as July 21, 1864, Colonel Charles Wainwright, commander of the V Corps artillery, noted in his diary, "The new work at the plank road gets on slowly. I was right in my surmise that the rebels would not like it; they make it so hot for the workmen that it has already been christened 'Fort Hell' by the men."[17]

Life was "hot" for the Confederate soldiers too, who would soon refer to their own earthen shelter as "Fort Damnation."

Some identify Fort Mahone with "Fort Damnation," but veterans of the fight reserve that appellation for the sector of fortifications between Rives' Salient and the Jerusalem Plank Road. As one Rhode Island veteran wrote, "Fort Damnation was a title indefinitely applied to the rebel works opposite Fort Hell, and included Rives' Salient, and the works extending west from that toward the Jerusalem Plank Road; it did not include Fort Mahone as many suppose."[18]

This understanding is echoed in the following discussion by a soldier from the 31st Maine, IX Corps, writing of his own regiment's charge from "Fort Hell" in the spring of 1865:

> The Confederates had several forts, redans and batteries, near the Jerusalem Plank Road, that swept the approaches in every direction. Back of these were other forts and works, which could fire over the front ones or into them, as occasion might demand. In this vicinity, on the enemy's side, was Fort Mahone, Battery 28 or "Fort Damnation," Batteries 27, 26 and 25. The four last named were on Rives' Salient. There were others back of these. Here were the siege guns, light batteries, rifles, howitzers and mortars, all trained to repel assault. "Damnation" was nearly opposite "Fort Hell" and probably acquired its forbidding designation from the "boys" on that account.
>
> It may be well to say right here that a student of the official reports will be somewhat perplexed to know which particular redan was "Fort Damnation." For my part, it was fixed in my mind that Fort Mahone enjoyed that distinction, and consequently that our attack was upon Fort Mahone. Yet that seems improbable, as the official surveys place the latter fort some four hundred yards to the south of the Plank Road, while I am certain that we struck the fort or redan in near

17 Allan Nevins, ed., *A Diary of Battle: the Personal Journals of Colonel Charles S. Wainwright, 1864-1865* (New York, 1962), 439.

18 W. P. Hopkins, *The 7th Regiment Rhode Island Volunteers in the Civil War, 1862-1865* (Providence, RI, 1903), 238.

proximity to the Plank Road and that this was always spoken of after the event as "Fort Damnation."[19]

Since "Fort Hell" did not exist when Chamberlain made his famous charge, why did he employ the designation in the title of his memoir? Perhaps he was confused, or perhaps his intent was to offer a general point of reference with which others could connect, given the site's subsequent notoriety. It is not unreasonable to conclude he also wanted to enhance the drama and glory of the moment by associating the engagement with a location that came to be known as a cauldron of fire and brimstone—a fiery place of Hell and Damnation.

Whatever the reason, Chamberlain's speeches and writings during the final years of his life linked his charge with "Fort Hell," the Jerusalem Plank Road, and Rives' Salient. A long and distinguished series of Chamberlain biographers picked up on his lead, embracing the viewpoint in writings spanning more than half of a century, including but not limited to Willard M. Wallace (*Soul of the Lion: A Biography of General Joshua L. Chamberlain,* 1995), Alice Raines Trulock (*In the Hands of Providence: Joshua L. Chamberlain & the American Civil War*, 1992), Mark Nesbitt (*Through Blood and Fire: Selected Civil War Papers of Major General Joshua Chamberlain,* 1996), Edward G. Longacre (*Joshua Chamberlain: The Soldier and the Man,* 1999), and Diane M. Smith (*Chamberlain at Petersburg: the Charge at Fort Hell,* 2004).[20]

With one exception, these authors dedicated only a few pages at most to Chamberlain's brief experience at Petersburg on June 18, 1864. The exception is Smith's book, which is entirely devoted to the subject. Its extensive annotations and the fact that it purports to present an accurate account from Chamberlain's pen gives *Chamberlain at Petersburg* an aura of authority. In terms of shaping current understanding of what actually transpired at Petersburg on June 18, Smith's narrative seems to have fully carried the day. Chamberlain's wounding and Rives' Salient are fused in modern consciousness. Numerous

19 T. P. Beals, "In a Charge Near Fort Hell, Petersburg, April 2, 1865," in *War Papers Read Before the Commandery of the State of Maine, Military Order of the Loyal Legion of the United States,* 70 vols. (Portland, ME, 1902), vol. 2, 106.

20 Willard M. Wallace, *Soul of the Lion: A Biography of General Joshua L. Chamberlain* (Gettysburg, PA, 1995), Alice Raines Trulock, *In the Hands of Providence: Joshua L. Chamberlain & the American Civil War* (Chapel Hill, NC, 1992), Mark Nesbitt, *Through Blood and Fire: Selected Civil War Papers of Major General Joshua Chamberlain* (Mechanicsburg, PA, 1996), Edward G. Longacre (*Joshua Chamberlain: The Soldier and the Man* (Conshohocken, PA, 1999), and Diane M. Smith, *Chamberlain at Petersburg: The Charge at Fort Hell* (Gettysburg, PA, 2004).

Joshua L. Chamberlain's "Promoted on the Spot" marker located on E. South Boulevard near Fort Mahone Street, Petersburg, VA.
Author

websites, for example, promote as historical fact the idea that he was wounded there, including www. nps.gov (which is perplexing since other NPS documents support the Baxter Road site).[21]

On November 8, 2014, the Rives' Salient location as the site of Chamberlain's wounding and "on the spot promotion" acquired a patina of authority when the Virginia Department of Historic Resources erected a Medal of Honor Recipients marker at the intersection of East South Boulevard and Fort Mahone Street near South Crater Road.[22] Few have asked whether this site is anywhere near Chamberlain's actual position when he fell on the fateful day of June 18, 1864. Despite his own testimony, did Chamberlain ever set foot on the ground upon which the Union V Corps later built Fort Sedgwick?

This book will carefully examine the evidence that Chamberlain and his contemporaries left in the historical record to reach conclusions on all these issues.

21 See www.nps.gov/pete/learn/historyculture/joshua-chamberlain.htm.

22 Historical Marker Database: Joshua L. Chamberlain Promoted "On the Spot" (2014), www.hmdb.org/marker.asp?marker=79063. GPS coordinates: 37° 12.364' N, 77° 22.898' W.

CHAPTER 1

SMOKE, CLOUDS, AND CONFUSION:
The Pitfalls of Embellishing Clouded Hindsight

NUMEROUS authors have placed Col. Joshua Lawrence Chamberlain's wounding at Rives' Salient. If the hypothesis is correct that he was never there, what is the source of the misinformation?

The short answer is Chamberlain's own clouded hindsight combined with creative embellishment by other authors during late 20th and early 21st centuries. What follows is the story of how history was rewritten when an intelligent, honorable and reliable man attempted to recollect and reconstruct memories that were not entirely clear to him. Subsequent writers, uncritically trusting the veracity of Chamberlain's statements, proceeded to repeat and amplify his errors.

Aside from "Lines before Petersburg, June 18, 1864,"[1] a letter of protest to General Ulysses S. Grant, in which the colonel questioned his orders to attack the front of the enemy's main works, Chamberlain did not leave a contemporaneous account of his movements or activities that day. The only official report of the action of Chamberlain's 1st Brigade comes from Colonel William S. Tilton, who assumed command of the unit on the evening of June

---

1 Joshua L. Chamberlain, "Lines Before Petersburg, June 18, 1864," in L. C. Bateman, "The Hero of Gettysburg," *Lewiston Evening Journal* (September 1-6, 1900), 5.

18. The lack of real-time documentation from Chamberlain himself is not surprising given the fact that the battle nearly killed him.

Although he must have spent a great deal of time thinking about the matter, we do not have any record of specific comments by Chamberlain concerning his whereabouts at Petersburg on June 18, 1864, for a span of nearly two decades after the engagement. He apparently did not revisit the battlefield until the end of January 1882, upon his return from a winter trip to Florida. He recorded his impressions in a letter to his sister, penned on January 29. In that account, he described having spent four hours trying to identify the spot where he had fallen on June 18, leading his charge against the Rebel works:

> All is changed there now. What was a solid piece of woods through which I led my troops is now all cleared field, & the hillside so smooth there is now grown up with little clumps of trees. . . . At last, guided by the railroad cut & the well-remembered direction of the church spires of the city, I found the spot—or a space of 20-30 feet within which I must have fallen. . . . I looked down & saw a bullet, & while stooping to pick it up, another & another appeared in sight & I took up six within as many feet of each other and of the spot where I fell.[2]

The impression that the ground was decidedly unfamiliar to Chamberlain immediately strikes the reader. Everything was changed. Woods were gone; little clumps of trees had sprung up on clearings. Features of the terrain were not proving to be reliable guides. In such a situation it would have been difficult to ascertain whether the unfamiliarity was due to changes made to the land by its owners over ensuing years (cutting down the woods, for instance), or because the location was misplaced.

Because of his unfamiliarity with features of the topography, Chamberlain resorted to using the railroad cut and the "well remembered direction of the church spires of the city" to lead him to the spot where he fell, reportedly within 20 or 30 feet. But the church spires at Petersburg are perhaps two miles from Chamberlain's supposed Rives' Salient attack position, and a mile and a half from the Baxter Road position. The similarity of perspective between the two sites, which are both southeast of the town, makes it difficult to fathom how

2   Joshua L. Chamberlain to Sarah Brastow Chamberlain Farrington, in Jeremiah F. Goulka, *The Grand Old Man of Maine: Selected Letters of Joshua Lawrence Chamberlain* (Chapel Hill, NC, 2004), 109-110.

one could ever hope to achieve such accuracy in pinpointing a precise location based on distant landmarks alone.

The letter to his sister Sarah adds nothing of substance to our understanding of where Chamberlain fell, partly because the methods of inquiry employed are questionable, but more significantly because the letter makes no reference to specific place names, such as Rives' Salient or Fort Sedgwick. The letter and an 1888 request that Chamberlain made to Horatio Warren, one of his regimental commanders at Petersburg, for his recollections of that fateful day show that Chamberlain was thinking about these events over a protracted period.[3]

In 1899, thirty-five years after his assault at Petersburg, Chamberlain compiled the memoir that he entitled "The Charge at Fort Hell." This document remained unpublished and largely forgotten in the Special Collections Library at Duke University until 2004, when Diane Smith made it the basis of her book, *Chamberlain at Petersburg.* The actual text of Chamberlain's manuscript makes no specific reference to Rives' Salient, Fort Sedgwick, or "Fort Hell." Only the title alludes to this location (although Chamberlain does make an oblique reference to these locations by his mention of artillery fire upon his brigade from Confederate Fort Mahone, which was to the Union left of Rives' Salient.)[4]

In September 1900, Chamberlain was featured in an article written by a reporter from the *Lewiston Evening Journal,* a local newspaper in his home state of Maine. In that piece Chamberlain provided his most detailed and colorful personal recounting of the events that had transpired thirty-six years earlier. It is important to reproduce it nearly in its entirety in order to fully understand this critical event and his memory of it:

> During that summer, I had been assigned to a splendid brigade of six regiments, and on the morning of the 18th, I charged with this force and carried the enemy's advanced position in front of Petersburg, known as "Fort Hell." There I had three batteries sent to me to hold my position, which was in close proximity to Rieeves' (sic) Salient, so called, [which] was the enemy's main entrenched line. . . . With this force, I was more than a mile in advance of our army on the extreme right (sic). At this moment, an aide

3 Horatio N. Warren to Joshua L. Chamberlain, July 7, 1888, in Joshua Lawrence Chamberlain Papers, box 4, folder: "Reminiscences to Chamberlain," Library of Congress.

4 Chamberlain, "The Charge at Fort Hell," 9.

dashed up and gave me a verbal order from the commanding general to charge and carry the enemy's main works in my front. To say that I was astonished would be putting it mildly. I couldn't believe it possible that they meant for me to do this with only one brigade. . . . I immediately drew my note book and wrote a letter to the commanding general, stating the situation and asking if there was a mistake in the order to charge. I gave this note to the aide and told him to carry it to General Grant at once, which he did. It was an audacious thing for me to do, and after the message was gone, I began to realize that I had risked my shoulder straps. It was a virtual disobedience of orders to attack an enemy, which under any circumstances is a hazardous thing to do. I expected to be placed under arrest at once, so I communicated to my subordinate officers informing them of my probable immediate arrest and removal. . . .

In a short time, the staff officer who had taken my message to the general commanding the army returned. Instead of placing me under arrest, as I expected, he said that the general approved my course and the advice contained in my message. He also said the whole army would attack at once, but from my advanced position, it would be necessary for me to lead the assault. He asked when I would be able to attack, and I replied: "At one o'clock."

"Perhaps you would like to see that letter written to General Grant,"[5] continued Chamberlain. He confirmed that had kept a copy of it, and then produced it:

---

5   For the purposes of this discussion, "Lines before Petersburg" is taken at face value for what Joshua Chamberlain claimed it to be—a letter hand-written from the battlefield on June 18, 1864. It is used with the understanding that some have questioned its authenticity, based on Chamberlain's explanation of the circumstances of its origin and its purpose. Chamberlain specifically identified General Ulysses S. Grant as the source of the order for his brigade to assault the main lines of the enemy in his front, as well as the recipient of his letter of protest, and the one who personally approved the course of action that Chamberlain had recommended. General Grant was at City Point, more than ten miles away. How would Chamberlain have communicated with him? Telegraphy was probably not available on the front during the initial assault on Petersburg, and even if it were, how likely was it that the telegraph would have been used to transmit a two-page letter from a colonel? How much time would a courier require to travel to City Point and back? Chamberlain's description seems to suggest that the exchange was almost instantaneous ("In a short time the staff officer who had taken my message to the General commanding the Army returned.") Also, why would a brigade commander have been communicating directly with the General-in-Chief? Would it not have been a breach of protocol for him to have bypassed Generals Griffin, Warren, and Meade? Some also wonder where Chamberlain found the time to personally write a two-page letter, let alone to make a duplicate copy, in the midst of a hostile battle environment. And why were the original plus Grant's response not included in the official correspondence of the army?

Lines before Petersburg, June 18, 1864

I have just received a verbal order not through the usual channels, but by a staff-officer unknown to me, purporting to come from the General commanding the Army, directing me to assault the main works of the enemy in my front.

Circumstances lead me to believe the General cannot be perfectly aware of my situation, which has greatly changed within the last hour. I have just carried a crest, an advanced artillery post occupied by the enemy's artillery supported by infantry. I am advanced a mile beyond our own lines, and in an isolated position. On my right a deep railroad cut; my left flank in the air, with no support whatever. In my front at close range is a strongly entrenched line of infantry and artillery, with projecting salients right and left such that my advance would be swept by a cross-fire, while a large fort to my left enfilades my entire advance (as I experienced in carrying this position.)

In the hollow along my front close up to the enemy's works, appears to be bad ground, swampy, boggy, where my men would be held at great disadvantage under destructive fire.

I have got up three batteries and I am placing them on the reverse slope of this crest to enable me to hold against expected attack. To leave these guns behind me unsupported, their retreat cut off by the railroad cut, would expose them to loss in case of our repulse.

Fully aware of the responsibility I take, I beg to be assured that the order to attack with my single brigade is with the General's full understanding. I have here a veteran brigade of six regiments, and my responsibility for these men warrants me in wishing assurance that no mistake in communicating orders compels me to sacrifice them.

From what I can see of the enemy's lines, it is my opinion that if an assault is to be made, it should be by nothing less than the whole army.

Very respectfully,

Joshua L. Chamberlain
Colonel commanding 1st Brigade 1st Division 5th Corps

(Transcribed from photographed copy in "The Hero of Gettysburg," *Lewiston Evening Journal*, September 1, 1900.)

I expected trouble to grow out of it, but trouble came in another form. . . .

My horse had been shot from under me that morning at "Fort Hell," and many other officers had met with the same misfortune. Then, on foot, I prepared my men for the sweep down the slope and across the field, with fixed bayonets and arms at shoulder, ready to bayonet the rebels in their entrenchments.

At one o'clock, I sounded the signal, and moved my brigade in the lines of battle in front of my guns.[6] The moment they could do so, my batteries opened an awful fire over our heads. The enemy replied with every missile known to war at pistol range. We were also enfiladed by the heavy guns from Fort Mahone, or "Fort Damnation," as the boys called it. It was a case where I felt it my duty to lead the charge in person, and on foot. My flag bearer had been shot dead at once. I picked up the flag—a red Maltese cross on a white field—and with my entire staff went forward. At the foot of the slope between us and the rebel works we struck soft, spongy ground, where I saw that my men would be caught. Accordingly, I faced towards them and ordered an oblique to the left. As no mortal voice could be heard in such an uproar of fire, I was waving my sabre and flag in the direction I wished my men to take, when a Minié ball of the ten thousand that were darkening the air, struck me as I was half facing to give this command. The ball entered in front of the right hip joint, passing clear through my body and coming out [by subsequent surgical extraction] behind the left hip joint.

I was standing so firmly on the ground at the time that I did not fall at first. I thrust the point of my sword into the ground and balanced myself over the hilt and held myself in that position until the men of the first line had passed in charge. I knew that if they saw their leader fall it would discourage them, so with rigid features I held myself up although helpless in all other ways. They saw me standing there like a statue leaning on my sword, but did not dream that I had received a mortal wound. . . .

The loss of blood soon brought me to one knee, and finally to the ground. I knew it was a mortal wound, as all medical history said so. As fate would have it, I recovered, and today my case stands alone in the medical history of the world of a man recovering from this wound. [In truth, urethral injuries were seldom fatal. More than one-hundred cases have been reported of Civil War soldiers who suffered similar injuries, and four out of every five victims survived.[7]] . . . The storm and whirl of battle surged around me for a full hour while I was lying there. . . . In a little lull of the fight Major Bigelow, commanding one of my batteries, the 9th Massachusetts, in sweeping the field with his glasses, saw my shoulder straps and dispatched four men with a stretcher down through the struggling mass to take me off. . . .

The New York papers the next morning printed long notices and editorials giving full description of how I died. It was quite cheerful reading for a live man, I can assure you.

The commanding officer gave orders for eight men to be detailed to carry me sixteen miles on a stretcher to City Point. From there I was taken by steamer to Annapolis and placed in the Naval School Hospital, where I lay with convulsive chills

---

6   All other sources suggest the attack commenced about three o'clock in the afternoon.

7   Herr and McAninch, "Urological Injuries in the Civil War," 1090.

and at the point of death for two months. Strange as it may seem, I disappointed all the doctors, and in five months was back to my command, serving until mustered out at the close of the war. [8]

Chamberlain's spellbinding tale so enraptured his interviewer that the journalist lapsed into poetic expression of profound admiration:

> What a subject here would be for a great historical painter! The finest artist in America should paint him standing before the frowning guns of Petersburg with life blood streaming from a supposed mortal wound, and yet erect, rigid, with sternly set features balancing himself on his sword thrust into the ground, while his men are sweeping past in that awful charge and all unconscious that their beloved leader is exerting all his willpower and strength to conceal from them his condition. The brush of the artist never had a grander theme. It should be put on canvas or sculptured in marble and placed in the rotunda of the Capitol at Washington to show the world the stuff of which American patriots are made. As an example of inspiring patriotism, it would rank by the side of Leonidas and his three hundred Spartans. [9]

In October 1903, shortly after a second visit to Petersburg, Chamberlain presented a paper before the Commandery of the State of Maine, Military Order of the Loyal Legion of the United States (MOLLUS), entitled "Reminiscences of Petersburg and Appomattox." In it, he recounted the "impressions made upon me by a recent visit to Petersburg and Appomattox Court House, Virginia, the first and last battlefields of the final campaign of the Army of the Potomac and the Army of Northern Virginia." [10]

According to Chamberlain, his motive in undertaking the visit was to assure himself as to certain points on those fields, "The last visions of which had left my memory somewhat clouded . . . with the sudden overcast of my own early down-going amidst storm and disaster." [11]

Chamberlain readily admitted that he had not had the opportunity to revisit the site of his near-mortal wounding during the months and years immediately

---

8   Bateman, "The Hero of Gettysburg," 5.

9   Ibid., 6.

10   Joshua L. Chamberlain, "Reminiscences of Petersburg and Appomattox: October, 1903," in *War Papers Read Before the Commandery of the State of Maine, Military Order of the Loyal Legion of the United States*, 70 vols. (Portland, ME, 1908), 161.

11   Ibid., 161.

following the battle. In fact, he viewed this lack of opportunity in a positive light. The intervening 39 years, he thought, was "time enough to cool one's blood, so as to gather the various data for mature judgment, more reliable perhaps than confused recollections of personal experience."[12]

Frankly acknowledging the confusion of his recollections (as a consequence of battlefield shock and subsequent sepsis from a life-threatening gunshot wound to his pelvis that threatened his "early down-going amidst storm and disaster") and the clouding of his memory (with the passage of thirty-nine years), the seventy-five year old warrior and polished raconteur was attempting to reconstruct the events of June 18.

Importantly, note that from the outset Chamberlain's recall was not entirely confused. His memory seems both vivid and reliable in terms of what he was able to remember about the nature of the terrain, the directions of his movements, and the substance of his conversations with other officers.

What seems to have been lacking is a grasp of the larger context of the drama. The V Corps arrived at Petersburg less than twenty-four hours prior to its engagement there. The morning of the 18th found Chamberlain's brigade advancing against a newly entrenched opponent on the high ground east of the city. Within a matter of just a few hours, the stricken colonel, with a nearly-mortal wound, was being evacuated from the field in shock. He was then absent from the Army of the Potomac for five months. During that time, the V Corps had proceeded to move leftward, constructing first Fort Sedgwick (also known as "Fort Hell"), and then numerous other fortifications, in an effort to outflank the right of the Confederate line.

Chamberlain, understandably, may not have possessed an accurate grasp of precisely where he was on June 18, or of who was opposing him. Having learned, in retrospect, that Griffin's division had initiated the construction of Fort Sedgwick, and knowing that he was in a fierce fight in the vicinity, Chamberlain may have assumed he was part of the assault that took and fortified the ground that "became famous throughout the siege as the hottest point of contact of the hostile lines."[13] Having faced a formidable foe certainly makes defeat more palatable, and "Hell" and "Damnation" provide a splash of color to any tale of daring and danger.

12 Ibid., 164.

13 Ibid., 173.

In his later years, Chamberlain seems to have been driven to flesh out the larger context of the fateful engagement (and perhaps to burnish his own reputation) by doing some retrospective investigation. He may not, however, have been terribly thorough in his preparation: There is no reference to the official reports of his own army, or those of his Confederate foes; there is no mention of an extensive correspondence with fellow officers to clarify specific details; there is no evidence of his having spent time consulting historical maps that survive to this day.

During the 1903 visit, Chamberlain did go to the trouble of touring the battlefield with a local guide, consulting a lone, worn Confederate war map, collecting souvenir bullets, and exchanging reciprocal experiences with an anonymous old Confederate officer who may or may not have opposed him on the field of combat.[14] His role, however, seems to have been more one of a spectator and casual sightseer rather than that of a researcher, scholar, or detective.

With the benefit of the supplemental information acquired on the second visit, Chamberlain composed his speech for the enlightenment and entertainment of comrades and admirers at the MOLLUS assembly. Given the purpose of the manuscript, it is not necessarily the most reliable of historical primary source documents. In the "Reminiscences," he speaks of his proximity to the [Jerusalem] plank road.[15] He tells of his brigade having taken and fortified ground that afterwards became strongly entrenched under the name of "Fort Sedgwick."[16] He mentions having confronted the infantry of Kershaw's Mississippians, Georgians and South Carolinians, as well as Alabama "friends" from Longstreet's Corps—"companions of the symposium at Round Top the year before"—who had replaced Johnson's division in the trenches early the previous evening.[17] (Review of the historical record will show that Kershaw and Field relieved Johnson on the evening of June 18, not June 17.) Each of these points becomes highly debatable as one carefully considers the historical record.

14 Ibid., 177.

15 Ibid., 171.

16 Ibid., 173.

17 Ibid., 174.

As we shall see, the details of Chamberlain's own account of his actions on June 18 (terrain, direction and distance of movements, landmarks, artillery placements, etc.) conflict with his interpretation. Abundant external contemporaneous testimony from multiple other sources also seems to render untenable the scenario of an attack by Chamberlain's brigade on Rives' Salient from the south, along the Jerusalem Plank Road.

The evidence strongly suggests that Chamberlain's own false premise conceived the myth that has come down to us—a myth perpetuated through faithful repetition by a long line of biographers over many decades. Still, we must ask, "Have we missed something? Did the biographers perhaps have access to other information that supports the Rives' Salient scenario?"

For the answers to those questions, we must look more closely at what they have to say.

CHAPTER 2

HISTORY SOMETIMES REPEATS ITSELF:
And Historians Often Repeat Each Other

THE explicit pronouncements made by Chamberlain concerning his role in the attack at Petersburg were made many decades after the event. The ranks of Civil War survivors were thinning. Veterans, understandably, wanted to find a way to immortalize their deeds of valor so history would not forget them. Regimental histories proliferated, and numerous magazine and newspaper articles dealing with the Civil War appeared.

Chamberlain was interviewed for a feature article entitled "The Hero of Gettysburg," which was published in the September 1-6, 1900, "Illustrated Magazine" section of *The Lewiston* (Maine) *Evening Journal*. In that interview, the aging general explicitly stated that his attack originated from the future site of "Fort Hell":

> My horse had been shot from under me that morning at "Fort Hell" and many other officers had met with the same misfortune. Then, on foot, I prepared my men for the sweep down the slope and across the field, with fixed bayonets and arms at shoulder, ready to bayonet the rebels in their entrenchments. At one o'clock, I sounded the signal, and moved my brigade in lines of battle in front of my guns. The moment they could do so, my batteries opened an awful fire over our heads. The enemy replied with

every missile known to war, at pistol range. We were also enfiladed by the heavy guns from Fort Mahone, or "Fort Damnation," as the boys called it.[1]

Chamberlain's own book, *The Passing of the Armies*, was first published in 1915, one year after his death. According to a reviewer, it is "a poem in prose." The book is a memoir of his recollections during the final meeting of the two great armies, when he presided over the parade of the Confederate infantry at the formal surrender of Robert E. Lee's Army of Northern Virginia at Appomattox Court House on April 12, 1865. Four times in his memoir, Chamberlain mentioned the presence of his brigade at Rives' Salient:

Successive assaults on the enemy's lines were made as corps after corps extended leftward; but gallant fighting left little to show but its cost. Especially did we hold in mind the last of these made by the V Corps on the second day, when an assault was ordered by my fine veteran Brigade on the strong entrenchments at *Rives' Salient*, commanding the important avenue of communication, the Norfolk Railroad and Jerusalem Plank Road. By this time, it was too late; all Lee's army was up and entrenched.[2]

With what strange emotion I look into these faces [Kershaw's troops] before which, in the mad assault on *Rives' Salient*, June 18, 1864, I was left for dead under their eyes! It is by miracles we have lived to see this day, any of us standing here.[3]

Here passes steadily to the front as of yore the 7th Maine Battery, Twitchell, my late college friend, at the head: splendid recessional, for I saw it last in 1864 grimly bastioning the slopes above *Rives' Salient*, where darkness fell upon my eyes, and I thought to see no more.[4]

But where are my splendid six regiments of them which made that resolute, forlorn-hope charge from the crest they had carried fitly named "Fort Hell," down past the spewing dragons of "Fort Damnation" into the miry, fiery pit before *Rives' Salient* of the dark June 18th? Two regiments of them, the 121st Pennsylvania, Colonel Warner, and 142nd Pennsylvania, Colonel [Horatio] Warren, alone I see in this passing

---

1   Bateman, "The Hero of Gettysburg," 5.

2   Joshua L. Chamberlain, *The Passing of the Armies* (New York, 1915), 26.

3   Ibid., 264.

4   Ibid., 338.

pageant, worn, thin, hostages of the mortal. I violate the courtesies of the august occasion. I give them salutation before the face of the reviewing officer—the President himself—asking no permission, no forgiveness.[5]

Twice more, Chamberlain referred to the charge at "Fort Hell:"

The 121st and 142nd Pennsylvania . . . were all that was left to us of the dear lost old 1st Corps, and of my splendid brigade from it in Griffin's division, in the ever memorable charge of *"Fort Hell,"* June 18, 1864.[6]

Bigelow . . . of the 9th Massachusetts . . . with Mink's 1st New York and Hart's 15th, came to support the charge at the ominous *"Fort Hell,"* whence Bigelow, with watchful eyes, sent his brave men down through hissing canister, and enfilading shell, and blinding turf and pebbles flying from the up-torn earth, to bring back my useless body from what else were its final front.[7]

From these accounts, penned fifty years after the engagement at Petersburg, it is clear Chamberlain went to his grave claiming, and probably firmly believing, that he had assaulted Rives' Salient from "Fort Hell." Who could blame his biographers for perpetuating the story?

Willard M. Wallace's *Soul of the Lion: a Biography of General Joshua L. Chamberlain* (1960) places the target of Chamberlain's Petersburg attack at Rives' Salient, across open ground commanded by direct rifle and cannon fire and enfiladed by artillery fire from Fort Mahone (or "Fort Damnation"):

In the early morning attack by the V Corps, Chamberlain had dashed ahead with his brigade and captured a strongly defended position from the Confederates, which was subsequently given the name "Fort Hell." . . . He was in an exposed position far in advance of the main army and did not like the situation.[8]

Wallace goes on to discuss the colonel's famous letter of remonstrance to his commanding general, the fact that Chamberlain led his charge in person and

---

5   Ibid., 348.

6   Ibid., 146.

7   Ibid., 350.

8   Willard M. Wallace, *Soul of the Lion: A Biography of General Joshua Lawrence Chamberlain* (New York, 1960), 128-32.

on foot across soft sticky ground, his severe wounding, and his evacuation from the field by Bigelow's men. Wallace's sole source for the detailed account is "The Hero of Gettysburg" 1900 feature in the *Lewiston Journal*.

The most prominent modern-day exponent of the Rives' Salient interpretation was Chamberlain biographer Alice Rains Trulock, whose book *In the Hands of Providence: Joshua L. Chamberlain & the American Civil War* (1992) was widely read within the Civil War community. In it, Trulock described Chamberlain's brigade advancing on a Rebel battery several hundred yards south of the main Confederate works near the Jerusalem Plank Road.[9] Emerging from the woods across the railroad, the 1st Brigade is "raked by enemy guns in Fort Mahone, across the Jerusalem Plank Road to the west."[10] The target Confederate battery flees to avoid capture, "beating a hasty retreat into the narrow valley in front of Rives's Salient and then back to the protection of the Confederate works. . . . The location of the battery that the brigade had successfully silenced was near the place where the Union Fort Sedgwick, renamed 'Fort Hell' by the men, would be constructed."[11]

There are several problems and inconsistencies with Trulock's reckoning. Despite having set the center of the action at Fort Sedgwick and the Jerusalem Plank Road, to the south of Rives' Salient and a mile from the railroad, Trulock correctly locates Chamberlain's artillery batteries "at [his] right and rear, the deep railroad cut behind them [making their] escape difficult, should the assault fail and the Rebels counterattack."[12] If, as Trulock maintains, Chamberlain's brigade line stretched a quarter of a mile in length,[13] it would be physically impossible for its right flank to have been resting on the deep cut of the railroad while its left flank was simultaneously engaged near the Jerusalem Plank Road—nearly a mile distant. Similarly, it is difficult to reconcile Chamberlain's brigade being positioned near Fort Sedgwick and Rives' Salient, and being to the immediate left of Sweitzer, whose 2nd Brigade spent the afternoon and

---

9   Alice Rains Trulock, *In the Hands of Providence, Joshua L. Chamberlain & The American Civil War* (Chapel Hill, NC, 1992), 199.

10 Ibid., 200.

11 Ibid., 201.

12 Ibid., 202.

13 Ibid., 208.

evening of June 18 in front of Pegram's Salient to the north of the Baxter Road.[14]

In his 1994 history of the 149th Pennsylvania Volunteers, Richard Matthews described a field sloping down from the front of the Confederate works for 200 yards ending at a marshy stream, and then rising gently toward the Union lines to a flat level crest upon which the Union would subsequently erect Forts Rice and Sedgwick. The ground then sloped away to the east, only to rise again near the railroad about a mile away from the Confederate works.[15] The description, minus the references to Forts Rice and Sedgwick, is similar to a report written by General Ayres, who commanded the 2nd Division, to General Warren at 11:15 a.m. on June 18, describing his own position, which actually was in front of Rives' Salient:

> I have established my line to the left of General Cutler, across the railroad, on a crest in the open. I drove the enemy's skirmishers from it, and am now intrenching. Also shall establish batteries. The ground falls from the crest about 200 yards to a deep ravine. It rises from the other side gradually, about the same distance, to the first line of rebel works; still rising, you come to their second line. Their line runs beyond my left, which I have refused.[16]

According to Matthews, Chamberlain's horse was struck from beneath him by a 12-pound solid shot during the 3:15 p.m. main assault of the Confederate fortifications, and Chamberlain was severely wounded shortly thereafter. The charge was made under enfilading artillery fire which, wrote Matthews "probably" came from guns located at Confederate Battery #29 to the south at Fort Mahone. The reliability of his account is also suspect because of its placement of Sweitzer to the left and south of Chamberlain's 1st Brigade, and Cutler's 4th Division along the Jerusalem Plank Road behind Fort Sedgwick.[17]

---

14 Ibid.

15 Richard E. Matthews, *The 149th Pennsylvania Volunteer Infantry Unit in the Civil War* (Jefferson, NC, 1994), 181.

16 *OR* 40, pt. 2, 183.

17 Matthews, *The 149th Pennsylvania Volunteer Infantry Unit in the Civil War*, 183. Note this is contrary to Chamberlain's own account, which placed the event in the morning during his charge on the artillery battery at "Fort Hell." Ibid., 181-82. These relative positions of the units find no support in the historical documentation, but resurface later in Diane Monroe Smith, *Chamberlain at Petersburg: The Charge at Fort Hell, June 18, 1864* (Gettysburg, 2004).

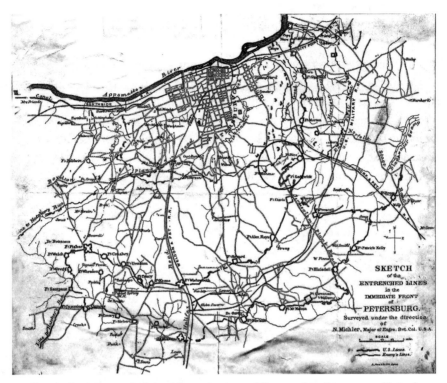

Chamberlain's map, which has blue and red pencil lines marking his supposed brigade line and the Confederate line of defense. *Library of Congress*

Mark Nesbitt's *Through Blood & Fire: Selected Civil War Papers of Major General Joshua Chamberlain* (1996) perpetuates the tradition of scholars who base their analysis and conclusions entirely upon Chamberlain's manuscripts and letters. Nesbitt places the attack in front of Rives' Salient from a point near the Jerusalem Plank Road.[18] Nesbitt's book includes detail about Chamberlain's personal map, which is housed in the Library of Congress. The vicinity of Rives' Salient on the folded map includes clear Union and Confederate battle lines hand-drawn in blue and red colored pencil—situated precisely in the front of Fort Sedgwick.[19]

18   Mark Nesbitt, *Through Blood & Fire: Selected Civil War Papers of Major General Joshua Chamberlain* (Mechanicsburg, PA, 1996), 132.

19   Nathaniel Michler, "Sketch of the Entrenched Lines in the Immediate Front of Petersburg," in Joshua Lawrence Chamberlain Papers (1828-1913), Manuscript Division, Library of Congress, Washington, D.C. ID No.: MSS15503, Box 7.

The source document for Chamberlain's mark-up was a postwar Michler map[20] similar to those included in a twenty-six page 1869 booklet entitled *A Guide to the Fortifications and Battlefields around Petersburg: with a Splendid Map From Actual Surveys made by the US Engineer Department.*[21] It is clear, however, Chamberlain's map is *not* one that he carried into battle on June 18. It has no topographical markings. It depicts Forts Sedgwick, Rice, Meikle and Morton, as well as the Military Railroad, all of which were constructed in subsequent weeks and months, while Chamberlain was fighting for his life in a military hospital in Annapolis, Maryland. The annotations were almost certainly added decades after the fact, and probably during one of Chamberlain's two excursions to Petersburg near the turn of the century. Thus, the map in and of itself proves nothing with regard to the precise location of Chamberlain's 1st Brigade on June 18, 1864.

In 2004, Diane Smith released *Chamberlain at Petersburg: The Charge at Fort Hell, June 18, 1864.*[22] In her book, she analyzed the largely forgotten and previously unpublished Chamberlain manuscript entitled "The Charge at Fort Hell," along with excerpts from the "Reminiscences of Petersburg and Appomattox" paper presented to MOLLUS by Chamberlain in October 1903. Extensive annotations amplify both manuscripts.

Smith logically assumes that, if one is attempting to fix the point of Chamberlain's charge, Chamberlain's own accounts should be the first and most important sources to be considered. Based on her reading of the Chamberlain manuscripts (in harmony with the interpretations of other Chamberlain writers who preceded her), Smith has Chamberlain's 1st Brigade separated from its division and far to the left by the Jerusalem Plank Road—more than a mile away from Sweitzer and the rest of the Army of the Potomac. There, from the vicinity of the future Fort Sedgwick (also known as "Fort Hell"), isolated and alone, Chamberlain and his brigade assault Rives' Salient,

---

20 Nathaniel Michler was a major of the Corps of Engineers in 1864. He was brevetted lieutenant colonel on August 1, 1864 and brigadier general on April 2, 1865, for his services during the Civil War. Many of the maps and surveys of Petersburg were done under his direction. Some of his maps were mass produced after the war.

21 *A Guide to the Fortifications and Battlefields around Petersburg, With a Splendid Map From Actual Surveys made by the US Engineer Department,* compiled by Jarratt's Hotel (J. B. Ege's Printing House, 1869).

22 Diane Monroe Smith, *Chamberlain at Petersburg: The Charge at Fort Hell, June 18, 1864* (Gettysburg, 2004).

the point along the inner defenses of Petersburg where the hastily constructed Harris Line joined the Dimmock Line of permanent fortifications, erected in 1863. The assault takes place from the south under murderous fire from fortifications at the salient itself, and from Fort Mahone to its left—works purportedly manned by veteran Confederate troops under Generals Charles Field and Joseph Kershaw, from Lee's Army of Northern Virginia.

Smith's extensive annotations of "The Charge at Fort Hell" include specific details (such as directions, distances, and place names) that are missing in the original accounts. Chamberlain, Cutler, and Ayres become "isolated from the rest of the Army of the Potomac, which at its nearest was a mile to the north." Sweitzer is positioned "well over a mile from Chamberlain's right," and Cutler "no less than three-fourths of a mile to the rear and left of the 1st Brigade." Chamberlain is found "squarely in front of and 300 yards away from "Battery No. 25" in an area known as Rives' Salient, [which] was the point at which the new Rebel line joined the formidable fortifications of the original Dimmock line," and "one-third of a mile forward of the area where Fort Sedgwick would be constructed during the ensuing siege."[23]

As explained in this book's Introduction, with a single exception, Chamberlain biographers have devoted only a few pages of their coverage to Chamberlain's brief experience at the Petersburg front on June 18, 1864. Smith's book, on the other hand, is a monograph entirely devoted to the subject. By virtue of its extensive annotations, and the fact that it presents a firsthand account from the pen of Chamberlain himself, *Chamberlain at Petersburg* seems eminently authoritative and definitive. In particular, it summarizes and expands the narrative of a long line of previous writers, beginning with Joshua Chamberlain himself.

Because Chamberlain's writings are so foundational to the idea of an attack against Rives' Salient by Chamberlain's brigade, it is important to take a fresh look at them in the hope of better understanding what Chamberlain actually told us. Unpacking that information will be our task in the next several chapters.

---

23 Ibid., 54-55.

CHAPTER 3

CHAMBERLAIN'S "CHARGE AT FORT HELL":
Orders and Objectives

A full understanding of Chamberlain's recounting of the orders he received, and the objectives contained therein, is crucial to understanding the events of June 18. A firm grasp of what he was trying to achieve goes a long way in helping us understand where he was, and against whom he fought. The benefit of hindsight allows us to reconstruct a more accurate picture than the one Chamberlain eventually pieced together out of the chaos and confusion of that fateful day.

According to Chamberlain, Griffin's orders assigned three objectives to him on June 18, 1864:

(1) Protect the artillery batteries attached to Griffin's 1st division, V Corps:

> Morning came with enemy artillery at close range. . . . Soon our batteries were advanced to reply to those annoying us. . . . The enemy seemed now contemplating to take our guns by a dash.[1]

---

1   Chamberlain, "The Charge at Fort Hell," 3.

Then General Griffin rode up and said, "We wish you would look out for these batteries here. They may try to take them." Col. Chamberlain replied, "Certainly, General; they shall not take them."[2]

(2) Dislodge a Confederate advanced light artillery position and accompanying skirmishers that were annoying and threatening the artillery batteries and infantry lines of Griffin's division:

I moved up close in rear of the guns [which were in the open field northwest of the Avery house, towards the Taylor property], covering my men as I could by taking advantage of the ground. . . . Many were falling, with no chance to strike back. Griffin and Warren rode up to me; Griffin spoke: "Those batteries out there must be dislodged. General Warren asks if you will do it. . . . We do not order it; we wish it if it is possible to be done. But it is a hard push up that open slope."[3]

(3) Attack and carry the batteries and works on his front—the inner line of defenses around Petersburg:

"The general commanding desires you to attack and carry the works in your front." "Does the General know where I am?" I asked. "Let me show you! They are the interior works, the main works at Petersburg."[4]

These three objectives were intended to be carried out within the local sphere of operation of Griffin's 1st Division. Note there was no mandate for Chamberlain to detach and make an end run around the 4th and 2nd divisions on the left flank of the Army, or to assault, alone, from the south to Rives' Salient.

How, then, did Chamberlain execute his orders and achieve Griffin's objectives? And what was the impact on June 18's operations and the story of his wounding?

2   Ibid., 3, 4.

3   Ibid.

4   Ibid., 6.

CHAPTER 4

OBJECTIVE ONE:
"Look Out For These Batteries Here"

T HE first of Griffin's objectives, and probably the easiest for Chamberlain to achieve, was the protection of the 1st Division's artillery. The following is from Chamberlain's "The Charge at Fort Hell":

> Morning came with enemy artillery at close range. . . . Soon our batteries were advanced to reply to those annoying us. The enemy seemed now contemplating to take our guns by a dash. . . . General Griffin rode up and said, "We wish you would look out for these batteries here. They may try to take them." "Certainly, General; they shall not take them" was the quiet assurance.[1]

Which batteries did Griffin have in mind when he gave this order, and where were they positioned? Griffin's own words—"These batteries here"—make it clear he was discussing the batteries of the V Corps attached to Griffin's 1st Division. As we shall see from what follows, in order for Chamberlain to do this, it would be necessary for his brigade to remain near the Baxter Road.

---

1 Chamberlain, "The Charge at Fort Hell," 3.

Setting the Scene—the Eve of Battle

After the failed Union assaults against entrenched Confederate lines at Cold Harbor in early June, General Warren initiated a restructuring of the V Army Corps pursuant to General Orders issued on June 5, 1864. Chamberlain was elevated to brigade command, and several of the corps artillery batteries were attached to the 1st and 2nd Divisions. An appreciation of this new organization, and how the individual units ended up where they did on June 18, 1864, is important to understanding the following:

The following reorganization of the Fifth Army Corps is hereby made:

First. The First Division will be commanded by Brigadier General C. Griffin. It will consist of General Bartlett's brigade, General Sweitzer's brigade, and the former Third Brigade, of the Fourth Division. This brigade will be commanded by Colonel Chamberlain. Colonel Bragg will rejoin his regiment. Three batteries will be attached to this division [the batteries of Phillips, Stewart, and Richardson].

Second. The Second Division will be commanded by Brigadier General R. B. Ayres. It will consist of his own brigade, the Maryland Brigade, Colonel Dushane, and the Heavy Artillery Brigade, Colonel Kitching. Three batteries will also be assigned to this division [the batteries of Rogers, Walcott and Rittenhouse].

Third. The Third Division will be commanded by Brigadier General S. W. Crawford. It will consist of the veteran brigade of Pennsylvania Reserve and the brigades commanded by Colonels Lyle and Bates.

Fourth. The Fourth Division will be commanded by Brigadier General L. Cutler, and will consist of the two brigades of Colonel Robinson and Colonel Hofmann.

Fifth. The remaining six batteries will constitute the reserve artillery of the corps [the batteries of Mink, Cooper, Breck, Bigelow, Hart and Barnes].

This order will go into effect at once, and each commanding officer will carry out his part of the changes ordered.[2]

2   *OR* 36, pt. 3, 613-14.

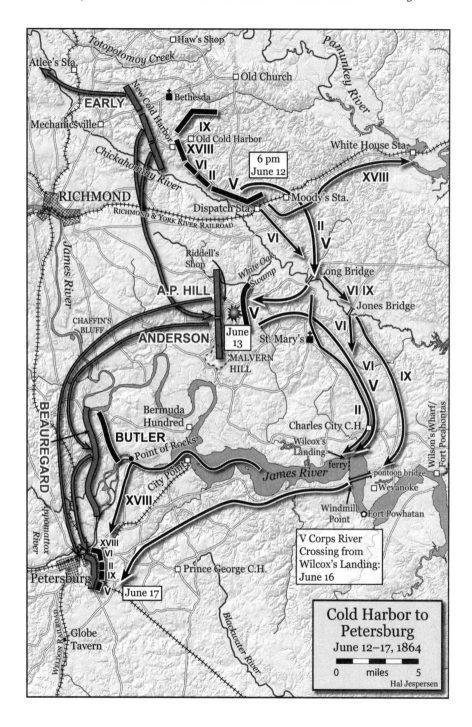

Cold Harbor to Petersburg
June 12–17, 1864

0   miles   5

Hal Jespersen

Through Special Orders No. 75, issued by Griffin on June 6, 1864, the newly arrived 187th Pennsylvania was combined with five depleted veteran Pennsylvania regiments—the 121st, 142nd, 143rd, 149th, and 150th, which had been transferred from the Third Brigade of Lysander Cutler's division. The strength of the 187th was about equal to the strength of the other five regiments combined. These six regiments formed Chamberlain's new command, which would be officially known as the 1st Brigade of the 1st Division.[3]

To complement the new assignment and increased responsibilities, General Warren sought a promotion for Chamberlain from colonel to brigadier general. "I wish you would make out a recommendation for the promotion of Colonel Chamberlain," Warren wrote Griffin on June 6. "I will forward it at once, so that it can take its chance with some others that are going to be forwarded."[4]

When General Ulysses S. Grant ordered the stealthy withdrawal of the entire Army of the Potomac from Cold Harbor on June 12, 1864 across the James River, the V Corps formed the vanguard. However, Warren and his corps veered off to the right at White Oak Swamp and Malvern Hill in order to screen the evacuation of the rest of the army and block any Confederate interference. The result of this detour and the longer distance involved in its march meant the troops of the V Corps were among the last of the 100,000- man army to make the crossing to the south side of the river on June 16.

During the evening and night of June 16-17, Chamberlain's brigade, with the rest of the V Corps, made a forced march of sixteen miles to reach the front at Petersburg, a major logistical hub about twenty-five miles below the capital at Richmond.[5] The corps began arriving on the morning of June 17. Prior to its arrival, heavy fighting by the Union II and IX corps had resulted in the capture of portions of the original 1863 Dimmock Line of permanent entrenchments on the eastern side of the city. During the night, the Confederates had thrown up a new line running nearly north and south along the eastern edge of the body of timber west of the Avery house, skirting the Norfolk Pike (Baxter Road)

---

3   *Ibid.,* 652.

4   *Ibid.*

5   John B. Horner, ed., *The Letters of Major Robert Bell* (Gettysburg, PA), 28.

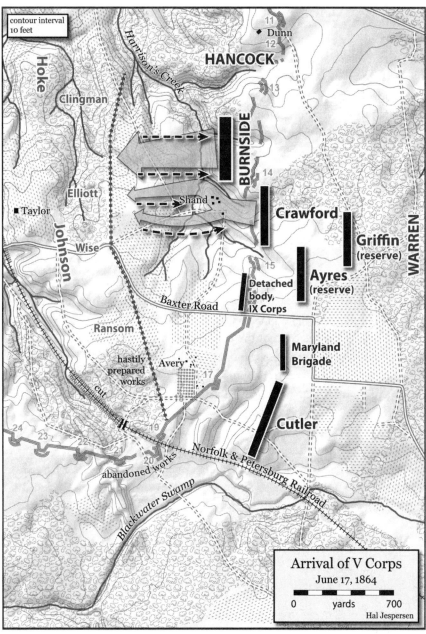

General Warren's V Corps arrived on June 17 and was dispatched to the left of the Union line. Cutler deployed with his flank along the Norfolk Railroad and the Blackwater Swamp. Burnside's IX Corps was in the process of mounting three assaults near the Shand property. Crawford supported the last of these advances that evening. Griffin and Ayres remained in reserve that day. Command of the II Corps, which assaulted farther north on the evening of June 16, was transferred from Hancock to Birney on the night of June 17-18.

where it made a bend, and then following the skirt of a large piece of pinewoods north of the pike.[6]

At 8:15 a.m. on June 17, Warren issued orders for Cutler to move his 4th Division to the front, followed by Brig. Gen. Samuel Crawford and his 3rd Division.[7] Cutler had the task of holding the corps' left flank on the swamp surrounding Blackwater Creek.[8] His 4th Division and the Maryland Brigade, which was detached from Ayres' 2nd Division, were in line east of the Avery house between the Baxter Road and the Norfolk Railroad.[9] The other three V Corps divisions massed to the right of Cutler, near the center of the Union line.[10] IX Corps divisions were now positioned on the V Corps' front in ravines surrounding the Shand house.[11] V Corps units formed behind enemy entrenchments that had been captured by General Burnside's men the previous night, with Griffin's 1st Division troops situated behind the lines of Crawford and Ayres.[12]

During the afternoon of June 17, General Orlando Willcox's 3rd Division, IX Corps, launched an attack against Confederate defenders but failed to break through. At dusk, General James H. Ledlie's 1st Division, IX Corps, assaulted the enemy's line at the edge of the large pinewoods north of the Baxter Road. Crawford's division was ordered forward to support the attack. Crawford's men became bewildered in the dark, stumbling between the two ravines surrounding the Shand house.[13] The men eventually reorganized, straightened their line, and advanced.

Troops from Ledlie's division of the IX Corps and Crawford's division of the V Corps both claimed to have captured an entire Confederate regiment, returning with many prisoners and the regimental colors. Ledlie claimed the

---

6   Washington A. Roebling, "Report of the Operations of the V Corps, Army of the Potomac, in General Grant's Campaign from Culpeper to Petersburg, as Seen by W. A. Roebling," journal entries for June 17-18, 1864, in Gouverneur K. Warren Collection, Roe Archives, New York State Library, Albany, New York.

7   *OR* 40, pt. 2, 128.

8   Ibid., 129

9   Roebling, "Report of the Operations of the V Corps," June 17.

10 *OR* 40, pt. 2, 125

11 Roebling, "Report of the Operations of the V Corps," June 17.

12 *OR* 40, pt. 2, 129.

13 Roebling, "Report of the Operations of the V Corps," June 17.

captured regiment was the 35th North Carolina, part of Matt Ransom's brigade, which was situated south of the Baxter Road.[14] Crawford, whose report for the day consists mainly of a strenuous protest to his superiors over stolen trophies of battle, claimed the captured colors belonged to the 39th North Carolina. This was impossible because the 39th North Carolina was fighting with the Confederate Division of the Gulf deployed many hundreds of miles south of Petersburg.[15] In any event, Ledlie and Crawford both withdrew, and the Union army did not hold any part of the enemy's fallback line at the edge of the woods behind the Taylor farm that night.[16] Crawford's division continued operating alongside the IX Corps during the next twenty-four hours.

Batteries of the V Corps, June 18, 1864

When V Corps commander Warren rode forward early on the morning of June 18, he found that the Confederates had fallen back once again during the night to a third and final entrenched position known as "the Harris Line," about one mile closer to Petersburg. The Federals observed the work of the enemy along this new line on the heights beyond the ravine through which the Norfolk Railroad entered the city.

According to the memoirs of Lieutenant Colonel Theodore Lyman, General George Meade's archivist and aide-de-camp, General Warren rode past the Shand house, crossed an oat field, and established his new corps headquarters in front and to the right of the Avery house, where a pinewood made a corner into open land. There was an oat field to the rear, and open untilled ground to the left of this position.[17]

Griffin's 1st Division remained massed behind woods near the Shand house. One of the first orders of business that morning was to deploy the artillery of the V Corps. "Some of Griffin's people advanced into the oat field," wrote Lieutenant Colonel Lyman, "and Phillips coming up with his battery [5th Massachusetts] Griffin called out to him: 'I want you to go in there with your guns; but you will be under fire there.' . . . Griffin went with him to choose a

---

14 *OR* 40, pt. 1, 532-33.

15 Ibid., 472.

16 Roebling, "Report of the Operations of the V Corps," June 17.

17 David W. Lowe, ed., *Meade's Army: The Private Notebooks of Lt. Col. Theodore Lyman* (Kent, OH, 2007), 212.

spot, but both were received by an unlooked for skirmish volley from the flank, and came back in a hurry!"[18]

Colonel Charles S. Wainwright commanded, as noted, the Artillery Brigade of the V Corps, consisting of twelve batteries. He kept a diary, and he wrote a contemporaneous official report. Together, these two documents enable us to determine the placement of the V Corps batteries on the morning of June 18 with precision.

Phillips', Richardson's, and Stewart's batteries had been assigned to Griffin's 1st Division, in the V Corps reorganization of June 5: "By 9:00 all the batteries were engaged. Griffin's three batteries, "E" Massachusetts [Phillips' 5th Massachusetts], "D" New York [Richardson's 1st New York Light.], and Stewart ["B" 4th U.S.] were on the left of the road to the Taylor house on open ground."[19]

Breck's, Mink's, and Cooper's batteries accompanied Cutler's 4th Division. Three other batteries—Barnes', Bigelow's, and Hart's—were unattached. In addition, three others—Rittenhouse's, Rogers', and Walcott's—were assigned to Brig. Gen. Ayres' 2nd Division on the left flank. Wainwright describes the deployment in considerable detail:

> June 18, at sunrise, Cutler's division advanced to the Avery house and the edge of the woods beyond. Breck's, Mink's, and Cooper's batteries were pushed forward with him and took position to the right of the woods along a ridge opening on the enemy's batteries and troops beyond the railroad. Soon after, Barnes', Bigelow's and Hart's batteries were brought up on the right of these and also opened. Meanwhile, Ayres' division, with Rittenhouse's, Rogers' and Walcott's batteries, passed around the left of Cutler and crossed the railroad. The three batteries went into position 900 yards in front of the great salient of the enemy's works and opened fire. Phillips', Stewart's, and Richardson's, were engaged in line with [Griffin's] 1st Division on the right of the [Baxter] road which crosses the railroad near the Taylor house, advancing as the infantry did until about 10 o'clock, when they had reached within 200 yards of the railroad and took a good position parallel to it, the right close to the above-mentioned dirt road, where they remained the remainder of the day.[20]

18 Lowe, *Meade's Army*, 213.

19 Nevins, *A Diary of Battle*, 424.

20 *OR* 40, pt. 1, 481-82.

The report of Captain Charles Appleton Phillips clarifies that Phillips', Stewart's, and Richardson's batteries remained left of the Baxter Road, advancing in line with Sweitzer's infantry brigade, which was advancing on the right of the road. Phillips' was the right battery of the three, and thus was closest to the Baxter Road:

> Griffin's division having been ordered to advance, Sweitzer's brigade was placed on the right of the road crossing the Norfolk and Petersburg Railroad and advanced across the railroad. The batteries of the division were placed on the left of the road, my own being the right battery, and advanced by battery evenly with Sweitzer's brigade. After advancing about 400 yards, we reached the crest of the ravine and remained there the rest of the day.[21]

Cooper's 1st Pennsylvania battery is a crucial point of reference. Wainwright locates it on a ridge at the edge of woods beyond and to the right of the Avery house, with at least six batteries farther to its right. Cooper's location can be even more precisely identified because an historic photograph of "Cooper's Battery in Front of Avery House" has survived, along with an accompanying description that links it to a position clearly marked on maps from the early days of the ensuing siege. This account was published in 1911:

> On the 18th our battery was advanced along with the corps to the position occupied by the battery in this photograph, and engaged the enemy in a battle on the afternoon of that day from the position occupied by the battery in this picture. . . . This position was occupied by us until possibly about the 23rd or the 24th of June, when we were taken farther to the left. The position shown in the picture is about 650 yards in front, and to the right of, the Avery House, and at or near this point was built a permanent fort or battery, which was used continuously during the entire siege of Petersburg— Battery XVII.[22]

Wainwright's *A Diary of Battle* explains that the six batteries not assigned to Griffin or Ayres were "strung along a farm road, and behind a hedge in front of the Avery house."[23]

---

21 Hewitt, ed., *Supplement to the Official Records*, 7, 277.

22 Henry Wysham Lanier, "Photographing the Civil War," in Albert Shaw, ed., *American Monthly Review of Reviews* (New York, 1911), vol. 43, 302-304.

23 Nevins, *A Diary of Battle*, 424.

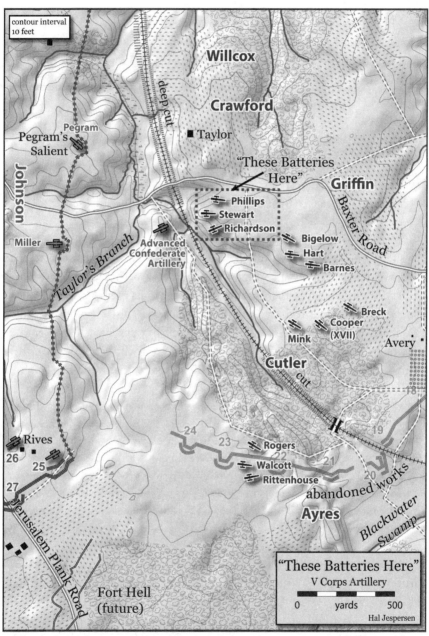

Chamberlain's first assignment was to protect artillery attached to Griffin's division (Phillips, Stewart, and Richardson) advancing south of the Baxter Road with Sweitzer's men north of it. The guns deployed 200 yards from the Deep Cut for the rest of the day. If Chamberlain moved left around Cutler and Ayres to the Jerusalem Plank Road, he violated his orders. (This map depicts the initial battery deployment. Many later moved, but all remained in the Taylor-Baxter Road vicinity. Mink ended up north of the Taylor ruins; Bigelow, Barnes, and Hart crossed the railroad, following Chamberlain's brigade.)

Therefore, on the morning of June 18, nine V Corps batteries were clustered between the Avery house and the Baxter Road. Three of these were positioned on open ground to the left of the Baxter Road, in close proximity to advanced enemy artillery placements, making them particularly vulnerable. They were the batteries assigned to the 1st Division—Phillips', Richardson's, and Stewart's. Griffin had been personally involved in their placement. Now they were at risk of being captured by a dash of enemy skirmishers from just across the "Deep Cut" of the railroad.

Griffin's orders to Colonel Chamberlain were to protect these three 1st Division batteries. In order for him to do this, it would be necessary for his brigade to remain near the Baxter Road.

The generally accepted scenario of Chamberlain's attack has him doing so along the Jerusalem Plank Road, his brigade moving south and west across a bridge over the railroad, probably just north of the Tatum property, near the old Confederate Battery 20, attacking toward Rives' Salient from the position soon to be occupied by Fort Sedgwick (or "Fort Hell"). In order for this to have happened, Chamberlain would have had to have marched one and one-half miles from a position north of the Baxter Road to the Jerusalem Plank Road via the Tatum farm. This, of course, would have taken Chamberlain far from his sphere of responsibility, and made it impossible for him to accomplish the task assigned to him by General Griffin. Would Chamberlain have gone so far out of his way to disobey orders?

The information available to us indicates that he did not do so. A study of Chamberlain's execution of Griffin's second order makes that point clear.

CHAPTER 5

OBJECTIVE TWO:
"Those Batteries Out There Must be Dislodged"

GENERAL Griffin's second discretionary order concerned the elimination of Confederate light artillery deployed in front of his division. Here is what Chamberlain wrote about this issue:

> Griffin and Warren rode up to me; Griffin spoke: "Those batteries out there must be dislodged. General Warren asks if you will do it. . . . We do not order it; we wish it, if it is possible to be done. But it is a hard push up that open slope."[1]

The obvious question raised by this discretionary order is the identity of the batteries General Griffin had in mind.

The guns to which Griffin referred comprised an advanced Confederate light artillery post positioned at close range on an open slope beyond, but near the "Deep Cut" of the Norfolk Railroad. This battery had been intentionally left behind during the Confederate withdrawal the previous night. Firing from higher ground and from a good location, the shells endangered Griffin's entire 1st Division. It is important to note that Griffin was not referring to the entrenched Confederate batteries located along the Harris Line. According to Chamberlain, "Morning came with enemy artillery at close range. . . . Soon our

---

1 Chamberlain, "The Charge at Fort Hell," 3, 4.

batteries were advanced to reply to those annoying us. . . . The enemy seemed now contemplating to take our guns by a dash."[2]

Chamberlain continued:

> When, on the evening of June 17, under the sharp attack of our II and IX corps, the enemy drew in the outer line of their defenses, they left on an outlying crest near the "Deep Cut" of the Norfolk Railroad, an advanced artillery post. . . . From this position on the 18th, they opened a strong slant fire on our division then drawn up for an assault in our immediate front north of the railroad.[3]

How did Chamberlain go about fulfilling his mandate to dislodge this advanced artillery post?

Moving forward behind Griffin's artillery batteries, Chamberlain sent his brigade to the left, parallel to the enemy's forward skirmish and artillery lines, under cover of a slight ridge and trees, toward the woods in front of the Avery farm. "I moved up close in rear of the guns, covering my men as I could by taking advantage of the ground. Many were falling, with no chance to strike back," recalled Chamberlain. "I rode up to my senior colonel and gave him orders to take the brigade to the left, not towards the enemy, but on a parallel line somewhat sheltered from the enemy's fire, and mostly from their sight, and *to gain a piece of woods on the right flank of the enemy's guns* [emphasis added] and wait for me."[4]

It is clear Chamberlain moved his brigade behind the V Corps artillery on a parallel line to the left, not toward the enemy. The movement took advantage of the ground and trees to shield the brigade from the enemy's fire and sight. This movement likely occurred behind a ridge on the plain between the Avery and Taylor farms. Griffin's three batteries were positioned there "in the open ground," wrote artillerist Wainwright, and another six batteries "were strung

---

2 Chamberlain, "The Charge at Fort Hell," 3.

3 Chamberlain, "Reminiscences of Petersburg and Appomattox," 170. Technically speaking, "slant fire" is when the artillery shot strikes the interior slope of a parapet, forming with it a horizontal angle not greater than thirty degrees. However, it can also be a reference to a difference in height between the artillery and its target, which would naturally affect the shell's trajectory. Chamberlain on June 18, 1864, was not behind a parapet, but the opposing advanced Rebel artillery post was on an elevated crest, and Chamberlain's brigade was lower than the enemy guns.

4 Chamberlain, "The Charge at Fort Hell," 3.

along a farm road, and behind a hedge to the front of the Avery house."[5] The objective of the movement was to gain a piece of woods to the left of the open plain, where the brigade would await Chamberlain's further orders.

Chamberlain, meanwhile, decided to make a personal reconnaissance. He recounted his experience in "The Charge at Fort Hell":

> Then I turned and gave rein to my horse, and headed straight for the rebel batteries. I had seen something, which looked not quite right, between us and the batteries; something I could not understand, looking, however like a line of rifle pits for infantry, in front of their guns. I wished to see what this was, and there was no way. I was not going to push my brave men up to it, and possibly have them annihilated there. I was riding, of course, at headlong speed. Soon I was aware of a tearing Tartar overtaking me, and rushing up to my side. "What in the name of Heaven are you going to do?" cries Griffin. "I am just going to look at that strange ground there" was the reply, without checking speed. "Then I am going with you," shouts Griffin.
>
> Meanwhile, the Rebels, seeing the strange embassy, had begun to burst shell right over our heads and almost in our faces. We were aware that people from both armies were looking on, astonished, not knowing what circus riding this was. "There, you see, General, what I feared. I was not going to put my men up here." It was a deep railroad cut, and earth thrown up high as a man's breast just below the range of the enemy's artillery. Their shot would skim the crest and mow men down like reaping machines. We both wheeled like a flash, with a half smile, strangely significant; he to his place with the center of his other brigades; I to my clump of woods, first taking a line to the rear, before bearing to my [division's] left where my brigade was crossing the railroad track at level grade. We followed a rough track up to the woods, and there formed in two lines, with two regiments as a flanking force to support me on the left.[6]

Several significant points surface in this detailed account. First, Griffin accompanied Chamberlain on the short reconnaissance. The commander would not have left his division to go on a long circuitous scout a mile to the left toward the Jerusalem Plank Road. Second, the two commanders headed straight for the Rebel batteries—not to the left. Third, the reconnaissance occurred on an open plain; people from both armies were able to look on,

---

5   Nevins, *A Diary of Battle,* 424. The road is depicted on the Gilmer Map running south from the Baxter Road past a barn. J. F. Gilmer, W. H. Stevens, C. H. Dimmock, "Map of the Approaches to Petersburg and their Defenses, 1863," Library of Congress.

6   Chamberlain, "The Charge at Fort Hell," 4.

which would have been impossible if Chamberlain was moving far to the left behind the woods in front of the Avery house. Fourth, Griffin wheeled and returned to his place at the center of his other brigades, which were apparently but a short gallop away. Lastly, the "strange ground" that had attracted Chamberlain's attention turned out to be a "deep railroad cut," which as we will see plays a key role in determining Chamberlain's location.

The "Deep Cut"

It is very important to fully understand the significance of the "Deep Cut." "Deep Cut," especially when preceded by the definite article "the," was a specific descriptor uniquely identifying the railroad cut in the area at and north of the Baxter Road crossing. It was used repeatedly as a landmark in the contemporaneous reports and regimental histories.

In describing the action of June 18, Major Roebling wrote about how General Cutler found the railroad running through a substantial cut as it turned sharply to the right near the Avery house, but he went on to mention another "very deep" cut near the bridge at the Norfolk Pike (Baxter Road) crossing. "After the men were got into it," penned the major, "it was hard to get them out again."[7] Thus, the proper designation "the deep cut" seems to refer specifically to this area around the Baxter Road Bridge.

The terrain near this cut north of the Baxter Road in 1864 consisted of cleared farmland. In contrast to the wooded area surrounding the shallower cut in front of the Avery property farther to the southeast, there were no trees at the Deep Cut north of the Baxter Road. This fits very well with Chamberlain's description: "The enemy's fire had an *unobstructed range over a clear slope of ground*, and *the deep cut* [emphasis added] between us forbade a straightaway rush."[8]

Thomas Parker, in his history of the 51st Pennsylvania, IX Corps (which would soon be stationed on the future site of Fort Morton north of the Baxter Road and opposite Pegram's Salient), estimated the depth of the Deep Cut at forty feet:

> The ground whereon the 51st rested was that occupied by Fort Morton a short time
> after. Between this line of pits and those of the rebels the railroad ran through a deep

---

7   Roebling, "Report of the Operations of the V Corps, Army of the Potomac," June 18, 1864.

8   Chamberlain, "Reminiscences of Petersburg and Appomattox," 171.

A modern photograph of the Deep Cut, north of the Baxter/Siege Road Bridge. *Author*

cut, forty feet deep, in the side of the hill, on which the regiment lay. The rebel works were on rather a more elevated position, with a deep and ugly ravine between the two lines. A creek ran through this ravine on the side nearest to the enemy. . . . The regiment, not knowing anything of this deep railroad cut, charged down to the very brink of it before they saw it, but having such headway on from running down the hill, they could not stop in time, and went headlong down the precipice before they came to a full stop, the enemy pouring volleys of grape and canister into their ranks, besides their whole line of musketry had full play at the same time on them. After reaching the bottom of the cut they could not get out, on account of the high perpendicular walls of earth on each side of the track.[9]

Private Henry Fitzgerald Charles of the 21st Pennsylvania Cavalry, fighting with Colonel Jacob B. Sweitzer's 2nd Brigade of Griffin's division near the Taylor property, estimated the cut there was about twenty feet deep:

> Soon we got on a little hill and got orders to charge down and take a deep cut of railroad. We started and took the cut but while going down, some of us had to go thru where some buildings were burned down. There was still plenty of fire and hot ashes and I got some fire in my shoes. My one foot was burned considerable but I did not dare to stop to take the fire out as they were feeding us plenty of grape and canister all around. We took the cut; it was about twenty feet deep, and the boys went down pell-mell and quite a number got hurt by the fellow's bayonet behind him. I stopped on top of the bank till they were straightened out and then I started out; just as I left the place, a shell struck and exploded everything to tinder. Had I stayed a minute longer, a

V Corps troops in the Deep Cut six weeks later, at the time of the explosion of Burnside's mine, as depicted in "The Siege of Petersburg—the Fifth Corps awaiting the order to advance, July 30th, 1864." *Frank Leslie's Illustrated History of the Civil War*

9   Thomas H. Parker, *History of the 51st Pennsylvania Volunteers* (Philadelphia, 1869), 564-5.

few grease spots would have [been] all that remained of me. My guarding Angel must have been protecting me all thru or I wouldn't be here now.[10]

Having discovered this significant impediment to his own direct forward progress, Chamberlain made a hasty retreat: "I [wheeled] to my clump of woods [which was nearby], first taking a line to the rear before bearing to my left where my brigade was crossing the railroad track *at level grade*."[11]

Note that Chamberlain's movement is first on a line to the rear, traveling east and away from the railroad cut. He is still with his division (and not off to the south near the Jerusalem Plank Road). Then there is some apparent confusion in his terminology. When he says that he moved to his left as he was riding away from the cut, he apparently meant to his own right, toward the south, which was toward the left of the Union advance, and to the left of Griffin's 1st Division line; Sweitzer was advancing on the right.

After this short gallop, Chamberlain found his brigade crossing the railroad track at level grade in or behind a clump of woods. This would have occurred just below the end of the Deep Cut, south of the Baxter Road and probably near the future site of Fort Meikle. The other cut, in front of the Avery house, where the track diverged away from the Confederate lines, was itself surrounded by woods. It was not on a "clear slope of ground." In order to get beyond that cut, Chamberlain's crossing "at level grade" would necessarily have been even farther south of the Avery property near the future Military Railroad. In that area there was no surrounding clump of woods. Thus, the terrain at the alternative cut and flat crossing does not fit Chamberlain's description. Further, Cutler and Ayres were operating in that sector.

Therefore, with the clear ground and the Deep Cut north of the Baxter Road prohibiting a straightaway rush, Chamberlain first moves his brigade left. After crossing the track in a flat area, he formed for battle in the relative concealment of the woods, planning to sneak up on the enemy, if possible. The brigade's leftward movement is then reversed, as it shifts back to the right, emerging from the woods to rush the right flank of the advanced Rebel light artillery battery on the treeless open slope on the west side of the railroad near the Deep Cut. Chamberlain accomplished his objective through a diversion around the obstacle that was the Deep Cut:

10 John Neitz, "The Civil War Diary of Henry Fitzgerald Charles" (1969, 2000), 8.

11 Chamberlain, "The Charge at Fort Hell," 5.

We followed a rough track up to the woods and there formed in two lines, with two regiments as a flanking force to support me on the left.

We were to advance as noiselessly as possible through the woods and on emerging, fire there a volley & make a rush upon the flank of the rebel guns, and overwhelm them if possible before they could recover their wits. The second line was to follow the first at a distance of 100 yards, till their line came to join with the first or replace it.

We made for the guns [to Chamberlain's right—they were flanking the Confederate battery's right]. Then a burst of artillery fire turned upon us with terrible effect. Down went my horse under me, a piece of case shot going through him; down went every one of my staff, wounded or unhorsed; down went my red Maltese cross, flag of our brigade; but on went everybody, on for the guns.[12]

Patrick DeLacy of the 143rd Pennsylvania, who would be awarded the Medal of Honor later in the war, wrote a letter to Joshua Chamberlain on December 28, 1903, two months after the general's presentation of his "Reminiscences" speech to the Maine MOLLUS assembly.[13] In that letter, DeLacy begged forgiveness for his tardiness in forwarding his recollections of the charge on June 18, 1864, explaining that he had wanted to be as accurate as possible in his accounting of events. Since he was writing thirty-eight years after the fact, it is obvious Chamberlain had solicited information from DeLacy, and had been hoping to use it in preparing his comments for the MOLLUS delivery.

In his handwritten letter, DeLacy referred to an enclosed typewritten report in which he recounted his recollections of that day. The typewritten report survives as an undated manuscript preserved in the Library of Congress. The 1903 date can be deduced from the obvious reference to it in DeLacy's letter, and from the handwritten postscript beneath the signature, in which DeLacy mentioned his tenure as President of the 143rd Regiment Association "for the past 38 years."

DeLacy's account is an important source of descriptive detail regarding the events of June 18:

---

12 Chamberlain, "The Charge at Fort Hell," 5.

13 Patrick DeLacy to General Joshua L. Chamberlain, December 28, 1903, in Joshua Lawrence Chamberlain Papers, Box 3, Library of Congress, 782-83.

In a few moments after this, you [Colonel Chamberlain] moved us to the left along and across the Norfolk Railroad, which I think was the name of the railroad, and into a woods, where the enemy soon found the range, and you were dismounted by a shell killing your horse and also killing three men and wounding seven others.[14]

Now, going back to the time your horse was killed, you moved us to the right, out of these woods, half wheeling the regiment first to the right, then to the left and forward so that the ridge in our immediate front protected us considerably from the artillery firing of the enemy until you had the front of the brigade well on to the top of this high ridge where an old rail fence ran along, with considerable brush and briars, which obscured our line to some extent from the enemy, and we laid down waiting for the order to charge.[15]

DeLacy makes it clear the direction of the march was first along and then across the railroad and then into the woods. The formation is in two lines with a flanking force on the left. The enemy's artillery detected and successfully targeted the brigade in the woods and killed Chamberlain's horse from beneath him. Chamberlain half-wheeled the regiment, first to the right then to the left and forward, shifting it to the right to move it out of the woods while still facing the enemy.

The assault was a success, the advanced Confederate light artillery battery dislodged, and a piece of high ground gained west of the railroad. According to Chamberlain:

The batteries limbered up and got off down the slope under cover of their main entrenchments [on the Harris line]. . . . We only got their ground, and drove away the guns. . . . The enfilading fire was so heavy we had to get a little below the crest we had carried and prepare to hold it against attempts to recover it.[16]

By a pardonable ruse of occupying their attention, we crossed the railroad south of the cut, gained a clump of woods on the flank of their guns, and by a sharp and hot, but short, encounter, realized our commander's wish. We carried everything. But we

---

14 Patrick DeLacy to General Joshua L. Chamberlain (typewritten), December 28, 1903, in Joshua Lawrence Chamberlain Papers, Box 4, "Reminiscences to Chamberlain," Library of Congress, 3.

15 DeLacy, "Reminiscences to Chamberlain," 3.

16 Chamberlain, "The Charge at Fort Hell," 5.

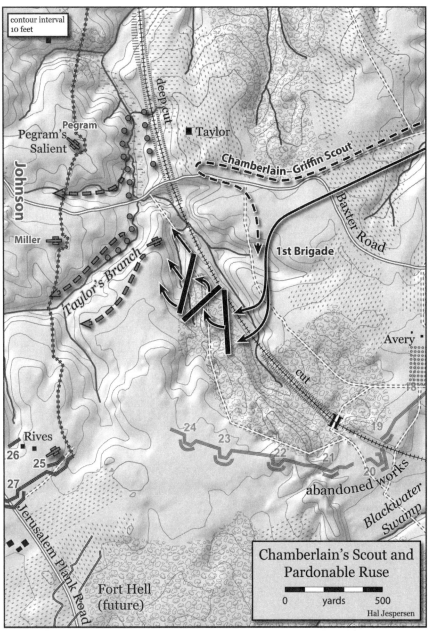

After personally scouting the Deep Cut on horseback with General Griffin (shown here by the dashed line), Chamberlain undertook a deceptive strategy. He would bypass the cut by moving his brigade to the left under the cover of trees and low terrain, then cross the track on flatter ground and maneuver through the woods back toward the right, with the goal of storming the battery on the crest by surprise. The gray dots and dashes indicate retreating Confederate skirmishers and artillery.

found it a more perilous place to hold than to carry, for we were greeted by a storm of shot and shell from the enemy's main works at the salient, under which we should lose more men than we did in carrying the position. I therefore drew the men back to gain the shelter of the crest.[17]

The captured position was the crest from which the advanced battery of enemy guns had been directing a slant fire against Griffin's batteries and the 1st Division from west of the railroad cut. Chamberlain's brigade awaited further orders sheltered behind the crest. Bigelow's battery would later ascend it about 4:00 p.m. after trotting 220 yards down a farm road. (It is important to keep in mind that the major assault on the entrenched Harris Line is still in the future.)

Chamberlain has successfully accomplished his objective of dislodging a Confederate skirmish line and an advanced light artillery battery just west of the Deep Cut of the Norfolk Railroad near the Baxter Road crossing. He achieved his goal by the ruse of moving around the right flank of the enemy position to drive the battery away. He will now take shelter behind the crest, awaiting further orders. Chamberlain had one more order left to obey: attacking the Confederate lines stretching in front of Griffin's 1st Division.

This task was at the core of what happened to Chamberlain on June 18, history's telling of it, and my own search for the truth of what happened that day.

17 Chamberlain, "Reminiscences of Petersburg and Appomattox," 171.

Chapter 6

Objective Three:
"Attack and Carry the Works in Your Front"

GENERAL Griffin's third order to Chamberlain had the most impact on the day's events. From Chamberlain's pen:

> A staff officer came out and gave me the order, "The general commanding desires you to attack and carry the works in your front." [Chamberlain replied] "They are the interior works, the main works at Petersburg, and am I to attack alone?"[1]

Author Diane Smith interpreted Chamberlain's phrase to mean he was to attack and carry the heavy permanent Dimmock Line fortifications. This would require transporting Chamberlain's 1st Brigade away from the Baxter Road area and the rest of Griffin's division down to Rives' Salient and the Jerusalem Plank Road, and perhaps even to the left of Cutler's and Ayres' divisions. In attacking there, alone and isolated from its division, the 1st Brigade encounters a formidable opponent of epic stature. "Rives' Salient was the point at which the new Rebel line joined the formidable fortifications of the original Dimmock Line," explained Smith, who continued:

> Chamberlain's position was roughly one third of a mile forward of the area where Fort Sedgwick would be constructed during the ensuing siege. This said fort soon earned

---

1 Chamberlain, "The Charge at Fort Hell," 6.

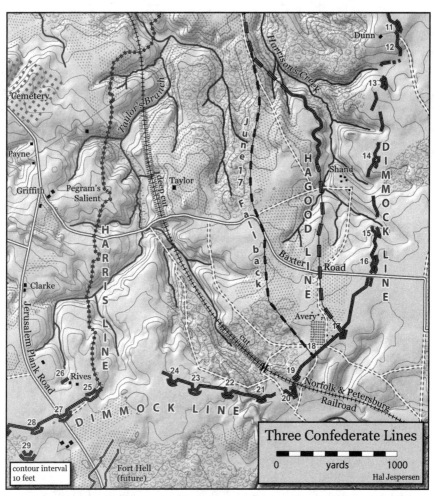

On June 15, 1864, Brigadier General William "Baldy" Smith's XVIII Corps swept over the Rebel earthworks on a 3.5-mile section of the eastern front of Petersburg's outer line of defenses, capturing Batteries 3 and 5–11 and prompting a Confederate retreat to a weaker defensive line along Harrison's Creek (known as the Hagood Line). As additional corps of Union troops continued to concentrate strength and press their attacks, General P. G. T. Beauregard's relatively small contingent of Confederate defenders fell back, first to a line along the eastern face of woodlots to the north and south of the Baxter Road on June 17, and finally, during the early morning hours of June 18, to an inner line west of Taylor's Branch laid out by Col. D. B. Harris, the chief engineer of Beauregard's army. The Harris Line would become the permanent Confederate position on the eastern front throughout the ensuing siege.

the name "Fort Hell." Thus, the 1st Brigade's fate was the same as that of the units to its left, Cutler's 4th Division and Ayres' 2nd Division. They had the unenviable positions as the only Army of the Potomac attackers on June 18 that assaulted the formidable works the Rebels had completed in 1863. And, by the time Chamberlain, Cutler, and Ayres made their mid-afternoon attack on the Rebel fortification, the enemy's parapets and artillery were fully manned by newly arrived elements of the Army of Northern Virginia.[2]

Chamberlain's use of the term "interior works," however, does not demand this extreme interpretation. Colonel Wainwright, commanding the Union V Corps artillery, and General William N. Pendleton, commanding the Confederate artillery, refer respectively to an "inner line" and to an "interior line" that had been hastily thrown up by the retreating forces commanded by General P. G. T. Beauregard. The line, which was incomplete on June 18, extended south from the Appomattox River via Hare House and Blandford Cemetery. It terminated at the Rives house. General Lee, explained Wainwright, "was putting up an *inner line* of works, and not having them finished this morning, fought us pretty stiffly all the way back."[3]

General Pendleton described this part of the line as follows:

General Beauregard having with his limited force on the 17th engaged the enemy in very large numbers on the east of Petersburg, and maintained the same contest, unequal as it was, so successfully as to preserve the city, found himself however, unable to hold the extended outer line of works on that side, and therefore during the night fell back to an *interior line* extending from the Appomattox in a direction between the Hare house and Blandford Cemetery to the Rives' house. This new line [was] selected mainly by the lamented Col. D. B. Harris.[4]

Chamberlain did indeed face a daunting challenge. Having captured a crest on the west side of the Norfolk Railroad, which had been occupied by Confederate light artillery and skirmishers, Chamberlain was now being asked to assault the breastworks of an enemy dug in for a "last-ditch" effort to defend Petersburg. However, the task was no more demanding than that assigned to any of the other Union brigades or divisions attacking along the newly

2   Smith, *Chamberlain at Petersburg*, 54.

3   Nevins, *A Diary of Battle*, 424.

4   *OR* 40, pt. 1, 755.

entrenched Harris line. With this understanding, there is no geographical constraint demanding that Chamberlain's brigade travel south and west nearly a mile toward Rives' Salient in order to assault the permanent Dimmock fortifications.

The Launching Point

What was the launching point for this Chamberlain attack? In "Lines before Petersburg, June 18, 1864," the Maine officer wrote the following:

> I am advanced a mile beyond our own lines and in an isolated position. On my right a deep railroad cut; my left flank in the air, with no support whatever. In my front at close range is a strongly entrenched line of infantry and artillery, with projecting salients right and left, such that my advance would be swept by a crossfire, while a large fort to my left enfilades my entire advance. . . . In the hollow along my front close to the enemy's works, appears to be bad ground, swampy, boggy.[5]

Chamberlain's account, as set forth in the previous chapter, described his moving left along the railroad to a flat area south of the Deep Cut, where he crossed, "wheeled his brigade to the right and attacked the artillery outpost on its right flank, occupying its position on a crest west of the railroad. The right flank of Chamberlain's brigade was now on the opposite side of the "deep cut" itself. Chamberlain estimated the distance of the enemy works at "not less than 300 yards from this point," the same distance specified by Thomas Chamberlain in his history of the 150th Pennsylvania.[6] Proximity of his right flank to the Deep Cut and proximity to the Rebel lines are two key points in determining the location of this action.

The Deep Cut ended just south of the Baxter Road crossing. This is the same cut that Chamberlain had scouted with Griffin while riding across an open plain. In order to have his right flank positioned on this cut, he must necessarily have been situated behind a crest at the approximate site of the future Fort Meikle, or to its right, where the enemy works would indeed be several hundred yards to his front ("at close range").

5   Chamberlain, "Lines Before Petersburg, June 18, 1864.

6   Chamberlain, "The Charge at Fort Hell," 6; Thomas Chamberlain, *History of the One-hundred and fiftieth regiment, Pennsylvania Volunteers* (Philadelphia, 1905), 261; DeLacy, "Reminiscences to Chamberlain," 4, of the 143rd Pennsylvania, estimated the distance as 400-500 yards.

The alternate scenario promoted by author Smith and others demands that the 1st Brigade's right flank was on the second cut in the woods to the south of the Avery house, with its left extending across the captured permanent Confederate Dimmock fortifications between Batteries 20 and 22. In this location, the brigade would have been situated behind Ayres' division and several hundred yards behind the batteries of Rittenhouse, Rodgers, and Walcott, which themselves were 900 yards from Rives' Salient.[7] No one would describe this as "close range." In no case could Chamberlain's brigade be assaulting from the future site of Fort Sedgwick, near the Jerusalem Plank Road, where there is no proximity to the railroad whatsoever.

Chamberlain also describes a hollow along his front, close to the enemy's works, that he described as "swampy, boggy." Multiple tributaries of Taylor's Branch are to the right of the future site of Fort Meikle. Note that there is no swampy ground of any kind south of Rives' Salient on the divide between the Taylor's Branch and Blackwater Creek watersheds.

Two Ravines

Beginning on the brow of a slight elevation 300 yards from the Rebel forts, Thomas Chamberlain described the subsequent advance of the 150th Pennsylvania, part of Colonel Chamberlain's 1st Brigade, across a little hill separating two ravines moving toward the base of the formidable earthwork that was subsequently blown up by General Burnside's famous mine. Here is Thomas Chamberlain's description:

> To the 150th naturally fell the duty of leading the way as skirmishers for the brigade, and Major Jones was ordered at a given signal—the firing of a certain battery—to move rapidly across the first ravine in front to the brow of a rising ground beyond, from which—if the supporting lines followed closely and in good order—he was to advance precipitously across a second ravine and press on until he struck the rebel works. These were to be carried, if possible; or, if that could not be accomplished, the nearest elevation was to be held and fortified. At the signal—which was given about four p.m.—Major Jones's command sprang nimbly through the hollow to the summit of the little hill, and seeing the long line of the 187th Pennsylvania following in admirable array, with the other supports close upon their heels, dashed swiftly into the second ravine and up its farther slope to the very base of the formidable earthwork

7 OR 40, pt. 1, 481-82.

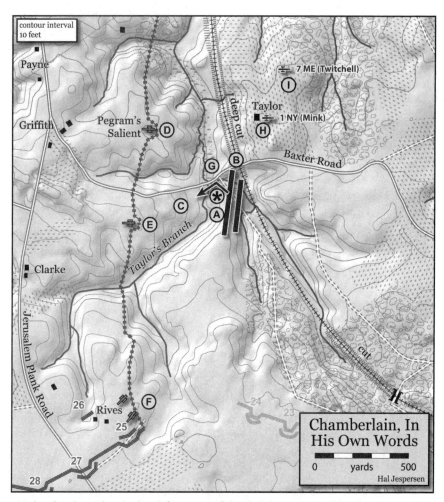

Colonel Joshua Chamberlain left a series of detailed descriptions of his location on the battlefield on June 18, 1864, in several of his personal accounts:

A. "on an outlying crest"; "drew the men back to gain the shelter of the crest." (RPA 170-71)
B. "on my right, a deep railroad cut." (LBP)
C. "I must advance not less than 300 yards from this point." (CFH 6)
D-E. "projecting salients right (D) and left (E)" (LBP)
F. "a large fort to my left enfilades my entire advance." (LBP)
G. "in the hollow along my front . . . bad ground, boggy, swampy. (LBP)
H. "Mink was across the railroad cut firing into the ice house to my right front." (CFH 5)
I. "Twitchell . . . grimly bastioning the slopes above." (POA 338)
Circled Star: "on the borders of a marsh or bog . . . I made a half face to the left and gave the command, 'Incline to the left.'" . . . I felt a sharp hot flush." (CFH 10-11)

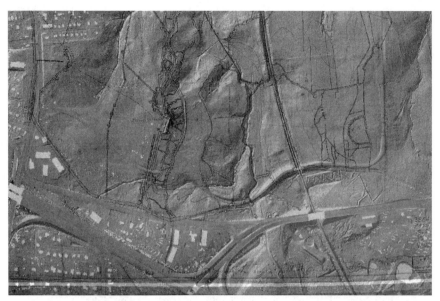

This is the 1865 "Manuscript Michler" map superimposed on a modern LIDAR map showing the peninsula between two branches of Taylor's Creek in front of the Horseshoe, and the Deep Cut of the railroad north of the Baxter Road bridge. "Map of defenses of Petersburg, Virginia, showing the position of General Lee and his staff during the attack on Fort Stedman, March 25, 1865," Library of Congress, Geography and Map Division (#99446547). The LIDAR map is courtesy of the Petersburg National Battlefield.

which was subsequently blown up by Burnside's famous mine. During this time the enemy was not idle. The forts and connecting intrenchments were strongly manned, and from every point dominating the scene of the assault came shot and shell and rattling grape and canister, coupled with a murderous fire of musketry, against which no troops could make an effective stand. While the 150th escaped with comparatively little loss in passing the last ravine, owing to its formation as skirmishers, no sooner had the 187th and the succeeding line of smaller regiments gained the top of the rising ground, already mentioned, than they began to melt away under the merciless storm of iron and lead.[8]

Based upon this account, the direction of the 1st Brigade's assault could only have been northwest, in the direction of the fortified position at Pegram's

8   Thomas Chamberlain, *History of the One-hundred and fiftieth regiment, Pennsylvania Volunteers* (Open Library version), 213, 214.

(or Elliott's) Salient, and the movement was across a little crest or ridge between two ravines of Taylor's Branch.

This description also matches the place I had been searching for on my first visit to the National Battlefield at Petersburg—the spot where "Griffin's division struck with more élan," as "Sweitzer's and Chamberlain's blue clads stormed across the ridge separating the two branches of Poor Creek [Taylor's Branch]."[9] The location has to be near the Baxter Road.

Furthermore, Thomas Chamberlain, quoting Sergeant Frey, reveals that Colonel Chamberlain's brigade mounted two separate assaults in its effort to capture the Rebel works on June 18, the second commencing at 6:00 p.m.—the very time of Sweitzer's third assault:

> We are now ordered to fall back to the foot of the hill, and slide back to avoid the bullets as much as possible. We lay at this place all afternoon under a hot June sun, exposed to a constant fire of shot and shell and Minié balls. At six in the evening the corps was formed for a last charge to carry the enemy's works and capture Petersburg, and we were moved a short distance to the right, behind a high bluff, in front of which was one of the enemy's forts with earthworks stretching to the right and left connecting with other forts in the line of defense. The fort in our front was the same that was blown up some time afterwards.[10]

Several features speak against a Rives' Salient location for this attack. The most obvious is the unambiguous allusion to Pegram's Salient, the future site of the Crater. In addition, one must consider the odds that a 1st Brigade regiment would be mounting a second assault at 6:00 p.m., the precise time of Sweitzer's attack, had it been operating independently, without their fallen brigade commander (Chamberlain was by this time wounded), from an isolated position near the Jerusalem Plank Road in front of Rives' Salient. Such a scenario is unlikely, at best. Instead, the evidence strongly points to participation by one regiment of Chamberlain's brigade in the evening assault by Sweitzer's brigade near the Baxter Road.

Any discussion of Chamberlain's attack needs to address Federal artillery support that was provided. The artillery's activities, especially its positioning on the field, provides additional evidence of where Chamberlain attacked.

9 Bearss and Suderow, *The Petersburg Campaign: The Eastern Battlefields*, 125-26.

10 Thomas Chamberlain, *History of the One-hundred and fiftieth regiment, Pennsylvania Volunteers* (Google Books version), 262.

CHAPTER 7

WHERE WERE THE GUNS?
Chamberlain's Artillery Support

ONE of Chamberlain's command decisions called for artillery support. "I saw that we could use artillery to advantage," he explained. "I sent back to Griffin or Warren, a mile, I should think— for some artillery.[1] Before long," he continued, "up came Bigelow and Hart, followed by Barnes. Mink was across the railroad cut firing into the icehouse to my right front.[2]

Bigelow's 9th Massachusetts Battery

Captain John Bigelow's 9th Massachusetts battery, which had played such a prominent role on July 2, 1863, at Gettysburg, advanced along the Baxter Road that morning, and continued forward behind the brigades of Chamberlain and Hofmann in the early afternoon. Bigelow's official report of the day is

1   Based on this statement and her interpretive paradigm, Diane Smith concluded that the rest of the Army of the Potomac was at least a mile north of Chamberlain's brigade when he was planning his attack. Smith, *Chamberlain at Petersburg*, 55. However, the reference to Griffin and Warren's headquarters at the Avery house being "back" a mile could just as well (and more plausibly) indicate its location a mile to Chamberlain's *rear*, or the *east* of his position.

2   Chamberlain, "The Charge at Fort Hell," 5. The three batteries specifically assigned to Griffin's 1st Division in the June 5 reorganization (Phillips', Stewart's, and Richardson's) remained on the east side of the railroad throughout the day. However, reserve artillery firepower was available to Chamberlain on the west side of the railroad with the arrival of the unattached batteries of Captains Bigelow, Hart and Barnes.

well-written and provides insight about the issue under discussion, namely, where did Chamberlain attack at Petersburg? Here is the portion of Bigelow's report that is pertinent to our discussion:

> June 18. Accompanied the corps in its advance and was first engaged with the enemy from the Baxter Road. Afterwards, followed the charge of the line in the afternoon, in the rear of Chamberlain's brigade, 1st Division, and Hofmann's brigade, 4th Division, to within 400 yards of the enemy's line as they advanced. Retained the position after the line withdrew. Occupied it June 19 and 20, each day being engaged with the enemy.[3]

Bigelow clearly notes that his battery simultaneously followed the advance of Chamberlain's brigade on the left of the 1st Division, and Hofmann's brigade on the right of the 4th Division. This could not have been possible if Chamberlain detoured far to the left flank of the V Corps, moving behind the 4th Division and Ayres' 2nd Division. If he had done that, then the only way to interpret Bigelow's report is that Hofmann and Bigelow accompanied Chamberlain there. There is absolutely no evidence that this ever happened.

Levi Wood Baker's *History of the 9th Massachusetts Battery* provides additional detail, found in a quote from artilleryman George Mader:

> Noon brought us an hour's rest. We had moved close to the line of action across the Norfolk Railroad; the roadbed was a deep cut, crossed by a wooden, rough-looking bridge. This bridge we crossed, to halt immediately upon the other side. . . . I passed a few remarks about the railroad alongside of which we were resting.[4]

Baker's account continues with the recollections of Captain Bigelow, 24 years after the event:

> June 18 finds us before Petersburg. . . . We were ordered to the left and to take position on a road running southeast from Petersburg—the Suffolk Plank Road [Baxter Road] . . . We only used sixteen rounds, when we were ordered to another position. We crossed the Norfolk Railroad on a bridge covered with poles [the bridge had burned

---

3   John Bigelow, Ninth Massachusetts Artillery Report of Operations from June 13-July 30, 1864, in Hewitt, ed., *OR Supplement*, 7, Addendum Reports, OR 40, pt. 1, 229.

4   Levi W. Baker, *History of the Ninth Massachusetts Battery* (South Framingham, MA, 1888), 123-24.

earlier in the morning], and halted in a place that was swept by the enemy's guns; soon countermarched, and lay behind a slight ridge till 4:00 p.m., when we are ordered in again. Three batteries start, one halts, and only the 9th Massachusetts and 15th New York, Capt. Hart, go in. We trot down a wood road one eighth of a mile that was swept by a fire of musketry, down a slope, through a ravine, up another slope going in battery before we reach the summit, and running our guns by hand to the front, until our range is clear. We open immediately and vigorously, firing as fast as possible. The infantry are swarming back through our line, and it looks like a repulse.

You will recall we followed General Chamberlain's charge on the gallop up the hill. We stopped at the crest, about on a line and 300 yards from the enemy's works; we fired across an intervening depression. As General Chamberlain charged across this in order to reach their line of works opposite us, they received a raking fire from a masked battery in a clump of trees. Some of them became demoralized and fell back; many came in through our [9th Massachusetts] battery. I tried to find out from the stragglers whether any infantry remained in our front to protect us against a counter charge, as the railroad cut in our rear prevented our getting away.[5]

It is clear from this information that Bigelow's 9th Massachusetts Battery advanced along the Baxter Road and then crossed the railroad on a hastily reconstructed wooden bridge covered with rough poles at a Deep Cut. The logical question, then, is which bridge did Bigelow use to cross his battery?

There are two, or perhaps three, possibilities. At the Baxter Road itself, the ground surrounding the bridge was clear. There was no tree cover along this portion of the Baxter Road, and there were no intervening crests between the position and the main Confederate line. At the curve of track along the shallower cut west of the Avery farm, on the other hand, where Cutler's men had been working through the morning to rebuild a bridge for the crossing of artillery, there was a thick patch of forest to shield the position from enemy sight and hostile fire. There were also intervening slopes protecting the ground, which would become the site for Union entrenchments and artillery placements of a more permanent nature in the weeks and months to follow.

When Bigelow found himself in a place "swept by the enemy's guns" on the west side of the bridge, he ordered a countermarch behind a slight ridge, which suggests he most likely crossed the Deep Cut at the Baxter Road. There, after stopping to rest alongside the railroad behind a ridge for an hour or two, the artillery battery trotted about 220 yards down a farm road before its men ran

5 Baker, *History of the Ninth Massachusetts Battery*, 125-27.

their guns by hand up a slope to a summit about 300 yards from the enemy's works. This position was close to the railroad cut, which later prevented their retreat in the repulse that followed.

The distances here are crucial. Given that the railroad bed diverges from the Confederate line as it moves southward, there is no way the batteries could have moved 220 yards (about 1/8th of a mile) from either of the lower bridges to arrive at a summit just 300 yards from the enemy's works.

Whether Bigelow's movement was toward the south from the Baxter Road crossing, as strongly suggested by his own account, or northward from the bridge repaired by Cutler's 4th Division infantry, the crest to the right of the future Fort Meikle location appears to be the only site on the battlefield that simultaneously meets all of the required conditions. It is certain that no terrain fits the description anywhere near Rives' Salient far to the left.

Chamberlain's own contemporaneous report in the "Lines before Petersburg" confirms his supporting artillery's proximity to the deep railroad cut:

> I have got up three batteries and am placing them on the reverse slope of this crest to enable me to hold against expected attack. To leave these guns behind me unsupported, their retreat cut off by the railroad cut, would expose them to loss in case of our repulse.[6]

Mink's 1st New York Battery H

In "The Charge at Fort Hell," Chamberlain also mentions that Captain Mink's Battery H, 1st New York Light Artillery was on the opposite (east) side of the railroad cut firing into an icehouse on his right front.[7] Mink had moved to the right of the Taylor house, north of the Baxter Road, at noon. Augustus Buell, chronicled the history of artillery units of the Army of the Potomac in *The Cannoneer*:

> Having gained the railroad along the whole front of the V Corps, about noon the 2nd and 4th Divisions, with a portion of the 1st, being established beyond it, Mink's Battery was moved to the edge of this cut, to the right of the Taylor House, engaged

---

6   Chamberlain, "Lines Before Petersburg, June 18, 1864."

7   Chamberlain, "The Charge at Fort Hell," 5.

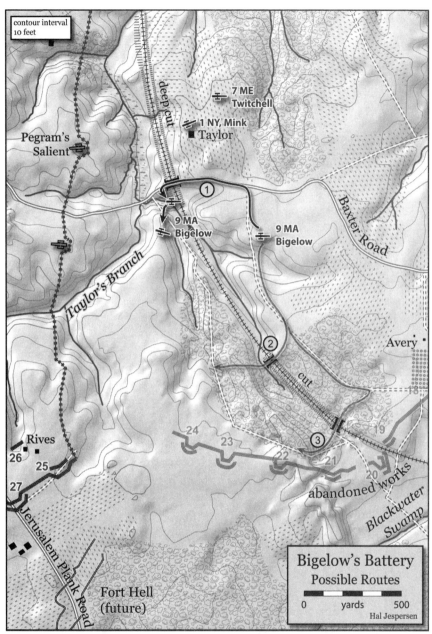

Captain John Bigelow's 9th Massachusetts battery supported Chamberlain's mid-afternoon assault. The battery crossed the Norfolk Railroad on a bridge. This map shows the only three potential bridge crossings. As readers will determine once they finish this chapter, only one span matches the historical description. None of the potential routes allow for an approach near the Jerusalem Plank Road and Rives' Salient.

two of the enemy's guns immediately in his front at 500 yards and kept them silent nearly all the time. Bigelow's and Hart's Batteries were taken across the railroad and halted behind the crest with Chamberlain's brigade of Griffin's division, while slight lunettes were being thrown up on the crest held by our skirmish line. At 3 to 4 p. m., when the general attack was made, these batteries were shoved up on the crest and opened on the enemy's works as our troops passed down into the intervening ravine. Barnes's Battery was soon after brought over and posted about 75 yards to the left of the others. The attack failing, the batteries covered the withdrawal of our troops. The position held by Mink's, Bigelow's and Hart's Batteries was within easy canister and musketry range of the enemy's works, and all suffered severely. Their practice was excellent, and reflected great credit on their officers and men. After dark Barnes, Bigelow and Hart were withdrawn. After June 19, Mink's Battery remained in position near the Taylor House until the morning of June 24.[8]

Captain Mink's report on this action supports Buell's *Cannoneer* account:

June 18, engaged the enemy before Petersburg, Va., advancing by battery with the other batteries of the brigade under fire of the enemy's artillery. At 4:00 p.m. we threw up lunettes and placed the battery in position on the right of the V Corps nearly opposite the reservoir; fired a number of shots into the enemy's works, cutting down their work around two of their guns in such manner as to give our sharpshooters command of their pieces.[9]

Clearly Chamberlain places Mink on his right flank, close enough to positively affect his advance. Mink was to the right of the Taylor house, north of the Baxter Road, engaging guns (most likely at Pegram's Salient) 500 yards to his front. Mink's own report places him on the right of the V Corps (and not on its far left, at Rives' Salient). Mink was nearly opposite the reservoir, which was west of the Blandford Cemetery. This may be even farther to the right than the location of the Taylor House. Mink's, Bigelow's, and Hart's batteries were somewhat grouped, all being within range of canister and musketry of the same enemy's works to Chamberlain's front. This line of evidence overwhelmingly indicates that Chamberlain's brigade was near the Baxter Road, not Rives' Salient, when he was planning his infantry assault.

8   Augustus C. Buell, *The Cannoneer: Recollections of Service in the Army of the Potomac* (Washington, DC, 1890), 232.

9   *OR* 40, pt. 1, 488.

The Icehouse

Chamberlain's reference to an icehouse on his "right front" is very significant. There are multiple references to an icehouse near the Baxter Road, but none in the vicinity of Rives' Salient.

Lieutenant William Lapham, Twitchell's battery, IX Corps, noted that there was a large and well-filled icehouse at the Taylor plantation, which apparently had served as a hotel before the Confederates burned it down:

> On the 23rd [of June], our division moved to the left and our battery took a position near the Taylor House. . . . The Taylor House near which we were stationed, had formerly been a hotel, but when we went into position, the buildings had been burned. . . . There was a large and well filled icehouse, and when we made our advance, this icehouse was between our lines near where our corps joined the Fifth. It was a treasure worth contending for, and one day after quite a skirmish, in which we lost several men, we succeeded in bringing it within our picket line. This ice lasted us nearly two weeks, the two corps sharing it alike. A portion of it was taken to the hospitals. So vexed were the Johnnies at its loss that they fired upon everyone who approached it.[10]

Lapham placed the house of ice near the juncture of the IX and V Corps lines, after both corps had moved toward the left in the days following the attack of June 18. A Michler map places this juncture of the V and IX Corps lines at the Baxter Road. Captain Twitchell's report of the position of his IX Corps artillery battery on July 9 also locates the left section on the front line across the railroad and near the icehouse.[11] This is consistent with Chamberlain's description of an icehouse situated on his right front after he had crossed the railroad.

Lieutenant Colonel Albert Monroe, the IX Corps' chief of artillery, wrote about the action that would transpire six weeks later in front of the Crater. In it, he described the locations of three sections of Twitchell's battery, one of which was to the left of a landmark icehouse:

---

10 William Berry Lapham, *My Recollections of the War of the Rebellion* (Augusta, ME, 1892), 132-33.

11 *OR* 40, pt. 1, 603.

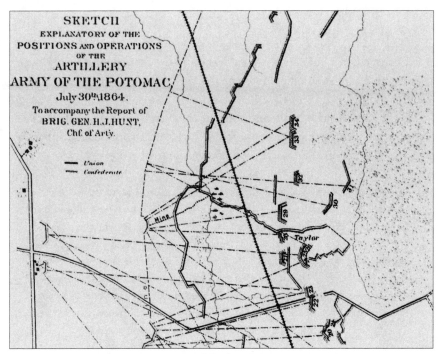

Twitchell's Battery 23, to the left of the Icehouse on July 30, 1864. *CW Atlas*

Twitchell's (Seventh Maine) battery, one section on the front line to the left of the icehouse bearing upon the ravine in front of the Third Division, one gun to the left of the Taylor house bearing upon the Petersburg road, and one at the right of the house.[12]

The three redoubts occupied by elements of Twitchell's battery (23, 27, and 28), are marked on Plate 64, "Batteries in Position before Petersburg Virginia on July 30, 1864," in the *Official Military Atlas of Civil War*. From Monroe's written description, the section situated left of the icehouse corresponds with Redoubt 23 on the map. The icehouse, if it was located to the right of this position, would have been to the north of the Baxter Road, although other information suggests the structure was more likely just to the south of it.

Icehouses were elaborate structures that were expensive to build. As such, they were uncommon, being found only on the properties of wealthy landowners, or associated with public houses, such as hotels. The buildings were typically placed on the north face of a slope, where the ground was most

12 *OR* 40, pt. 1, 599, 600.

protected from the heat of the sun. There was an outlet at the bottom to allow drainage of melted water from the base of the shaft, often into a stream. An icehouse was always placed on high ground because the outlet had to be above the water table. From a distance, it had the appearance of a grassy knoll.[13]

After he crossed the railroad on the afternoon of June 18, Chamberlain discovered an icehouse to his right front. Mink's Federal battery was firing into it. Earlier in the morning, Mink had been with Lt. George Breck and Captain James H. Cooper right of the woods in front of the Avery house, south of the Baxter Road. Wainwright described his battery as being thrown forward and firing *up* the track to the *northwest*, driving the enemy out of a clump of woods *at the icehouse*.[14] By mid-afternoon, however, Mink had moved his battery to the right of the Taylor house north of the Baxter Road. From there, in order to target the same location, he would have been firing either directly across, or more likely down, the track to the *southwest*. Thus, the icehouse must have been situated west of the railroad between Mink's two locations. We know it was to the right of the woods in front of the Avery house, close enough to the Taylor plantation to have been easily accessible to the hotel workers who once operated there.

The Gilmer Map of 1863 shows two man-made structures on a slight ridge in the fork between two branches of Taylor's Creek just south of the Baxter Road several hundred yards from the Taylor house. This location on a peninsula between two streams would seem an unlikely place to locate a house or barn, but it would be a good site for an icehouse.

A modern LIDAR (Laser Light Detection and Ranging or Light Radar) image shows two interesting topographical features in approximately the same location, which National Park Service cultural resources personnel believe may represent the remains of the Taylor icehouse. Further exploration is planned to determine whether this indeed represents the ruins of an icehouse.[15] If so, it would provide yet another strong piece of evidence linking Chamberlain's attack to the vicinity of the Baxter Road and the Taylor property.

---

13 Elizabeth A. Gillispie, "An Examination of an Ice House at Old Town Plantation," in Electronic Theses & Dissertations (2012), Paper 624, 32.

14 *OR* 40, pt. 1, 481-82.

15 Julia Steele, Cultural Resource Manager, Petersburg National Battlefield, Personal Communication, February 11, 2015. Perhaps prophetically, early excavations of the site yielded muddy discarded bottles of Ice House brand beer!

The Attack from the Center

Wainwright personally witnessed Chamberlain's charge while he was mounted atop the knoll where Hart and Bigelow were stationed. He watched until Chamberlain's men began falling back.[16] At this time Wainwright was commanding twelve artillery batteries, nine of which were clustered around the Baxter Road. It is simply implausible under any scenario to believe Wainwright would have wandered off with Chamberlain's brigade to the Tatum farm, the Jerusalem Plank Road, and the area of the future Fort Sedgwick and leave the center of his command behind and alone at such a crucial time.

Whether Wainwright could see it or not, when Chamberlain fell in the ravine to the front of the 9th Massachusetts Battery, the severely wounded colonel was removed from the field by Captain Bigelow's men.[17] John Bigelow provides independent corroboration:

> While engaged in stopping [the retreat of] the infantry, word was brought to me that General Chamberlain lay in our front, badly wounded. I sent word to the ambulance to take the stretcher and bring him in, my informant acting as guide.[18]

Bigelow's battery occupied a position near the Deep Cut of the railroad, and Chamberlain himself was probably initially evacuated into that very same cut that Lieutenant Colonel Lyman describes as being full of V Corps casualties.

Trying to assess where Chamberlain actually fell, and the likely distances and terrain over which the stretcher bearers traveled, turned out to be more important than I initially believed.

16 Nevins, *A Diary of Battle*, 426.

17 Chamberlain, "The Charge at Fort Hell," 13.

18 Baker, *History of the Ninth Massachusetts Battery*, 125-27.

CHAPTER 8

FACTS MATTER:
Major Roebling's Rule

MAJOR Washington A. Roebling served as a staff officer to General Warren. Roebling kept a diary that is the closest thing we have to a report from the perspective of the V Corps' high command on June 18, 1864. It offers a great deal of information for our purposes, especially about distance and terrain that further our analysis.

According to Roebling: "The reason of Griffin and Crawford [advancing] so much closer lay in the fact of the R. R. cut being much closer to the lines there, and the ground they had to advance over was steeper, so that the rebels fired over."[1]

Roebling places Ayres' 2nd Division on the extreme left of the V Corps, perpendicular to the old line of Rebel works (probably batteries 22-24), with half of his troops left, or south, of the old Rebel line. Cutler's 4th Division was on Ayres' right, having advanced with its left flank hugging the Norfolk Railroad up to the rightward (northwesterly) curve of the line, where the division had to cross it. Griffin was straddling the Baxter Road, advancing toward the Deep Cut of the Norfolk Railroad at the Baxter Road crossing.

Major Roebling continued:

---

1 Roebling, "Report of the Operations of the V Corps," June 18, 1864.

Griffin's [1st Division] and Crawford's [3rd Division] skirmishers had now advanced over the open fields on each side [south and north] of the Norfolk Pike [Baxter Road] up to the railroad cut, the bridge over which was gone; the cut here was very deep, and after the men were got into it, it was hard to get them out again.[2]

Roebling tersely summarized the results of the 3:00 p.m. attack along the V Corps front in a dozen words: "there was a repulse with a loss of 1600 men killed and wounded." He did, however, provide a specific and insightful analysis of the reasons for the relative success or failure of the various V Corps divisions that afternoon:

The nearest approach to carrying the enemy's line was in Griffin's front; some of the men were shot there within 20 feet of the enemy's line; Cutler carried a slight crest between his position and the enemy's, which he held. . . . The least advance was made in Ayres' front where the ground was perfectly level and fairly swept by the rebel fire. The reason of Griffin and Crawford [advancing] so much closer lay in the fact of the R. R. cut being much closer to the lines there, and the ground they had to advance over was steeper, so that the rebels fired over. . . The line [that night] in front of Griffin and Crawford was not more than 150 yards from the enemy's line.[3]

Roebling's observations concerning the June 18 assault (which we can dub "Roebling's Rule") can be summarized as follows: A shorter attack across favorable terrain offers the best chance of success, while a longer attack across flat terrain offers a greater chance for failure.

In his "Reminiscences," Colonel Chamberlain claimed to have nearly reached the Confederate defenses:

When you picture that field, air and earth cross-cut with thick-flying, hitting, plunging, burying, bursting missiles, you will not wonder that we did not succeed in bayoneting the enemy at their guns inside their works. You will rather wonder that some of my men got near enough to fall within twenty feet of them.[4]

---

2   Ibid.

3   Ibid.

4   Chamberlain, "Reminiscences of Petersburg and Appomattox," 173. It is important to note that several reports coming from within Sweitzer's brigade claimed the same thing (i.e., Parts of that brigade, attacking in conjunction with Chamberlain's command, also made it close to the enemy works before being thrown back. 21st PA (55 yards): Oliver B. Knowles to General Joshua L. Chamberlain, December 15, 1865, Library of Congress, Joshua Lawrence

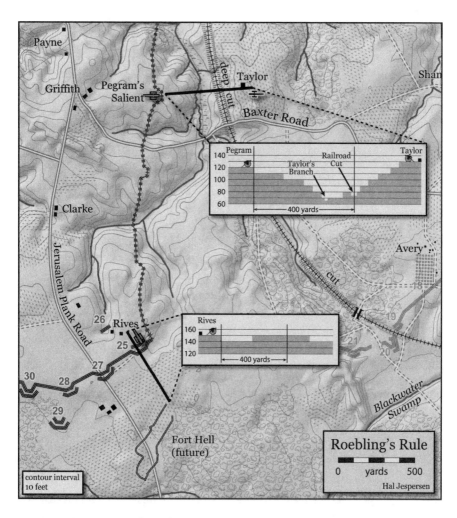

Here is a recap of the basic facts that put Chamberlain's attack near the Baxter Road rather than a mile to the left against "Fort Hell" and Rives' Salient:

1) Chamberlain claimed that his brigade approached within 20 feet of the enemy's works;

Chamberlain papers, box 4, folder: Reminiscences to Chamberlain; 155th PA (20 feet) - OR 40, pt. 2, 183 (Official Reports of Gen Griffin/Warren); 155th PA (20 feet) - 155th Regimental Association, Under the Maltese Cross, Antietam to Appomattox, The Loyal Uprising in Western Pennsylvania, 1861-1865, Campaign 155th Pennsylvania Regiment (Pittsburgh, PA, 1910), 295-296.

2) Reports from Sweitzer's brigade made similar claims;

3) Major Roebling's report states that Griffin's division (Chamberlain and Sweitzer) was the most successful of any division in Warren's corps that day and came within 20 feet of the Confederate trenches (which corroborates the claims of observers from both the 1st and 2nd brigades);

4) The railroad cut angles west as it runs north, or progressively closer to the Rebel line of works that ran generally north-south;

5) Major Roebling offered a pair of cogent reasons for the success of Griffin's advance. First, the relative safety offered by the railroad cut meant that these Union troops (Chamberlain and Sweitzer) began the assault closer to the enemy lines than other troops, so the distance they had to cover under fire was shorter. Second, the ground over which they advanced was steeper, so much of the Rebels fire passed over their heads;

6) Neither "Fort Hell" nor Rives' Salient nearly a mile away are close to the railroad cut, and the ground in front of these Rebel positions is not sloped;

7) The terrain in front of "Fort Hell" and Rives' Salient was similar to the terrain on General Ayres' front, where no significant advance could be made because of topographical constraints and enemy fire coming from behind the permanent fortifications at that point in the line.[5]

Given the overwhelming weight of this evidence, it would have been impossible for Chamberlain to have accomplished what he did detached from Griffin's division and attacking alone a mile farther left away from the rest of the Army and nowhere near the railroad cut.

Unlike Chamberlain, Ayres was operating opposite Rives' Salient, but to the east of it, not to the south of it. Unable to advance, Ayres assumed a

---

5   According to Roebling, Ayres moved his division behind Cutler's left "along the old line of fortifications, and there formed, with about half of his troops being to the left of the old [Dimmock] line. . . . The enemy's lines seemed to form a salient opposite Ayres where their new line joined the old one. . . . In front of Ayres, the enemy had such a sweep that his line had to be reformed under a heavy fire of artillery and musketry." Roebling, "Report of the Operations of the V Corps," June 18, 1864. Roebling's account is a nearly perfect description of Rives' Salient.

Major General Gouverneur Warren and staff, V Corps,
Army of the Potomac, at the Avery House. LOC

defensive posture. If Chamberlain had moved past Tatum's farm toward the Jerusalem Plank Road, where he could see the guns of Fort Mahone, he would have been even farther to the left (farther south, and farther west) than Ayres. The ground there was even flatter, and the distance from the railroad cut even farther. If Ayres could not advance with his division because of unsuitable topographical constraints and the defending enemy, it seems unlikely Chamberlain would have successfully assaulted with a single brigade, under more severely adverse conditions.

The criticality of terrain and distance was evident to others on the field. General Meade had dispatched Lt. Col. Theodore Lyman to spend the day with General Warren, with instructions to report back promptly and frequently. Generals Griffin and Crawford came often throughout the day to the V Corps headquarters at the Avery house to consult with General Warren.[6]

6 Lowe, *Meade's Army*, 211, 213.

At 3:30 p.m., Lyman and the others "rode into the open plain" to see the troops go up. It is instructive to consider what it might have been possible for them to see from this open plain. The viewscape opens to the northwest, toward the Baxter Road and Pegram's Salient. Observation of activity to the southwest, at the Jerusalem Plank Road and Rives' Salient, would not have been possible because of intervening ridges and trees.

Lyman's account specifically mentions Colonel Chamberlain:

> The advance was chiefly by the brigades of Chamberlain and [Hofmann] on the left[7]. . . . The men moved up without spirit, receiving a withering fire, and fell back behind the first crest, Chamberlain desperately wounded. The railroad cut, which offered protection, was full of our wounded. About us came plenty of Minié bullets, cutting up the dust, and of shells and case there was no end. Of the wounded brought past us there was an uncommon proportion of terrible artillery lacerations.[8]

Warren's own correspondence provides clarification, confirming that the mid-afternoon attack that he and Lyman observed from their vantage near the Avery farm was at the center of the V Corps line, and not on the far left:

> The center of my line (the only part I could see) got well under way at 3:15 p.m. It received a very heavy fire, and after carrying one ridge had to halt there. . . . We met a heavy fire, and have suffered considerably from it. The railroad cut is a great obstacle.[9]

It is interesting to note that Lyman described bullets and artillery shells fired by the Confederate defenders peppering the ground where the commanders were observing the assault from positions well to the rear. This suggests a straight and clear line of fire from the Confederate defenses, through the assaulting line to the observation point on the open plain northwest of the Avery house. The direction of fire must have been from west to east. If the attack had been launched from "Fort Hell" along the Jerusalem Plank Road, on

---

7   The reference to "the left" is potentially confusing. It could refer to Hofmann's brigade of Cutler's division being on the left of Chamberlain's brigade. On the other hand, it might be intended to distinguish the attack of Chamberlain and Hofmann, which occurred to the left of the Baxter Road from the other portion of the V Corps assault under Sweitzer and Crawford, which occurred on the right side of that same road just a few hours later.

8   Lowe, *Meade's Army*, 213-14.

9   OR 40, pt. 2, 180.

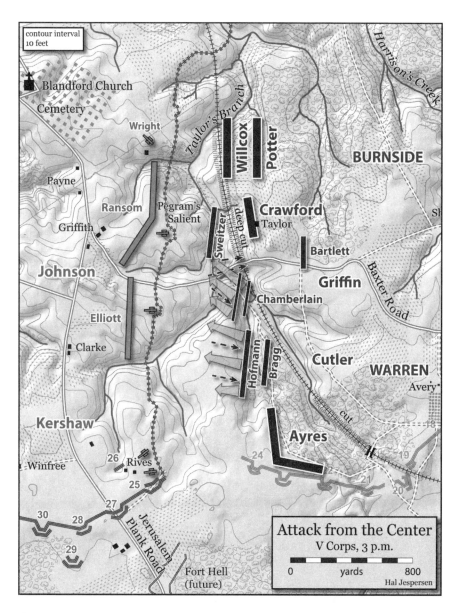

contour interval
10 feet

Blandford Church
Cemetery

Wright

Willcox

Potter

BURNSIDE

Harrison's Creek

Taylor's Branch

Payne

Ransom   Pegram's
Griffith   Salient

Sweitzer

deep cut

Crawford
Taylor

Bartlett

Johnson

Griffin

Chamberlain

Baxter Road

Elliott

Clarke

Hofmann

Bragg

Cutler

WARREN

Avery

Kershaw

Winfree   26   Rives
25

Ayres

24

cut

18

19

27

30   28

29

Jerusalem Plank Road

Fort Hell
(future)

Attack from the Center
V Corps, 3 p.m.

0   yards   800

Hal Jespersen

the other hand, the Confederate line of fire would have been aimed primarily toward the south, nearly perpendicular to the direction required to reach the observers on the open plain near the Avery headquarters. Furthermore, most of such a barrage, even if it was properly directed, would have been absorbed by the hundreds of intervening yards of woodland between Rives' Salient and the Avery site.

Lyman also noted that during the repulse Chamberlain's line retreated to the protection of the railroad cut, which was close behind the action. (This was not the case at the Fort Sedgwick location along the Jerusalem Plank Road).

There are other reports for the events of June 18 and beyond that add weight to the V Corps command report and the relevant aspects of Chamberlain's testimony regarding a Baxter Road attack. The report from Chamberlain's own brigade was very instructive on this point, and we turn to it next.

CHAPTER 9

A TWIST OF IRONY:
Sweitzer's Position Holds the Key

NONE of the original brigade commanders in General Griffin's 1st Division submitted official reports for the action on June 18, 1864. Joshua Chamberlain's severe injuries kept him on the sidelines for nearly half a year. The commander of Griffin's 2nd Brigade, Col. Jacob Sweitzer, was mustered out of military service with the rest of his 62nd Pennsylvania on July 13, 1864, less than one month after the fight. Finally, Col. Joseph Bartlett's brigade was held in reserve and did not participate in the June 18 assault. Colonel William S. Tilton initially served under Colonel Sweitzer as the regimental commander of the 22nd Massachusetts and the 2nd Massachusetts Sharpshooters. He was elevated to command Chamberlain's brigade on the evening of June 18 after Chamberlain was shot down, and it fell to Tilton to pen the official report covering the actions of the two engaged brigades of Griffin's 1st Division.

There are two components to Tilton's report (the only "contemporaneous" report submitted from Griffin's division at the brigade or division level for the June 18th action) that directly concern us. The first regards his perspective as the commander of the skirmishers deployed in front of Sweitzer's brigade, as follows:

June 18, at 5 a.m. broke camp and marched to the front, stacking arms in rear of II Corps, where we made coffee. At 8 a.m., the brigade advanced to the front and left to take up a line before the enemy's works on new ground. My regiment was detailed to skirmish to the front and drive in the rebel pickets. I deployed in an open field near Colonel Avery's house, with my right resting on the Norfolk Turnpike Road. We pushed forward to the Norfolk Railroad, which crossed the pike and to a ravine beyond, where the right of my line, being more exposed than the left, was driven back. The left, however, under Major Burt, held its own, having shelter in rear of a crest. I thereupon strengthened my right with 100 men from the Sixty-second Pennsylvania; went in again, when I succeeded in driving the rebel skirmishers out of the ravine into one beyond. About 12 m., Sweitzer's brigade moved toward and took position in this last ravine, all the regiments but one being on the right of the [Baxter] road. The 1st Brigade, Colonel Chamberlain, then advanced to the ravine and took position on the left of Colonel Sweitzer's brigade. This was done under a very heavy fire, and the brigade lost more than 200 men, including Colonel Chamberlain, who was wounded. Thus, we remained right under the enemy's works until just before dark, when I was ordered to take command of 1st Brigade.[1]

According to Tilton the skirmishers of the 22nd Massachusetts pushed forward in the early morning hours of June 18 through an open field near the Avery house left (south) of the Baxter Road (Norfolk Stage Road), driving in the Rebel pickets. The skirmishers fought their way across the railroad cut, into a ravine of Taylor's Branch to the west of the cut, and then into a second ravine beyond that.

The 21st Pennsylvania Cavalry, the unit in which my ancestor served, was probably the largest contingent in Sweitzer's brigade. The other regiments in the brigade had suffered heavily during Grant's Overland Campaign, but the 21st Pennsylvania Cavalry had only recently joined the Army of the Potomac at Cold Harbor. Ten old and new regiments joined the army on June 2, 1864, adding 3,727 men to the army. "The largest of these regiments," according to a General Report to the Secretary of War, "were the Twenty-first Pennsylvania [Cavalry] (dismounted), 950 men, Fourth Delaware, 503 men, and the Fourth New Hampshire, 500 men."[2]

The 21st Pennsylvania Cavalry lost 55 men to all causes at Cold Harbor, leaving the regiment with, officially at least, some 900 men at the beginning of the Petersburg Campaign. The regiment was exceedingly large, comparable in size to the 187th Pennsylvania Infantry in Chamberlain's brigade, each regiment being relatively fresh commands of approaching 1,000 men each. Their

1   OR 40, pt. 1, 455-58.

2   Ibid., 36, pt. 1, 87.

presence significantly augmented the strength and vigor of the battle-worn brigades to which they were attached.[3]

Colonel Tilton observed that all of Sweitzer's regiments except one advanced to the right (or north) of the Baxter Road. The 21st Pennsylvania Cavalry (dismounted) almost certainly was part of this main battle line contingent because the Keystone regiment was the largest and freshest available to Sweitzer. Holding it back would have made no sense.[4] Henry Fitzgerald Charles, a private in the 21st Pennsylvania Cavalry, recalled that the regiment passed through an area where some ruins were still smoldering. The buildings had been set afire that morning, just before the descent of the 21st Pennsylvania Cavalry into the Deep Cut.[5]

Oliver B. Knowles was a major in command of the 21st Pennsylvania Cavalry on June 18. In December 1865, Knowles (who would muster out the following July as a brevet brigadier general), wrote a letter to Chamberlain in which he leaves no question as to the precise whereabouts of his own regiment and, by association, of Chamberlain's entire brigade. Knowles and the 21st Pennsylvania Cavalry advanced north of the Baxter Road toward Pegram's Salient (the future site of the Battle of the Crater). "On the 18th June, the day you were so fearfully wounded," began the 22-year-old Knowles,

> we made several desperate charges on the works in front of Petersburg. Immediately in front of my Regt. was the redoubt which our forces afterwards so unsuccessfully attempted to blow up ("Burnside's mine"). By actual measurement, we got within 55 yards of this work, but the fire was too fearful to advance further. On that day, the left

---

3 "Examination of the Return of Casualties in the Union Forces for the Cold Harbor Campaign, June 2-15, 1864," in ibid., 170. The 187th Pennsylvania was nearly the same size as all five combined older regiments in Chamberlain's brigade. This may have been the case with the 21st Pennsylvania Cavalry and Sweitzer's brigade. DeLacy, "Reminiscences to Chamberlain," 6.

4 The nine hundred men of the 21st Pennsylvania probably held the left flank of Sweitzer's main battle line as it advanced to the *right* of the Baxter Road. Upon reaching the ravine, the men of the regiment may have shifted somewhat to the left, replacing skirmishers from the 22nd Massachusetts and 62nd Pennsylvania, who had earlier advanced across the railroad from the south of the Baxter Road, driving off the Confederate skirmishers and clearing the ravine. Those two battle-weary units were subsequently moved to the rear where, together with the 4th Michigan, they formed the 2nd Brigade's reserve line for the 6 p.m. attack.

5 Neitz, *The Civil War Diary of Henry Fitzgerald Charles*, 8. This an obvious reference to the Taylor ruins north of the Baxter Road, which is explored in more depth in Chapter 16.

of my Regiment connected with the right of your Brigade after we crossed the Norfolk & Petersburg R.R., so you may understand the position.[6]

Finally, we have the report of Major John Lentz, 91st Pennsylvania, which explicitly states that Sweitzer's main battle line comprised the 32nd Massachusetts, 21st Pennsylvania Cavalry (dismounted), 155th Pennsylvania, and 91st Pennsylvania, all under the command of Colonel E. M. Gregory.[7]

All this evidence places the 21st Pennsylvania Cavalry on Sweitzer's main battle line north of the Baxter Road. There, the line of Sweitzer's 2nd Brigade advanced across the railroad tracks and pushed to the ravine beyond, occupying it sometime after noon, having driven the enemy to his entrenchments about a quarter of a mile west of the railroad. Sweitzer's brigade hastily threw up breastworks immediately beneath, and about 150 yards distant from, the enemy's works at Pegram's Salient. According to Tilton, Chamberlain then advanced his brigade into the same ravine, taking up a position on the immediate left of Sweitzer's brigade. It was in that action that Colonel Chamberlain received his nearly-fatal wound.[8]

An anonymous letter from a member of the 21 Pennsylvania Cavalry's Company F appeared in the July 1, 1864, edition of *The Tribune*, the daily newspaper of the city of Johnstown, Pennsylvania. The letter provides a description of the three engagements of Sweitzer's brigade at the front of Petersburg on June 18:

> On the morning of the 18th, we were moved to the front, to relieve the Ninth Corps, then engaged with the enemy. We soon became engaged, and our brigade (the Second) made three successful charges, driving the rebels from the Petersburg and Suffolk Railroad. In the first charge our regiment lost heavily, having charged over a hill and

6   Oliver B. Knowles to General Joshua L. Chamberlain, December 15, 1865, Library of Congress, Joshua Lawrence Chamberlain papers, box 4, folder: Reminiscences to Chamberlain.

7   OR 40, pt. 1, 461. The 4th Michigan Infantry was also a part of the brigade, but its three-year enlistment was due to end within a matter of hours and, in consideration of this, Colonel Sweitzer had promised to hold the Wolverines back unless the situation became dire. Martin N. Bertera and Kim Crawford, *The 4th Michigan Infantry in the Civil War* (East Lansing, MI, 2010), 225-6. Samuel Bates' *History of Pennsylvania Volunteers, 1861-1865*, vol. 2, 192, says that Lentz's 91st Pennsylvania regiment had to shift to the *left* at dusk on June 18, in order to charge the enemy on the hill where the mine was subsequently sprung. This places the right of Sweitzer's brigade significantly north of the Taylor ruins.

8   OR 40, pt. 1, 455-56, 459, 461.

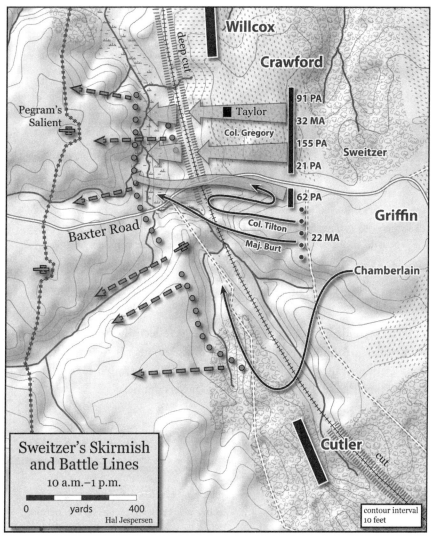

The 22nd MA deployed as skirmishers left of the Baxter Road. Major Mason W. Burt led the left contingent, and Col. William S. Tilton, commanding the regiment, was on the right. After pushing to the railroad and a ravine beyond, Burt held his own, having shelter behind a crest. Tilton's skirmishers were more exposed and driven back. Tilton strengthened his right with 100 men from the 62nd Pennsylvania and went in again, driving Rebel skirmishers out of the ravine and into another beyond. Colonel E. M. Gregory led Sweitzer's main battle line (21st PA, 91st PA, 155th PA, 32nd MA) in its advance north of the Baxter Road, moving first to the railroad cut, and then to the ravine beneath the enemy works at Pegram's Salient. The 21st Pennsylvania Cavalry formed the left of Sweitzer's line in the ravine, and later connected with the right side of Chamberlain's brigade (after having relieved and replaced the 22nd MA and 62nd PA, which had done the initial skirmishing on the left). Note: The gray dots represent Rebel skirmishers, and the gray dashes and arrows show their retreat in the face of the Union advance.

through an open field which the rebel batteries commanded. In our company (F) there were six wounded, two of whom have since died. In the second charge our Lieutenant Colonel was wounded and sent to the rear. In the third charge our company had one wounded.

Arriving at the top of the hill in the third charge, we very suddenly came to a halt. The rebel skirmishers had retired and immediately in our front was a long line of breastworks and a very strong fort commanding them. We here formed a line of battle, with the 62nd Pennsylvania Volunteers supporting us. Night closed on us, and we dug with our bayonets and threw up with our tin cup something of a breastwork to protect us from the bullets of the Rebel sharpshooters. Being poorly supported, we lay there, momentarily expecting to be driven back by the rebels, who lay behind their secure breastworks in numbers three to our one. However, on the following morning we were relieved by the 3rd Division of our Corps, and we moved back on the railroad—a deep cut in the road affording us good shelter from the grape, canister and musket balls of the Rebels which fell like hail around us. Here we rested all day and part of the ensuing night, when we were moved to the rear about one mile, where we found our division, the first, massing for some purpose.[9]

The second part of Colonel Tilton's report reflects his perspective as acting commander of the brigade that had been Chamberlain's for just twelve days until the time of his wounding. In this section, Tilton recapitulates earlier events before moving on to what transpired under his command:

I have the honor to report the part taken by this brigade [Chamberlain's 1st Brigade] from the day I took command, June 18, 1864, until the end of the fifth epoch, July 30, 1864: At about 12 m. on the 18th of June, the 2nd Brigade had advanced down the Norfolk Turnpike [Baxter] Road and crossed the railroad to a ravine, which was immediately under the enemy's works, and the 1st Brigade, then under command of Colonel Chamberlain, went forward soon after and formed upon the left of Sweitzer's brigade.

There it was [on the left of Sweitzer, near the Baxter Road], just before dark, that I was placed in command with orders to charge when troops on my right and left did. In making the [earlier] movement, which was done under a heavy fire, the loss had been severe. Colonel Chamberlain was wounded. I immediately proceeded to reconnoiter

9 Anonymous (July 1, 1864), "Letter from Company F, 21st Pennsylvania Cavalry," *The Tribune*, Johnstown, Pennsylvania. Company F (one of twelve in the regiment) suffered eight casualties in those three attacks, the highest number sustained in that company on a single day during the entire war. Among the wounded was my ancestor Samuel's brother Abraham, one of three Smith brothers serving together in the 21st Pennsylvania Cavalry.

the ground, and communicate with the brigade commanders upon my right and left. Colonel Hofmann on the left, commanding a brigade in Cutler's division, assured me of his co-operation at the right moment. The 83rd Pennsylvania, 44th New York, and 16th Michigan regiments, of Bartlett's [3rd] brigade, were now sent me as a support. I removed the 187th Pennsylvania, which had formed my second line, to the left of my front line, and placed Bartlett's three regiments in my second line, with orders to intrench and clear up the bushes in their front. After waiting anxiously the movement of the brigade on my right, I finally received notice that it had been suspended.[10]

Where was the 1st Brigade on the evening of June 18, when Colonel Tilton assumed command? Tilton makes it clear the brigade's position was last mentioned in the preceding sentence: "There it was," i.e., "on the left of Sweitzer's brigade." The 1st Brigade had taken position in a ravine under the enemy's works on Sweitzer's left in the afternoon, and it had remained in that same ravine, in the same position relative to Sweitzer's brigade, until nightfall, after Chamberlain was wounded and Tilton put in command. It is also clear that Tilton assumed command of the 1st Brigade "Just before dark." Sunset occurred in Petersburg that evening about 8:30 p.m., or roughly five hours after Colonel Chamberlain's wounding and well after Sweitzer's 6:00 p.m. charge. According to Tilton, the brigades of Chamberlain, Sweitzer, and Bartlett remained near the Baxter Road throughout the day. Chamberlain was severely wounded immediately to the left of Sweitzer, probably just to the south of the Baxter Road.

Chamberlain's brigade was on the left of Griffin's division, somewhat in the center of the V Corps line. Colonel Hofmann, holding the front line of General Cutler's 4th Division, was on Chamberlain's left, and General Ayres' 2nd Division was on the left of Cutler. Colonel Bartlett's 3rd Brigade, part of Griffin's division and previously held in reserve, was close enough to the front to be able to come to the support of the 1st Brigade that evening if needed. If Chamberlain had been nearly a mile farther left in front of Rives' Salient along the Jerusalem Plank Road as so many other writers have claimed, then Hofmann, Bartlett, and Sweitzer had to have been there with him—or all of these reports are wrong. Time, space, and reason (when using terrain and historical documents) do not allow for a long detour to the Jerusalem Plank Road and Rives' Salient.

10 Ibid., 456-57.

Implications of the Subsequent Movement to the Left
of the Three Brigades of Griffin's Division

As noted, when Colonel Tilton assumed command of Chamberlain's 1st Brigade just before dark on June 18, it was situated left of Sweitzer and immediately to the right of Colonel Hofmann's brigade of Cutler's division.[11] The right flank of Lieutenant Colonel Michael Wiedrich's 15th New York Heavy Artillery, 3rd Brigade, Ayres' division, connected with Colonel Hofmann' s brigade, and Wiedrich's left flank connected with Colonel Nathan Dushane's 2nd Brigade (the "Maryland Brigade") of Ayres' division.[12] Thus, the V Corps line, from left to right, consisted of Ayres 2nd Division, Hofmann's brigade, Chamberlain's brigade, Sweitzer's brigade, and some elements of Crawford's 3rd Division (probably the 13th Massachusetts and 88th Pennsylvania.)

Chamberlain launched his attack in two lines, with the 187th Pennsylvania following behind the front line of veteran regiments, comprised of the 121st, 142nd, 143rd, 149th, and 150th Pennsylvania. When Tilton assumed command, three regiments of Bartlett's 3rd Brigade were sent forward as support. Tilton removed the 187th Pennsylvania, which had lost heavily, from the second line and replaced it with Bartlett's 83rd Pennsylvania, 44th New York, and 16th Michigan regiments and ordered them to entrench. The 83rd Pennsylvania also relieved the advanced skirmishers of the 150th Pennsylvania. These regiments remained in their new works until the night of June 20.[13]

On June 19 at 4:00 a.m., Tilton withdrew his 1st Brigade and took up a new line behind Bartlett's brigade. About dark the following day, Tilton moved farther to the rear near V Corps headquarters at the Avery house. In his personal journal, General Warren explained that Griffin's withdrawal from the center on the night of June 20 was done in preparation for a planned extension of the V Corps line farther left the next day, when Griffin was ordered to take his division to the Jerusalem Plank Road.[14]

---

11 Ibid., 456-57.

12 Ibid., 471-72.

13 OR 40, pt. 1, 456-57; 462-68; Thomas Chamberlain, *History of the One-hundred and Fiftieth Regiment, Pennsylvania Volunteers,* 264-65.

14 OR 40, pt. 1, 453-54, 456-57.

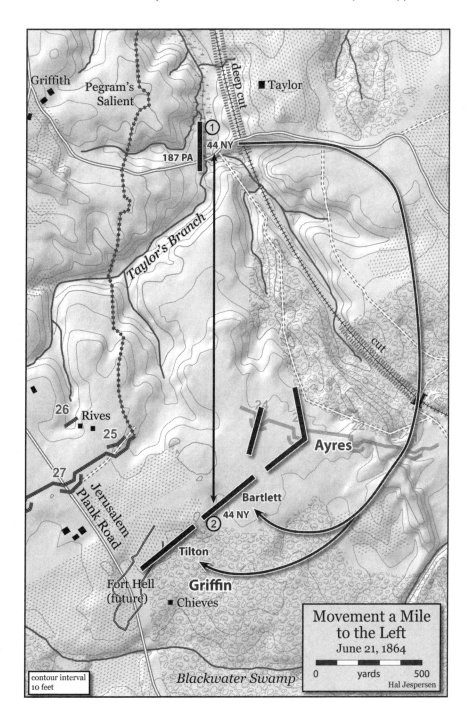

Griffith

Pegram's
Salient

deep cut

Taylor

①
44 NY

187 PA

Taylor's Branch

cut

26
Rives
25

24

23

22

Ayres

27

Jerusalem Plank Road

Bartlett

②   44 NY

Tilton

Fort Hell
(future)

Griffin

Chieves

Movement a Mile
to the Left
June 21, 1864

contour interval
10 feet

Blackwater Swamp

0   yards   500

Hal Jespersen

During this shift to the left on June 21, Colonel Tilton was ordered to move the brigade to a position on the left of General Ayres. When he reached that point, Tilton discovered that Bartlett was already there, which prompted General Griffin to direct Tilton to move even farther to the left, so that the 1st Brigade's left flank eventually rested on the Jerusalem Plank Road, with its right running toward Bartlett's left.[15]

Significantly, the 44th New York of Bartlett's brigade, which had been holding the position of the 187th Pennsylvania of Chamberlain's brigade from June 18 to 20, found itself moving about a mile in order to take up its new position to the left of Ayres.[16] In this new location, it was still a quarter-mile (estimated length of the 1st Brigade line, which would form to the left of Bartlett) to the right of the Jerusalem Plank Road. (This move makes no sense if Chamberlain had already taken the ground at the future site of Fort Sedgwick, and had made his attack on Rives' Salient near the Jerusalem Plank Road.)

"After this battle," recalled Lieutenant Patrick DeLacy of the 143rd Pennsylvania, Chamberlain's brigade, "we were moved away and around to the left where we took position with our left resting on the Jerusalem Plank Road. Here we threw up a line of breastworks and erected "Fort Hell" under the engineer corps."[17] "Away and around to the left" suggests a movement of substantial distance toward the Jerusalem Plank Road, which would also have been unnecessary if the 1st Brigade had already moved there and taken the ground of "Fort Hell" on June 18.

DeLacy's account dovetails nicely with the situation described by Major Roebling in his "Report of the Operations of the V Corps:"

> June 20th, Monday: The pickets of General Ayres were advanced a little on the left so that they could see the Jerusalem plank road. [Apparently the left flank of the Army of the Potomac was not close enough even to be able to see the road on June 18 and June 19.] Steps were taken to hold the line with as small a force as possible so as to have a force free to operate further to the left. During this night General Griffin was withdrawn from his position in the line, Generals Cutler and Crawford each stretching a little. The standard set up was that 2500 men per mile would be sufficient to hold the lines. Desultory firing kept up all day, with occasional stampedes during the night.

15 Ibid., 457.

16 Ibid., 467-68.

17 DeLacy, "Reminiscences to Chamberlain," 12.

Arrangements were being made for the extension of our lines toward the left across the plank road.[18]

Griffin did not march his division left to the Chieves house[19] and the Jerusalem Plank Road until June 21:

> June 21st, Tuesday: General Griffin moved around to the Cheeves (sic) house, massing his division near there. At the same time Gen. Birney, then commanding the 2nd Corps, moved across the plank road near the Williams house, intending to advance up the plank road on the western side of it; in course of the day they had a line formed, Gibbon on the right; his right resting on the plank road at a point 200 yds in advance of the present fort Davis. In the afternoon Gen. Meade rode past Griffin's HdQrs at the Cheeves (sic) house, and made a fuss because his division was massed there yet. They accordingly moved up at once without much opposition to the edge of the timber overlooking the field south of the rebel line. Their left rested on the plank road at Fort Hell, and right connected with Ayres; there was a gap between Gibbon's right and Griffin's left, across the plank road, which however was controlled by our artillery. All quiet that night.[20]

This new location of the 1st Division would become the site upon which "Fort Hell" would be erected. Samuel Bates, in telling the story of the 91st Pennsylvania of Sweitzer's brigade, is very clear on this point:

18 Roebling, "Report of the Operations of the V Corps," June 18, 1864.

19 There are many confusing variations on the spelling of this family name. "Chieves" is used on the 1863 J. F. Gilmer "Map of Approaches to Petersburg and their defenses," *Official Military Atlas*, Plate 40. This map was drawn by Confederate engineers before the war came to Petersburg in earnest, and probably reflects the correct spelling. The "Chieves" spelling also appears on the U. S. Corps of Engineers map prepared for the Court of Inquiry in the Mine Explosion, which can be found as Appendix 65 *Official Military Atlas*, Plate 64, and on the 1952 Hanson map of "Troop Movement Maps, Petersburg Campaign—Part of the Master Plan Petersburg National Battlefield." Major Nathaniel Michler, Chief Engineer for the Union Army, disseminated maps with the spelling "Chevers": "Vicinity of Petersburg, August 28, 1864," "Map of the Environs of Petersburg from the Appomattox River to the Weldon Rail Road Showing the Positions of the Entrenched Lines occupied by the Forces of the United States during the Siege," and "Map of Petersburg and Five Forks." Michler also made at least one map on which he employed the spelling "Cheevers" ("Map of the Siege of Petersburg, 1864-5"). Major Washington Roebling utilized yet another variant—"Cheeves"—which we see in the quotation above.

20 Roebling, "Report of the Operations of the V Corps," June 18, 1864.

On the morning of the 21st, the regiment having moved on the previous evening down the Suffolk [Baxter] Road, the left wing, under Captain Sellers of Company G, was detailed as skirmishers, and advancing on the enemy's breastworks, the left resting on the Jerusalem Plank Road, drove the rebel skirmishers up to the ground on which Fort Hell was afterwards built.[21]

If Chamberlain had taken and held that ground on June 18, why would Sweitzer's skirmishers have been needed to retake it on June 21? The movement to the left by Griffin's three brigades several days after Chamberlain's assault is yet another blow to the theory of a June 18 attack on Rives' Salient from the Jerusalem Plank Road.

After researching the Union reports and terrain issues, I decided it was time to delve into the other half of the equation at Petersburg—the Confederates fighting on the opposite side of the battlefield. What did they have to say about the June 18, 1864 location and nature of the Union effort?

---

21 Bates, S. P. *History of the Pennsylvania Volunteers,"* vol. 2, 192.

CHAPTER 10

THE CONFEDERATE VIEW:
Bushrod Johnson Speaks

ACCORDING to Lieutenant James A. Gardner, Battery B, 1st Pennsylvania Light Artillery (Cooper's Battery), on June 18, 1864, "the division of the Confederates which was opposite us was that of General Bushrod Johnson." However, he continued, "as the Army of Northern Virginia, under General Lee, began arriving on the evening of June 18th, it would be impossible for me to say who occupied the enemy's lines after that."[1]

Major General Bushrod Johnson commanded a division in P. G. T. Beauregard's Department of North Carolina and Southern Virginia. Lieutenant Gardner was correct. On June 18, Johnson's command straddled the Baxter Road. Just as Gardner was studying the Rebels, Johnson was observing and recording the movements of the enemy opposing him, which consisted primarily of General Griffin's 1st Division of Warren's V Corps.

Johnson's observations are preserved in a diary entry that survives as an Addendum Report to the Army Official Records. It is instructive to compare his perspective with those recorded by the Union commanders opposing him. In general, the accounts are parallel and complementary, which speaks well for the accuracy of the reporting on both sides that day.

---

1 Lanier, "Photographing the Civil War," 303. Lieutenant Gardner provided a long description of a picture provided by Lanier.

General Johnson began his observations by describing an artillery duel that opened between 7:30 and 8:00 a.m., as Union forces were observed advancing on his front:

[In the] morning the atmosphere grew thick. The sun was dim and red, and the light was obscured after sunrise. My lines were not formed until near sunrise. . . . Enemy seen advancing 7:30 a.m., [the] delay being quite astonishing, and at that hour [we] opened first gun from section of Pegram's battery on right of Baxter Road. Miller's section on right and Pegram's four Napoleons on left joined in fire. . . . The enemy's line, about one brigade of Yankees [on the] crest of hill east side of Taylors Creek in front of Taylor's house, was driven by flank at double-quick to Wise's left to the woods by artillery alone. . . . Enemy massed in the woods [and] brought up four batteries . . . on edge of woods. [They] opened first battery about 8 o'clock. All these batteries commenced 10 o'clock from their new position on right of road.[2]

Note the striking similarities between Johnson's account (above) and Major Roebling's observations from the Union side of the line:

It was daylight before he [Cutler] started; a fog concealed our movements. . . . I returned to Cutler with orders for him to advance, keeping his left on the Norfolk road, because at the Avery house the road appeared to run nearly west. As soon as the line of battle appeared west of the Avery house, the rebels opened from a rifled battery on the crest this side of Petersburg; an entrenched line was also apparent there with men standing on the parapet. The Maryland Brigade [detached from Ayres' division] was on the right of Cutler, and attempted to cross the open field, but the artillery fire compelled them to edge off to the left under cover of the woods.[3]

---

2 Bushrod R. Johnson, "Diary of Bushrod Johnson," Hewitt, OR Supplement, Volume 7, Addendum, 277-8. That early morning, Brigadier General Henry A. Wise's Rebel brigade, mentioned above in Johnson's account, was on the extreme right of Bushrod Johnson's Confederate divisional line near the Jerusalem Plank Road. D. Augustus Dickert, *History of Kershaw's Brigade* (Newberry, SC, 1899), 380. "[Joseph] Kershaw's brigade relieved that of General Wise, taking position on extreme right, resting its right on the Jerusalem Plank Road, and extending towards the left over the hill and across open fields. Wise had some hastily constructed works, with rifle pits in front. These later had to be relieved under a heavy fire from the enemy's battle line."

3 Roebling, "Report of Operations of the 5th Corps," June 18, 1864. The "Maryland Brigade" was commanded by Colonel Nathan Dushane, of Ayres' division, and comprised the 1st, 4th, 7th, and 8th regiments and the Purnell (Maryland) Legion.

The Maryland Brigade was deployed on open ground on Cutler's right flank, opposite the left flank of Wise's brigade. The woods mentioned by Johnson and Roebling were front of the Avery farm and provided some degree of concealment for the advance of Cutler's main force.

About 10:00 a.m., Union skirmishers and sharpshooters (almost certainly Colonel Tilton's 22nd Massachusetts from Sweitzer's brigade), as well as skirmishers from Samuel W. Crawford's division, advanced west, driving Confederate advanced skirmishers from the slope in front of the Taylor house, back to the Confederate reserve skirmish line on the west side of Taylor's Branch. In the early afternoon, blue battle lines descended the slope into the railroad cut, fighting their way to the creek and driving the Rebels back to their interior works.

Two Union charges followed, one between 3:00 and 4:00 p.m., and the other between 6:00 and 6:30 p.m. The Confederate observations of the mid-afternoon charge share uncanny similarities with what we know of the assaults by the brigades of Chamberlain and Hofmann, while the evening attack resembles the assault of Sweitzer's brigade of Griffin's 1st Division.[4]

The First Charge (3:00 – 4:00 p.m.)

According to General Johnson:

At about 4 p.m. enemy's skirmishers advanced on road of Taylor's Branch, and drove in our skirmishers to their works. The enemy made a charge in two lines of about one brigade near Elliott's right artillery. Our artillery and the 18th and 26th South Carolina regiments promptly repulsed them, except about 300 who sought shelter in the ravine on that part of our front. General Elliott sent out two companies and drove them off. A raking fire of one of Slaten's guns, followed by the fire of two companies moved forward from our lines by Brigadier General Elliott promptly drove them from their cover.[5]

---

4   Civil War commanders did not synchronize their watches.

5   Johnson, "Diary of Bushrod Johnson," 278; Bushrod R. Johnson, "UPR: Report of Major General Bushrod R. Johnson, C. S. Army, commanding Johnson's division, of operations June 16-18, 1864," The Siege of Petersburg Online website. Elliott was Brigadier General Stephen Elliott, the commander of a brigade of South Carolina units. Slaten's guns was a reference to Captain W. S. Slaten of the Macon (Georgia) Light Artillery.

In keeping with Bushrod Johnson's emphasis on the role of artillery in turning the tide of the advance, Lt. Col. Lyman, Meade's aide, reported "an uncommon proportion of terrible artillery lacerations" in the wounded being evacuated to the rear. Chamberlain personally got bogged down in the swamp. However, elements of the 150th Pennsylvania, acting as skirmishers, "sprang nimbly through the hollow to the summit of the little hill" on the peninsula between the two branches of the creek, and "dashed swiftly into the second ravine and up its farther slope to the very base of a formidable earthwork" known as Pegram's Salient.

Johnson's "road of Taylor's Branch" refers to the farm road running between the two branches of the creek south of the Baxter Road. Several obvious similarities appear when Johnson's report is compared with accounts from observers in Chamberlain's brigade on June 18:

Colonel Chamberlain: "We followed a rough track up to the woods, and there formed in two lines."[6]

Colonel Horatio Warren, 142nd Pennsylvania: "General Chamberlain ordered the old troops to go forward in the front line and that the supporting line, composed of the new regiment, should follow us at a distance of about 150 feet. . . . At three o'clock the order was given and our men dashed over the brow of the hill and down through the ravine."[7]

Lieutenant Colonel Thomas Chamberlain, 150th Pennsylvania: "At the signal—which was given at about four p.m.—Major Jones' command sprang nimbly through the hollow to the summit of the little hill, dashed swiftly into the second ravine and up its farther slope to the very base of a formidable earthwork."[8]

As noted earlier, Lieutenant Colonel Theodore Lyman, General Meade's aide-de-camp, observed the battle with General Warren's staff from the V Corps headquarters near the Avery house. At 3:30 p.m., he wrote,

The advance was chiefly by the brigades of Chamberlain and Hofmann on the left. . . . The men moved up without spirit, received a withering fire, and fell back behind the

6   Chamberlain, "The Charge at Fort Hell," 5.

7   Horatio N. Warren, *Two Reunions of the 142nd Regiment, Pa. Vols.* (Buffalo, NY, 1890), 34-36.

8   Thomas Chamberlain, *History of the One-hundred and fiftieth regiment, Pennsylvania Volunteers* (Open Library version), 213.

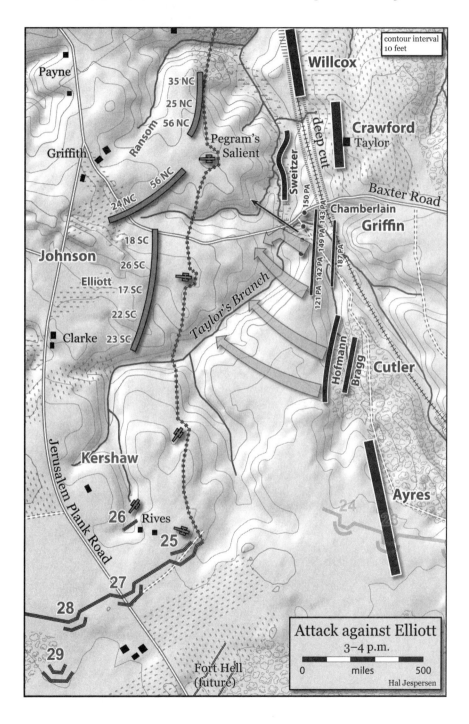

Payne

35 NC

25 NC

56 NC

Ransom

Pegram's
Salient

Griffith

56 NC

24 NC

18 SC

Johnson

26 SC

Elliott

17 SC

22 SC

Clarke   23 SC

Taylor's Branch

Jerusalem Plank Road

Kershaw

26   Rives

25

27

28

29

Fort Hell
(future)

Willcox

contour interval
10 feet

deep cut

Crawford
Taylor

Sweitzer

150 PA

Baxter Road

Chamberlain

Griffin

121 PA 142 PA 149 PA 143 PA

187 PA

Hofmann

Bragg

Cutler

Ayres

24

Attack against Elliott
3–4 p.m.

0   miles   500

Hal Jespersen

first crest, Chamberlain desperately wounded. The railroad cut, which offered protection, was full of our wounded.[9]

Bushrod Johnson's description can only apply to the Chamberlain-Hofmann charge because there were no other Federal brigades assaulting his front in any formation during the mid-afternoon on June 18.

The Federal brigade described in Johnson's account assaulted Elliott's artillery and his 18th and 26th South Carolina regiments. In the account below discussing the second charge early that evening, Johnson noted Elliott's brigade was just south of the Baxter Road. If Chamberlain was attacking Elliott from a position to the left of Sweitzer, he could not have been facing the Confederate divisions of Kershaw and Field at Rives' Salient, having already gained ground for his guns on what would later become Fort Sedgwick ("Fort Hell").

The Second Charge 6:00-6:30 p.m.

General Bushrod Johnson offered his perspective of the fighting:

At about 6 ½ o'clock in the evening the enemy appeared in line of battle on the north-side of Baxter Road, in front of Pegram's Battery of four guns. A conflict immediately commenced with the artillery and infantry. Soon five enemy's colors were counted, perhaps but the regiments of one brigade. [They] commenced entrenching in edge of woods below brow of hill north of Baxter's Road, and were soon under cover with skirmishers advanced. They gained the cover of the hill and established trenches in the edge of the woods some two-hundred yards in front of Ransom's Brigade.

At the same time about one brigade on the south side of the Baxter Road charged up to within 100 yards . . . exposed to nine rounds of canister, and the direct and flank fire from Elliott's brigade, which inflicted severe losses and drove them back...[10]

W. G. Carter detailed Sweitzer's advance from the Union vantage:

Our lines of battle were soon up, and at 6:00 p.m. a charge was ordered. The 155th Pennsylvania, 32nd Massachusetts, and 21st Pennsylvania formed our brigade line, the 62nd Pennsylvania and 22nd Massachusetts and 4th Michigan remaining behind (the

---

9 Lowe, *Meade's Army*, 213.

10 Johnson, "Diary of Bushrod Johnson," 278; Johnson, "UPR: Report of Major General Bushrod R. Johnson."

latter's time being out). The 1st Brigade, under Col. Chamberlain, was to move upon our left. Our regiment [the 22nd Massachusetts], which had been sent out all day as skirmishers, was ordered to remain behind. A part of the regiment, however, failed to obey the order and 'went in.' Forward went our brigade. . . . The 1st Brigade failed to move forward; Colonel Chamberlain [had been] wounded. . . . Our brigade received all the fire on its flanks that should have been taken by the 1st Brigade.[11]

Meade's staff officer, Theodore Lyman, also left us his perspective:

6 p.m. Another assault; chiefly on the right by Sweitzer's brigade, Crawford's division and parts of the IX Corps. Warren drew his sword and, with shut lips, walked a few paces forward to look. He turned back, and, with a sad air, said "It's just the same as before!"[12]

Commonalities in these accounts include the time of the attack, its location, and the size of the assaulting force. Sweitzer ordered the assault at 6:00 p.m., and Johnson observed it at "about" 6:30 p.m. The action was north of the Baxter Road in front of Pegram's battery. Colonel Tilton recalled that all of Sweitzer's regiments with the exception of one (the 4th Michigan, whose term of enlistment was nearly over), advanced to the right (north) of the Baxter Road, and several regimental histories from Sweitzer's brigade mention having advanced to the crest from which position Ambrose Burnside's IX Corps would later dig and explode the mine. This, of course, was the ground in front of Pegram's Salient. (This topic will be explored further in Chapter 13.) Johnson counted five Union flags, "perhaps the regiments of one brigade." J. C. Elliott of the 56th North Carolina, fighting 150 yards left of the salient, noted seven Union flags massed on a hill within 200 yards of him. Part of Chamberlain's brigade and Crawford's division may have also participated.

Thomas Chamberlain's *History of the 150th Pennsylvania* suggests that at least part of Joshua Chamberlain's brigade did in fact advance with the 2nd Brigade toward Pegram's Salient during this early-evening attack:

We are now ordered to fall back to the foot of the hill, and slide back to avoid the bullets as much as possible. We lay at this place all afternoon under a hot June sun, exposed to a constant fire of shot and shell and Minié balls. At six in the evening the

---

11 W. G. Carter, *Four Brothers in Blue*, 440.

12 Lowe, *Meade's Army*, 214.

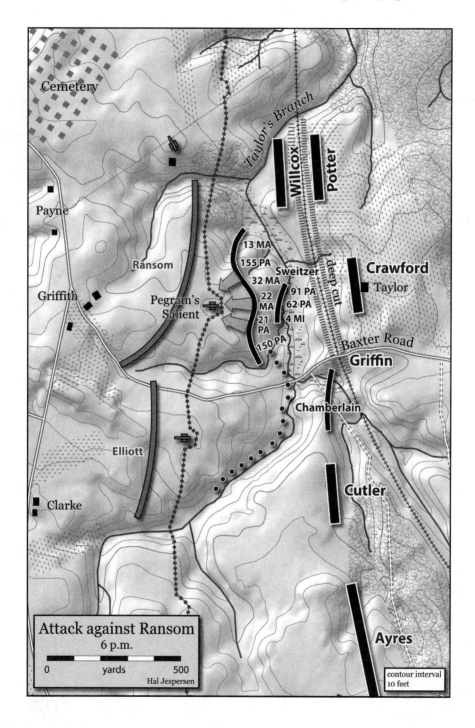

Cemetery

Payne

Ransom

Griffith

Pegram's
Salient

Elliott

Clarke

Taylor's Branch

Willcox

Potter

13 MA
155 PA
32 MA
Sweitzer
22
MA
21
PA
150 PA

91 PA
62 PA
4 MI

deep cut

Crawford

Taylor

Baxter Road

Griffin

Chamberlain

Cutler

Ayres

Attack against Ransom
6 p.m.

0   yards   500

Hal Jespersen

contour interval
10 feet

The 6:oo p.m. fight was north of the Baxter Road before Pegram's battery in the area later known as the "Horseshoe." The attacking regiments mainly belonged to Sweitzer's brigade (the 150th PA from Chamberlain's brigade also claimed participation, and Theodore Lyman said some from Crawford's division and the IX Corps were also present). The dots south of the Horseshoe indicate parts of Chamberlain's brigade and Cutler's division that did not retreat after the attack, but remained west of the creek into the night.

corps was formed for a last charge to carry the enemy's works and capture Petersburg, and we were moved a short distance to the right, behind a high bluff, in front of which was one of the enemy's forts with earthworks stretching to the right and left connecting with other forts in the line of defense. The fort in our front was the same that was blown up some time afterwards.[13]

The flag of the 150th Pennsylvania may well have been one of the five to seven counted from the Confederate side. The presence of part of the 1st Brigade in the 6:00 p.m. charge by Sweitzer's troops may also explain the comment by Henry Fitzgerald Charles of the 21st Pennsylvania Cavalry, "we got all mixed with another regiment on the brow of the hill."[14]

Johnson's report is consistent with the scenario of Chamberlain and Hofmann attacking Elliott, and Sweitzer (and some of Crawford's men) attacking Ransom. Johnson is consistent with the placement of Chamberlain's 1st Brigade to Sweitzer's left, just south of the Baxter Road, and is in harmony with nearly all other known accounts penned about the action that day.

Besides corroborating Union reports suggesting Griffin's two attacking brigades were operating together near the Baxter Road, Johnson's report addresses the issue of when Army of Northern Virginia units relieved his lines at Petersburg: "During the night [following the action of June 18], my command was relieved by Field's Division and part of Kershaw's."[15]

Joshua Chamberlain, however, wrote that these Confederate divisions arrived the previous evening, and that he had confronted them while attacking Rives' Salient. This also offered yet another avenue of investigation.

13 Tom Chamberlain, *History of the One-hundred and Fiftieth Regiment, Pennsylvania Volunteers*, 262.

14 Neitz, *The Civil War Diary of Henry Fitzgerald Charles*, 12.

15 Johnson, "UPR: Report of Major General Bushrod R. Johnson."

CHAPTER 11

SILENT CONFEDERATE WITNESSES:
Joseph Kershaw and Charles Field

JOSHUA Chamberlain believed that he had faced Joseph Kershaw's and Charley Field's veteran divisions from Lee's Army of Northern Virginia at Petersburg on June 18, 1864, and that they arrived at the front the evening prior to his attack. He made this clear in his 1903 MOLLUS speech, "Reminiscences of Petersburg and Appomattox":

> My guide assured me [the enemy's works] were now little changed from their old appearance as on the day of our assault. He added that the Confederates regarded this as the strongest part of their lines. It was easy to trace the entrenchments of the infantry—Kershaw's Mississippians, Georgians and South Carolinians, and on their right some of our old Alabama friends—companions of the symposium at Round Top the year before, troops of Longstreet's Corps who had come early in the evening before, and taken the place of Johnson's division there.[1]

Chamberlain maintained the same outlook near the end of his life, as evidenced by his recollection in *The Passing of the Armies*: "With what strange emotion I look into these faces [Kershaw's troops] before which, in the mad assault on Rives' Salient, June 18, 1864, I was left for dead under their eyes! It is by miracles we have lived to see this day, any of us standing here."[2]

---

1 Chamberlain, "Reminiscences of Petersburg and Appomattox," 174.

2 Chamberlain, *The Passing of the Armies*, 264.

As we learned in the previous chapter, Confederate sources document that the line opposing Warren's Union V Corps (and thus Chamberlain) was comprised of elements of Bushrod Johnson's division, which was part of General Pierre Gustave Toutant Beauregard's command, not the Army of Northern Virginia. Union sources also put Johnson's men on the line that day, as evidenced by the recollection of Lieutenant James A. Gardner that opened the previous chapter.[3]

Are these sources mistaken? Did Chamberlain, along with Generals Cutler and Ayers, share the unenviable distinction of being among the only Army of the Potomac attackers on June 18 to assault the formidable works the Confederates had completed in 1863, manned by newly arrived elements of Lee's army?[4]

Several questions must be addressed in order to resolve the conflicting claims. First, when did troops from the Army of Northern Virginia arrive in front of the V Corps? Second, where did they deploy? Finally, were any of Lee's troops actually engaged on June 18?

General Beauregard's Initial Defense of Petersburg

General Beauregard assumed command of the Department of North Carolina and Southern Virginia on April 18, 1864. One of the main tasks assigned to him was to guard Richmond's southern approaches. He made his headquarters at Petersburg, which had formidable fortifications on the Dimmock Line, stretching for some ten miles from the Appomattox River east of town to the same river on the west. These fortifications were reinforced with 55 batteries along the course of the line. What Beauregard lacked, was troops. His roughly 18,000 men were not enough to occupy this extensive line and other points in his department.

General Grant intended to strike the Confederacy at several points simultaneously, in an effort to prevent the South from using its interior lines to send troops in one sector to reinforce threatened positions elsewhere. One of those thrusts was launched under the command of Major General Benjamin Butler, who was ordered to move his 30,000-man Army of the James up the

3 Lanier, "Photographing the Civil War," 304. Gardner's account appears in the previous chapter.

4 Smith, *Chamberlain at Petersburg*, 54.

James River, land his troops and strike at Richmond from the south, while Lee was busy fighting Meade's Army of the Potomac farther north. The main purpose was not to capture the Southern capital, but to sever the Richmond and Petersburg Railroad, a major logistical lifeline, forcing Lee to detach troops and thus weaken his army. Butler landed Federal forces at Bermuda Hundred on May 5 (the same day the Wilderness battle began), on the south bank, where he could threaten Petersburg. Beauregard, who turned in one of his finest performances of the war, stifled Union efforts and sealed Butler's command behind a line of entrenchments, ending the Bermuda Hundred campaign.[5]

A month later, on June 9, Butler led an expedition of some 4,500 men to attack Petersburg. By that time Beauregard had available a mere 2,200 militia from the First Military District in Petersburg, commanded by Brigadier General H. A. Wise, to defend this critical rail hub. The men were not primarily Confederate regulars, and included men too old to draft and boys too young for military service. Some were veterans, but others were civilian professionals, shopkeepers and others exempt from military service. Arming them with suitable firearms was one of the top challenges. Only Federal mistakes and a spirited defense saved the city in this First Battle of Petersburg.[6]

Major General William F. "Baldy" Smith's XVIII Corps with a division of cavalry (about 16,000 men) advanced against Petersburg on June 15, with Major General Winfield Hancock's II Corps following. The move forced Beauregard to make some hard choices. Besides the motley force described above, Beauregard's meager command consisted of only two divisions commanded by Major Generals Bushrod Johnson and Robert F. Hoke. Both were preoccupied with blocking Butler's progress at Bermuda Hundred.

Beauregard decided he had no choice but to abandon the Dimmock Line fortifications on the east side of the city south of the Appomattox River, and fall back toward Harrison's Creek. He also made the bold decision to strip the Howlett Line at the Bermuda Hundred and move Hoke's and Johnson's divisions south to defend Petersburg. For three days this small force of about 14,000 men was all that stood between the city and Smith's corps and the heavy

---

5 Surprisingly little has been written about this campaign. Among the best is William Glenn Robertson, *Backdoor to Richmond: The Bermuda Hundred Campaign* (Baton Rouge, LA, 1987).

6 For an excellent account of the June 9 battle, see William Glenn Robertson, *The First Battle for Petersburg: The Attack and Defense of the Cockade City, June 9, 1864* (El Dorado Hills, CA, 2015), and the chapter, "Lions in the Way," 50-78.

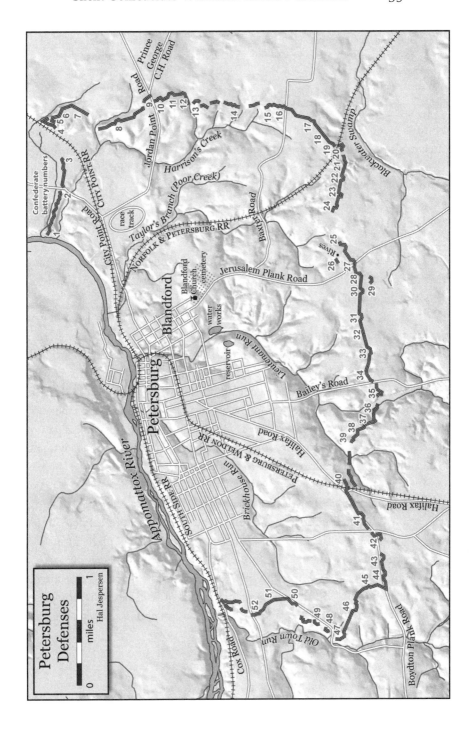

Petersburg
Defenses

0 miles 1

Hal Jespersen

The Dimmock Line, constructed between 1862 and 1864, was a ten-mile arc of artillery batteries and connected infantry earthworks constituting Petersburg's outer defensive perimeter. It surrounded the city on three sides, the Appomattox River forming the northern barrier of protection.

---

reinforcements en route from the Army of the Potomac. The approaching threat triggered urgent appeals to General Lee that Grant had crossed the James River, and was just outside Petersburg. Lee doubted the reports until it was nearly too late to save the city.

Arrival of Troops from the Army of Northern Virginia

Confederate sources confirm that Bushrod Johnson's division, straddling the Baxter Road, constituted the main Rebel presence opposing the V Corps on the left flank of the Union army on June 18, 1864.

In his "Instructions issued June 17, 1864, for the contraction of lines before Petersburg," General Beauregard directed: "General Johnson's line will cross the Baxter Road nearly at right angles, thence running to the Jerusalem Plank Road, and from that point following the original lines. He will extend as far west as his numbers permit." In a message from Petersburg on June 18 at 11:30 a.m., Beauregard added, "Occupied last night my new lines without impediment."[7]

The continued presence of Beauregard's beleaguered troops on this part of the Rebel line into the morning of June 18 is good evidence Kershaw's and Field's divisions had not arrived there on the evening of June 17.

In fact, Confederate sources make it clear those two commands, belonging to James Longstreet's First Corps of the Army of Northern Virginia, remained at Bermuda Hundred until well after midnight. The corps' official diary notes that the movement of Kershaw and Field to Petersburg took place during the early morning hours of June 18: "June 18. At 3 a. m., Kershaw moves for Petersburg, followed by Field, [leaving] Pickett occupying the whole line [at Bermuda Hundred]." Beauregard noted the arrival of Kershaw's division in his sector at 7:30 a.m. on June 18, and of Field's division about 9:30 a.m. General Lee himself arrived at about 11:00 a.m.[8]

---

7   OR 40, pt. 2, 666, 668.

8   Ibid., 761, 668.

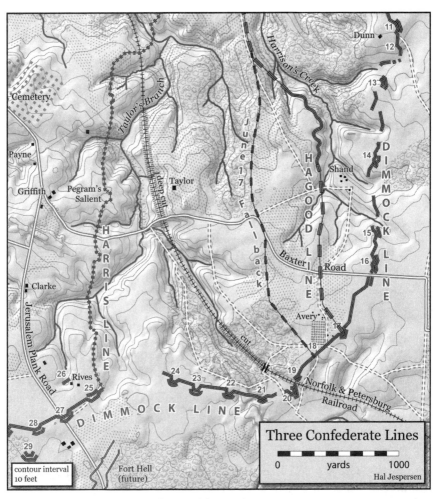

On June 15, 1864, General William "Baldy" Smith's XVIII Corps swept over a 3.5-mile section of Rebel works along the eastern front of Petersburg's outer line, capturing Batteries 3 and 5–11 and prompting a Rebel retreat to the weaker Hagood Line along Harrison's Creek. As more Union troops concentrated to press the attack, General P. G. T. Beauregard's small contingent of defenders fell back, first to a line along the eastern face of woods north and south of the Baxter Road on June 17, and then, on the early morning of June 18, to the inner Harris Line west of Taylor's Branch. The Harris Line would become the permanent Confederate position on the eastern front throughout the ensuing siege.

The Initial Deployment of Kershaw's and Field's Divisions

Writing two decades after the war, Beauregard recalled that Kershaw's division was placed on or behind the sparsely-manned Harris line, with its right flank situated near the Jerusalem Plank Road:

General Kershaw's division, which proved to be the vanguard of General Lee's army, reached Petersburg early Saturday morning, June 18th; it numbered about 5000 men, and, by my orders, was placed on the new line already occupied by our forces with its right on or near the Jerusalem Plank Road, extending across the open field and bending back toward the front of the cemetery.[9]

D. Augustus Dickert, the author of *History of Kershaw's Brigade*, was marching in Colonel John Henagan's brigade, which Kershaw commanded before he was elevated to lead the division. Dickert's account lends support to Beauregard's recollection:

> When we reached Petersburg, about sunrise, we found only Wise's Brigade and several regiments of old men and boys, hastily gotten together to defend their city, until the regulars came up. They had been fighting in the ranks, these graybeards and half-grown boys, for three days, and to their credit be it said, "They weathered the storm" like their kinsmen in Wise's Brigade. . . . Kershaw's brigade relieved that of General Wise, taking position on extreme right, resting its right on the Jerusalem Plank Road, and extending towards the left over the hill and across open fields. Wise had some hastily constructed works, with rifle pits in front. These later had to be relieved under a heavy fire from the enemy's battle line.[10]

Once relieved from the front, Wise's brigade disappears from the record of the events of the day.

Field's division, which consisted of five brigades (Bratton's, Law's, Anderson's, Gregg's, and Benning's), arrived two hours later and took up a position on Kershaw's right.[11] Beauregard would recall that Field did not actually begin deploying his troops until "somewhere between 12:00 m. [noon] and 1:00 p.m."[12]

General Bratton's report makes it clear that, upon arrival, his brigade first went into position on the south side of Petersburg: "On the next morning

9 P. G. T. Beauregard, "Four Days of Battle at Petersburg," in Robert U. Johnson and Clarence Buell, *Battles and Leaders of the Civil War*, 4 vols. (New York, 1884), vol. 4, 543.

10 Dickert, *History of Kershaw's Brigade*, 380. The other three brigades in the division were led by Brigadier Generals William Wofford, Goode Bryan, and Ben Humphreys.

11 *OR* 40, pt. 1, 761.

12 P. G. T. Beauregard, "Four Days of Battle at Petersburg," in *B&L*, vol. 4, 543.

(18th) we were relieved by troops from Pickett's division and moved across the Appomattox to Petersburg and were put in position on the line about Battery Number 34."[13]

Thus, Lee's two divisions were initially deployed to strengthen and extend the right flank of Beauregard's line. Field's division occupied Dimmock fortifications on the south side of Petersburg between Battery 34 and the Jerusalem Plank Road, where his left connected with Kershaw's right. Kershaw's line extended from the Jerusalem Plank Road toward the Baxter Road and the Blandford Cemetery to the north. The lines of the two divisions joined in the general vicinity of Rives' Salient.

Subsequent Movement of Field's Division to the Left

Field's division did not remain on the Dimmock Line south of Petersburg for long, however. By the end of the day, Brigadier General John Bratton was leading his brigade to the left:

> At dark [on June 18] we [Bratton's Brigade] moved to the left and relieved troops on the new line covering the Baxter Road, my left resting on the battery under which the enemy afterward sprung a mine. The works here were very imperfect, and the sharpshooting was incessant and active. The enemy was found next morning [June 19] well intrenched close to our front, and could sharpshoot us from two lines.[14]

William Houghton of the 2nd Georgia, part of Benning's brigade, reported the arrival of his unit at the front line during the night of June 18, and their deployment behind the front line as follows:

> Hood's old division, commanded at that time by General Field, to which the writer belonged, arrived at the front line during the night of the 18th of June, and took

---

13 OR 40, pt. 1, 766. Colonel James Hagood of the 1st South Carolina, part of Bratton's brigade in Field's division, was a bit vague on the timing: "On June 18 we arrived at Petersburg and were put in trenches on the Baxter Road. From this time until July 21 we were constantly on duty and under fire." Ibid., 767.

14 OR 40, pt. 1, 766. Moving left at dark toward the Baxter Road and encountering the enemy the following morning is a common theme in reports from other brigades of Field's division. For example, R. F. Davis of the 7th Georgia, part of Anderson's brigade, also makes reference in his diary to having relieved Bushrod Johnson's division "at dark" on June 18. F. Davis, Co. E, 7th Georgia, diary excerpt supplied by Henry Persons.

position behind the line which had fought all day, and when light dawned we found that we were in close range of the enemy and without works, in an open field. With bayonets for picks and tin cups for spades we speedily threw up earthworks, which afterwards formed part of the famous line of defense.[15]

Even though Benning's brigade was initially placed in position on the Dimmock Line south of Petersburg during the morning of June 18, its members did not think themselves to have "arrived at the front line" until after nightfall, when they "took position behind the line which had fought all day." Houghton subsequently referred to the fact that his regiment, in its new position, was 100 yards west of the future site of the Crater—quite a way to the rear of what would become the Confederate front line during the ensuing nine-month standoff.

According to Joseph Pryor Fuller of the 20th Georgia, also part of Benning's brigade, the Georgians paused an hour in Petersburg, "where considerable excitement prevailed among the female population," and then moved to the extreme right of the line [Battery 34] for a short time, until relieved by men from Lt. Gen. A. P. Hill's Third Corps, after which they moved to the left to relieve Bushrod Johnson's division. When Field's division relieved Johnson, the brigades of Law and Gregg formed in front, with Benning fifty yards behind Law's brigade (under Colonel William Perry). They lay there unprotected for an hour or two and then marched up to the line and "went into the ground before daylight [on June 19]."[16]

Was Field's Division Engaged on June 18?

In a postwar paper presented to the Southern Historical Society, General Field mentioned skirmishing on June 17, but offered nothing to suggest an attack against his division on the 18th. His summary of the events of June 18 is brief and to the point: "I [went] on to Petersburg on the 18th. I took position in the trenches at Petersburg, my left resting at the battery afterwards blown up and known as the 'Mine.'" The First Corps diary entry for June 18, chronicling

---

15 W. R. Houghton and M. B. Houghton, *Two Boys in the Civil War and After* (Montgomery, AL, 1912), 128.

16 J. P. Fuller, diary entry, June 18, 1864, personal communication from Andy Johnson, January 31, 2015.

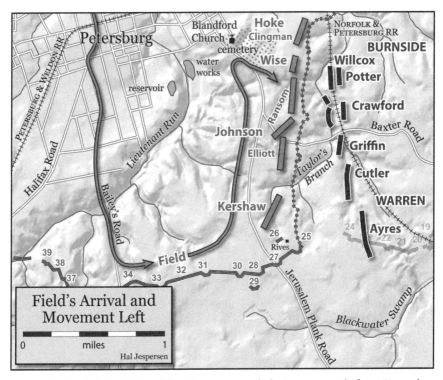

Field's Arrival and Movement Left

0   miles   1

Hal Jespersen

General Charles W. Field and his division started their move south from Bermuda Hundred sometime after 3:00 a.m. on June 18. They crossed the Appomattox River, paused an hour in Petersburg, "where considerable excitement prevailed among the female population," then occupied the extreme right of the Confederate line at Battery 34 for a short time. The deployment may have occurred as late as noon or 1:00 p.m. At dark on the evening of June 18, the division moved to the left and relieved troops on the "new line covering the Baxter Road," where the left of Bratton's brigade "rested on the battery under which the enemy afterward sprung a mine" (Pegram's Salient). Benning's brigade took position during the early morning hours of June 19, in an open field "behind the line that had fought all day," 100 yards west of the future site of the Crater.

the movements of Kershaw's and Field's divisions, included no mention of any action involving those two commands, noting only a feeble attack in the afternoon on Elliott's brigade of Johnson's division, which itself was not even a part of the First Corps.[17]

17 Charles W. Field, "Campaign of 1864 and 1865," *Southern Historical Society Papers*, 52 vols. (Richmond, VA, 1876-1943), vol. 14, 549; *OR* 40, pt. 1, 761. The lack of an attack against Field's division on June 18 correlates with other sources. According to William C. Jordan of the 15th

On February 17, 1879, military historian and attorney John C. Ropes (whose brother Henry, of the famous 20th Massachusetts, was killed at Gettysburg) presented a paper to the Military Historical Society of Massachusetts titled "The Failure to Take Petersburg on June 16-18, 1864." "Field's division," he noted, "was placed at Rives's Salient, on Kershaw's right and where the Jerusalem Plank Road enters the works, and still farther to the right A. P. Hill's Corps was placed. Apparently neither Field nor Hill was engaged on the 18th."[18]

Thus, there is no credible evidence of any major engagement involving Field's division on June 18, which is further evidence against the idea that Joshua Chamberlain launched his famous attack against Rives' Salient.

Was Kershaw's Division Engaged on June 18?

Some evidence suggests skirmishers from Henagan's (formerly Kershaw's) South Carolina brigade, part of Kershaw's division, saw action and suffered light casualties on June 18, as explained by Augustus Dickert:

> Wise had some hastily constructed works, with rifle pits in front. These later had to be relieved under a heavy fire from the enemy's battle line. As the other brigades of the division came up, they took position on the left. Fields' Division and R. H. Anderson's, now of this corps, did not come up for some hours yet. . . . Before our division lines were properly adjusted, Warren's whole corps made a mad rush upon the works, now manned by a thin skirmish line, and seemed determined to drive us from our entrenchments by sheer weight of numbers. But Kershaw displayed no inclination to yield, until the other portions of our corps came upon the field. . . . After some hours of stubborn fighting, and failing to dislodge us, the enemy withdrew to strengthen and straighten their lines and bring them more in harmony with ours.[19]

Alabama, part of Law's (Perry's) brigade, "We went to Petersburg and worked on breastworks every night." W. C. Jordan, *Some Events and Incidents During the Civil War* (Montgomery, AL, 1909), 87.

18 J. C. Ropes "The Failure to Take Petersburg on June 16-18, 1864," in *Papers of the Military Historical Society of Massachusetts* (Boston, 1906), vol. 5, 181. Casualty lists also support this view. For example, a review of the official casualty lists for Anderson's Georgia brigade during the 1864 campaign does not show a single casualty for June 18, 1864. Henry Persons, Personal Communication, Dec. 7, 2014.

19 Dickert, *History of Kershaw's Brigade*, 380-81.

Dickert's account suggests the fighting might have been heavier than an exchange of fire among skirmishers. However, Colonel William Drayton Rutherford of the 3rd South Carolina (also part of Henagan's brigade), indicates otherwise. Writing in his diary on June 18, Rutherford mentioned only the withdrawal of the pickets, and that no attack was launched by Federal forces against that part of the Confederate line: "Arrived at Petersburg early in the morning. Our pickets driven in. The enemy masses in our front but does not attack."[20]

In keeping with the theme, Bryan's Georgians of Kershaw's division found Union works already thrown up within sixty yards of their own when it arrived at the front, which suggests the major assaults had already ended before their arrival. Bryan's brigade seems to have been preoccupied solely with building breastworks under the constant artillery and sniper fire that would come to characterize the ensuing standoff, as this report makes clear:

> The enemy had thrown up works within sixty yards of ours, and when we were placed there, the works were incomplete and we were compelled to complete them under the incessant fire of musketry and artillery, and on some parts of the line the works were begun without any protection whatever. The number of casualties occurring in the brigade at this place will give some idea of the difficulties which had to be contended against.[21]

Brigadier General Benjamin G. Humphreys, who commanded the Mississippi Brigade in Kershaw's division, wrote of his experience in a manuscript titled "Sunflower Guards." According to him, the enemy "halted at the railroad and concealed themselves." Humphreys made no mention of any significant engagement on his front. Here is some of what he wrote:

> I left the Richmond Hospital on the 15th of June and overtook my command at Frazier's farm and reached Petersburg and [went] into line on the Jerusalem Road on the right of General Clingman [Hoke's division] and relieved General Wise. Our division was greatly exhausted, but were cheered by the South Carolinians and Georgians as "fresh troops." We were soon busy constructing breast works, but the enemy "advance" made us lay down our spades. The enemy halted at the railroad and concealed themselves—other columns continued to advance as Grant extended his

---

20 William Drayton Rutherford, diary entry, June 18, 1864, supplied by Mac Wyckoff

21 *OR* 40, pt. 1, 768.

entrenchment to our right, the Confederate forces still arriving and confronting him. Lee was again between him and Richmond.[22]

The absence of any Confederate reports or recollections of an attack on the Dimmock fortifications between Battery 34 and the Jerusalem Plank Road, or of an assault near Rives' Salient at the junction of the Harris and Dimmock lines (where the lines of Field and Kershaw connected) is very significant. If Chamberlain's brigade had struck from the south along the Jerusalem Plank Road, advancing to within a handful of yards of the Rebel fortifications there, surely someone would have noticed.

Redeployment by Field and Kershaw to the Baxter Road Area

There is little or no doubt that Bushrod Johnson's division was the main Confederate force straddling the Baxter Road on the morning of June 18. Johnson's command—primarily the brigades of Stephen Elliott and Matt Whitaker Ransom (under the temporary command of Colonel Paul Faison)[23]—was the one attacked by Charles Griffin's division on the afternoon and evening of June 18. Johnson's division, according to reports from Bratton's, Benning's, and Anderson's brigades, and from Johnson himself, was not relieved by Field and Kershaw until these units from the Army of Northern Virginia were redeployed on the evening of June 18.[24]

However, the logistics of one division, much less two, redeploying and relieving another division is not a rapid or simple process. A good sense of what this entailed at the operational level is found in a pair of sources that cover the activities of the 56th North Carolina, Ransom's brigade, Johnson's division.

According to Captain Robert D. Graham, Company D, who wrote the history of the 56th North Carolina in Walter Clark's *Histories of the Several Regiments and Battalions from North Carolina, in the Great War 1861-'65*, the 56th took position on the crest of the first rise east of the Blandford Cemetery with

---

22 Benjamin G. Humphreys, "Sunflower Guards," in Claiborne Papers #151, Southern Historical Collection, Manuscript Department, Wilson Library, University of North Carolina at Chapel Hill, 25-26.

23 "Ransom's Brigade at Second Petersburg," *Raleigh Confederate*, June 23, 1864, www.beyondthecrater.com/resources/np/1864-np/jun-64-np/np-18640623-raleigh-confede rate-ransoms-brig-2nd-petersburg/.

24 Johnson, "UPR: Report of Major General Bushrod R. Johnson."

its right flank resting on the Jerusalem Plank Road. That part of the line crossed the future site of the infamous Crater, just north of the Baxter Road. The 56th North Carolina was at, or very near, the right flank of Ransom's brigade line.[25]

Elliott's South Carolina brigade was on the immediate right of the 56th North Carolina (a reversal of the relative positions as depicted on Howe's otherwise seemingly accurate map in *Wasted Valor*.)[26] The line of the 56th ran from the point at which it connected with Elliott's brigade, obliquely to the northeast, thus commanding a portion of Elliott's front, which faced due east. The North Carolina regiment was broken into two wings separated by a ravine that crossed the Confederate line and by Pegram's Virginia artillery battery.[27]

James Carson Elliott (not to be confused with the South Carolinian brigadier general with the same last name), also of the 56th North Carolina regiment, recorded his memories of the day's events in *The Southern Soldier Boy: A Thousand Shots for the Confederacy*. It is clear, from his description, that Lee's contingent had not yet arrived on the line by the morning of June 18:

> At daybreak on the 18th, we were standing in single file, half line of battle, when we heard Grant's massive columns charge on our skirmishers, and take the last ditch between them and Petersburg. Our artillery was all in position on our last line. Lee's army had not come and Grant only had a half line of tired and worn-out soldiers in his front, standing in an open field between him and Petersburg.[28]

Captain Graham's regimental history picks up the narrative with a description of the enemy advancing in splendid array, five columns deep, to make their first assault—a vain dash against Elliott's lines to the south—sometime after midday. The storm then shifts to the Confederate left (north) of Pegram's Salient along the front held by the 25th, 35th, and the left wing of the 56th North Carolina regiments, as Sweitzer and troops from the IX Union Corps advanced to the foot of what would come to be called the "Horseshoe" —that long curved salient of the Union line directly fronting Pegram's Salient.

25 Walter Clark, *Histories of the Several Regiments and Battalions from North Carolina, in the Great War 1861-'65*, 5 Vols. (Pub, date?), III, "56th Regiment," 362-64.

26 Howe, *Wasted Valor*, 126.

27 Clark, *Histories of the Several Regiments and Battalions from* North Carolina, 362-64.

28 James Carson Elliott, *The Southern Soldier Boy: A Thousand Shots for the Confederacy* (Raleigh, NC, 1887), 23-25.

As this action was unfolding, elements of Field's division were moving down from the north, advancing as far as Pegram's Salient and the ravine dividing the two contingents of the 56th North Carolina. According to Graham, "They [the Federals] thus [found] a double line ready for them, though crowded into unfinished works."[29]

An anonymous Confederate veteran from Brigadier General Archibald Gracie's brigade of Kershaw's division, writing six years later in *The Plantation* (an Atlanta weekly magazine), confirms the late afternoon arrival of Lee's reinforcements:

> About 3:00 p.m., the Federals, in three lines of battle, attempted to carry the works on our left. . . . Shortly after this, I was ordered to carry a message to General Hoke, then on the left of the line. Riding rapidly down the Jerusalem Road, I met the head of Longstreet's corps near the old Blandford church—General Lee was coming to our aid at last. The enemy discovered that we had been reinforced, and the battle of the 17th and 18th of June ended. We had defended Petersburg with not more than four thousand men against three army corps.[30]

James Carson Elliott picks up the narrative on this issue and provides important details:

> Then to our left, winding down a ravine, we saw Longstreet's column coming in, and soon came crowding up our ditch Anderson's division, South Carolinians and Georgians. Most of these regiments were very short, and I was eager to note what these battle-scarred veterans who had just been fighting for a month through the Wilderness thought of the situation. Tired from an all-night's march, but as soon as they got in position they stripped blankets and piling handfuls of cartridges on the breastworks got up on the parapet, took a look in front and said, "This is a good place; we would like for them to come on ten lines deep, so we won't waste any lead." Then they quietly sat down.[31]

---

29 Clark, *Histories of the Several Regiments and Battalions from* North Carolina, 364

30 Anonymous (1870, July 2), "Memorable Days," *The Plantation* (Atlanta), 374. www.beyond thecrater.com/resources/np/postwar-np/np-18700702-plantation-atlanta-gracie-brig-2nd-petersburg/.

31 Elliott, *The Southern Soldier Boy*, 23-25.

Captain Graham's account described an attack left (north) of Pegram's Salient, directed against a "double line" comprised of weary defenders from Bushrod Johnson's division newly reinforced by arrivals from Lee's Army of North Virginia. After fending off this assault, the left half of Ransom's brigade line was relieved by units from Field's division. However, due to the openness of the ground and the presence of the ravine that had to be crossed in passing Pegram's artillery battery at the salient, it was necessary to postpone the relief of the right wing of the 56th North Carolina until darkness could conceal the movement.[32]

Augustus Dickert left no doubt that Field's troops participated in the repulse of the afternoon Federal assault:

About four o'clock in the afternoon Meade organized a strong column of assault, composed of the Second, Fifth, and the Ninth Army Corps, and commanded in person, holding one corps in reserve. . . . The infantry then commenced the storming of our works, but Field's Division had come up and was on the line. . . . The battle raged furiously until nightfall, but with no better results on the enemy's side than had attended him for the last three days—a total repulse at every point. By noon the next day [June 19], Lee's whole force south of the James was within the entrenched lines of the city, and all felt perfectly safe and secure. Our casualties were light in comparison to the fighting done during the day, but the enemy was not only defeated, but badly demoralized.[33]

What are we to conclude from these accounts concerning Field's movement to the left? It is clear that veterans from Field's division arrived and strengthened Ransom's brigade line left of Pegram's Salient, the future site of the Crater, in the mid-afternoon hours, probably just as Sweitzer, Crawford, and Orlando Willcox of the IX Corps were advancing beyond the railroad and creek to the base of the "Horseshoe." When they arrived at the Harris line, Field's Army of Northern Virginia troops were exclusively north of Pegram's Salient and the ravine separating the two wings of Ransom's brigade. In this location there is no way Chamberlain's men could have confronted them on June 18.

---

32 Clark, *Histories of the Several Regiments and Battalions from* North Carolina, 365.

33 Dickert, *History of Kershaw's Brigade*, 380-81.

Meanwhile, the Federals were organizing a movement against the right wing of Ransom's brigade line, which was held by the 24th North Carolina and the right wing of the 56th North Carolina. These units were arrayed on the southern face of the "Horseshoe." Captain Graham described an unsuccessful early evening advance by Union forces against the 56th North Carolina followed by the arrival of Kershaw's division on the front line:

> Their troops are rapidly massed now in our immediate front, and rush to cover below us along the run at the foot of the steep hill. Just before sundown they advance up the slope, and it is with difficulty that the ardor of the men to fire at the first view of them is restrained; but they appreciate the order to wait until they can sight the belt-buckle as a target, when one or two well-directed rounds ends the business of the day, and it is thought with greater loss to them than on either our right or left, as this time they have been allowed to come in speaking distance. Thus, the day closes; but at the foot of this salient, the enemy, out of reach of shot and shell, has come to stay. . . . In the night Kershaw's division moved up our lines as we march out under a sharp musketry fire of the enemy, doubtless, from the commotion, expecting a counter-charge.[34]

The weight of this evidence corroborates Bushrod Johnson's contention that Kershaw's division did not move to relieve his front line (specifically those units to the right, or south, of Pegram's Salient) until after dark on June 18. Essentially all of Johnson's own troops remained in place until at least 3:00 p.m., and many of them stayed in the front line well beyond that, and likely into the night.

The late arrival of Field's veteran division on the line; the silence of Field and others in his division regarding any engagement with the Federals on the southern front on June 18; the outright denial by Colonel Rutherford of an attack on Kershaw's brigade near the Jerusalem Plank Road; the shifting movement of the Army of Northern Virginia infantry leftward, toward the Baxter Road during the course of the day (due to inactivity in the southern sector)—all of these elements bear silent witness to the fact that Joshua Chamberlain did not attack hardened veterans of Kershaw's and Field's divisions at Rives' Salient from "Fort Hell" along the Jerusalem Plank Road on June 18.

---

34   Clark, *Histories of the Several Regiments and Battalions from North Carolina*, 365-66.

Chamberlain and the other brigades of Griffin's division were not alone on the Union line that afternoon. Federal divisions commanded by Lysander Cutler and Romeyn Ayres, both of Warren's V Corps, were also advancing. What further light might their operations shed on our understanding of the location of Chamberlain's attack?

CHAPTER 12

WHERE WERE THEY DEPLOYED?
The Location of Cutler and Ayres

THE positions of Lysander Cutler's 4th Division and Romeyn Ayres' 2nd Division, both of Warren's V Corps, provide additional evidence of where Chamberlain attacked on June 18.

Diane Smith, author of *Chamberlain at Petersburg* and a leading modern advocate that Chamberlain attacked along the Jerusalem Plank Road, puts Chamberlain's brigade near that road at 1:00 p.m., "squarely in front of and some 300 yards away from Battery No. 25," and roughly one-third of a mile forward of the area where Fort Sedgwick, or "Fort Hell," would later be built. This is clearly incorrect when measured against the historical record.[1]

According to Smith, Cutler's and Ayres' divisions were deployed to the left of Chamberlain's brigade. In a subsequent annotation, she places Cutler, at midday, "in the woods near the Jerusalem Plank Road, no less than three-fourths of a mile to the rear and left of the 1st Brigade," with Ayres' division moving westward to meet a perceived growing threat on the V Corps' left. According to Smith's account, Chamberlain, Cutler and Ayres "were all isolated from the rest of the Army of the Potomac, which at its nearest was a mile to the north."[2]

---

1 Smith, *Chamberlain at Petersburg*, 54.

2 Ibid., 54, 55.

This theory creates a complicated series of dilemmas. Chamberlain supposedly was attacking from the future site of "Fort Hell," which straddled the Jerusalem Plank Road. Chamberlain's brigade frontage probably covered about one-quarter of a mile of ground.[3] Cutler's division was comprised of two brigades (Colonel J. William Hofmann and Brigadier General Edward Bragg), while Ayres' division had three brigades (Colonels Edgar Gregory, Nathan Dushane, and J. Howard Kitching). The extended frontage of these five brigades would have spanned a considerable distance to Chamberlain's left.

This raises four crucial questions: (1) Did their deployment extend west of the Jerusalem Plank Road? (2) If so, why was there a subsequent need for the V Corps to move left toward the Jerusalem Plank Road on June 21? (3) Was Cutler, at midday, three-fourths of a mile behind Chamberlain, as Smith believes, and therefore nearly a mile to the southeast of the Confederate works?[4] (4) Were Cutler and Ayres both east of the Jerusalem Plank Road? Fortunately, these and other contemporaneous records can help us answer these questions.

Cutler's Division

Major Roebling described Cutler advancing his division westward early on the morning of June 18, initially with his left flank hugging the Norfolk Railroad until the point at which the track began bending toward the north. There, he crossed the track and found skirmishers on the opposite bank of the cut to his right (possibly the same Rebels Chamberlain confronted when he attacked the advanced artillery position on the left of Griffin's division). Here is Roebling's account:

> I returned to Cutler with orders for him to advance, keeping his left on the Norfolk Road, because at the Avery house the road appeared to run nearly west. . . . As Cutler advanced it was discovered that the railroad ran through a deep cut turning sharply to the right, and that our whole line would have to cross it. A bridge across the cut was still in flames. On the right of Cutler's line the enemy's skirmishers were encountered on the opposite bank of the cut. A delay of some time was occasioned here before

---

3 Trulock, *In the Hands of Providence*, 208; Nesbitt, *Through Blood and Fire*, 130-131.

4 Smith, *Chamberlain at Petersburg*, 55.

Cutler's line was reformed on the other side of the cut and the enemy's skirmishers had been pressed back.[5]

According to artilleryman Wainwright, Cutler pushed forward at once to take possession of the Avery house, and then continued through a piece of wood beyond.[6]

The V Corps correspondence contains an order from General Warren, relayed by Major Roebling at 11:55 a.m., for Cutler to attack the enemy at noon, moving on the left flank of Griffin's division. There is also a report from Cutler dated 1:30 p.m. that he was situated on a crest about 600 yards from the enemy's works, with a plateau in front of him, and that Chamberlain was under the impression that he was supposed to move to occupy the crest where Cutler was sitting.[7]

Cutler's own report describes the attack that followed:

> At daylight on the 18th I was ordered to move on the enemy's works. The order was immediately executed. The enemy's first and second lines were found to have been abandoned during the night. . . . I pushed my skirmishers and line of battle forward across the Norfolk Railroad, and found the enemy on the crest beyond and in front of Petersburg. The enemy had set fire to the bridges across the railroad cut as they retired. I immediately rebuilt the bridge in my front to enable the batteries to come up. Having formed my command on the left of the railroad in two lines, I moved forward, my right resting on the road, and drove in the enemy's pickets on his works in front of town. . . . At 2:50 p.m., an order was received to advance on the enemy's works; at 3 o'clock an order saying the movement was general. I immediately put my command in position to advance and, at 3:20 p.m., moved forward, my 2nd Brigade (Colonel Hofmann) leading, supported by my 1st Brigade (Colonel Bragg). . . . My command suffered severely, both by direct and flank fire of both infantry and artillery, and though a part of both brigades got within about seventy-five yards of the enemy's works, they were unable to carry them. My men held the ground gained until dark, when, in obedience of orders, I withdrew the most advanced portions of my command and intrenched, connecting with Griffin on my right and Ayres on my left. After intrenching I

---

5   Roebling, "Report of the Operations of the V Corps," June 18, 1864.

6   Nevins, *A Diary of Battle*, 424.

7   OR 40, pt. 2, 187. This suggests that Cutler and Chamberlain were close enough to be communicating and cooperating.

remained in the same position to the close of the month [of July], on the last day of which a mine was sprung in front of the IX Corps and a little to my right.[8]

Additional detail is gleaned from Hofmann's report (also of Cutler's division):

The brigade was moved to the west side of the railroad, and formed in line of battle in a wood, the right of the brigade resting on the railroad, and subsequently moved to the front of the woods and in rear of a hill. At 3 p.m., the brigade was formed in line of battle on the crest of a hill, and moved forward to charge the works of the enemy, then about 700 yards in our front. In order to reach the enemy's works, it was necessary to cross a ravine about 200 yards in front of the works.[9]

These accounts clearly and consistently set forth that Cutler began his attack from a crest beyond the woods in front of the Avery house, 600-700 yards from the Confederate works, with his right resting on the railroad cut, and that his division was a short distance away from the future site of the Crater. There is no mention at all that Cutler moved his 4th Division toward the Jerusalem Plank Road.

Hofmann's Brigade Pushes Chamberlain to the North

Chamberlain summoned Captain John Bigelow, 9th Massachusetts Artillery, to support his 3:00 p.m. infantry charge. Bigelow had accompanied the V Corps in its advance throughout the day, being first engaged from the Baxter Road, then following the earlier charge in the rear of both Chamberlain's and Hofmann's brigades to within 400 yards of the enemy's line.[10] According to his testimony, the two infantry brigades were side-by-side, Chamberlain to the right, and Hofmann to the left.

Cutler's 4th Division was to the right of Ayres' 2nd Division, which was initially straddling the captured Confederate works running perpendicular to Rives' Salient. Ayres later refused his line along those same works to prevent a

8   OR 40, pt. 1, 473.

9   Ibid., 475.

10 Hewitt, ed., OR *Supplement*, 7, 229.

flank attack. At least some of Ayres' division occupied space north of the captured works that ran perpendicular to, and directly opposite, Rives' Salient.

Hofmann's 2nd Brigade was in the lead of the 4th Division's attack on June 18, with Brig. Gen. Edward S. Bragg's 1st Brigade in support. Hofmann's brigade consisted of seven regiments: 3rd Delaware, 4th Delaware, 76th New York, 95th New York, 147th New York, 56th Pennsylvania, and 157th Pennsylvania. The 4th Delaware regiment, which consisted of about 500 men, was attached to the Army of the Potomac at Cold Harbor on June 2, 1864.[11]

One of the members of the Delaware regiment, Lieutenant Henry Gawthrop, recalled in his diary the movement of Hofmann's brigade across the railroad and into dense woods. Beyond the abandoned works, "the 4th Delaware stormed two lines of undefended trenches until it reached the Norfolk and Petersburg Railroad." The Federal soldiers continued through what Gawthrop described as "almost impenetrable woods" until they emerged "in an exposed position and began to receive both musket fire and artillery shelling." The men went prone on the crest of a hill, which gave them some protection from the deadly fire. The Rebel line was about 500 yards distant, and when all was ready, Gawthrop and his comrades reorganized themselves for a bayonet charge.[12]

What makes this account unique and especially revealing is that the text is accompanied by a hand-drawn map showing the precise position of the 4th Delaware and Hofmann's brigade on June 18, 1864. Gawthrop's sketch map is primitive in comparison to maps drawn by the Corps of Engineers, but it is well proportioned and appears to convey the essential information accurately. The map shows Hofmann's brigade near the future site of Fort Meikle. The brigade's right flank is not more than 100-200 yards south of the Baxter Road. The line extended up toward the eastern branch of Taylor's Creek near the point at which the creek crosses the railroad track. It is opposite the salient later identified with the Otey battery on the Confederate Stevens map.[13]

11 *OR* 36, pt. 1, 87.

12 Lieutenant Gawthrop diary, as quoted and used in Justin Carisio, *A Quaker Officer in the Civil War: Henry Gawthrop of the 4th Delaware* (Charleston, SC, 2013), 67.

13 Ibid., 68, 69; W. H. Stevens, "Sketch of the Confederate and Federal Lines around Petersburg," in Library of Congress Civil War Maps, 2nd ed., 610. (This is a point of reference only. The Otey 13th Virginia Light Artillery Battery of the Army of Northern Virginia was not there on June 18.)

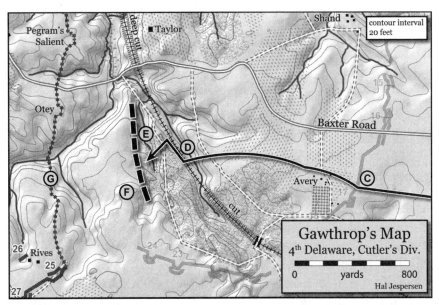

Lieutenant Henry Gawthrop's map shows the route taken to the front at Petersburg by the 4th Delaware Infantry of Hofmann's brigade (Cutler's division, V Corps), on June 18, 1864. The position of the battle line is quite precise and significant, for our purposes, because Chamberlain's brigade was situated to Hofmann's right. This map puts Chamberlain immediately south of the Baxter Road, with his right flank on the Deep Cut of the Norfolk Railroad—exactly where Chamberlain said it was. Gawthrop's labels: (C) abandoned works; (D) Norfolk and Petersburg Railroad; (E) lying down on the crest of a hill offers protection; (F) the knoll; (G) Confederate works, the assault's objective. The Otey designation is a reference point for descriptive purposes only, for the ANV battery had not yet arrived there on June 18. *Redrawn from Gawthrop's map of the 4th Delaware's movements related to the June 18, 1864 assault at Petersburg, Delaware Historical Society*

Further support for placing the right of Cutler's division at this relatively northerly location comes from Bates' *History of Pennsylvania Volunteers.* According to Bates, the 56th Pennsylvania of Hofmann's brigade charged "at a point a quarter of a mile south of the site afterwards selected for the mine," advancing to a position within 30 yards of the Rebel entrenchments. Pegram's Salient, the future site of the exploded mine, is one-quarter of a mile north of the salient here referred to as "Otey's battery." This is significant, because the presence of the 4th Division in this area pushes Chamberlain's brigade to the right. The two brigades could not have occupied the same space at the front. "The enemy had fallen back and thrown up a line of breast-works on the crest beyond the Petersburg and Norfolk Railroad, which shortened by several miles, his line of defense," explained Bates. "At three p.m., this new line was attacked by the whole corps, the 56th charging at a point a quarter of a mile south of the site afterwards selected for the mine."[14]

Gawthrop's account further sets forth that the 4th Delaware's line and the right of the 147th New York (another regiment in Cutler's division) gained a knoll about halfway between the crest of the hill, where the charge began, and the Confederate defenders. Gawthrop identifies this knoll as position "F" on his map, and it is somewhat north of Rives' Salient.[15] The implication is that the left flank of Hofmann's brigade advanced there. If so, Hofmann's thrust was along a line extending perhaps a quarter of a mile in length.

Gawthrop's decision to map Hofmann's location unknowingly provided us an important clue as to the whereabouts of Chamberlain's brigade on June 18. If Hofmann occupied the 400 yards between the "knoll" and the "Otey" redoubt, not much space remained south of the Baxter Road to accommodate Chamberlain on Hofmann's right. The adjacent 400 yards to the north of Hofmann straddles the Baxter Road. This area is where the Rebel line and the Norfolk Railroad are converging, which allowed Chamberlain to simultaneously have his right flank on the Deep Cut of the railroad, and yet be situated only "300-400 yards" from the Confederate works. It is the same ground that Chamberlain had reconnoitered with Griffin when they galloped across a clearing "straight for the Rebel batteries" that were situated across the "deep cut" of the railroad, near the Baxter Road. This is the ground that he carried by his "pardonable ruse" earlier that day of sneaking around to the left in the woods and then wheeling to the right to drive away the Confederate light artillery from the ridge crests.

In this location, straddling the Baxter Road, Chamberlain could have seen Captain Charles E. Mink firing on his right front from north of the Taylor house. He could have also keyed on a salient to his front—Pegram's Salient (later mistaking it for Rives')—while simultaneously receiving slant fire on his left flank from the "Otey" position and from Rives' Salient (later mistaking it for Fort Mahone).

The overwhelming weight of evidence describing the activities of Hofmann's brigade and Cutler's division consistently and compellingly demonstrates that neither unit was anywhere near the Jerusalem Plank Road or the future site of "Fort Hell" on June 18, 1864.

14 Bates, *History of Pennsylvania Volunteers*, vol. 2, 223.

15 Carisio, *A Quaker Officer in the Civil War*, 69.

Ayres' Second Division

Major Roebling also described the early morning movement of Ayres' division to the left, behind and around Cutler, to a position along the old line of rebel fortifications. There, the division went into formation with half of the force to the left of the old Confederate line (Batteries No. 20-24). Unlike Chamberlain, Ayres *was* opposite Rives' Salient, although to the east, not to the south:

> Ayres' division, in the meantime moved around behind Cutler's to his left, along the old line of fortifications, and there formed, about half his troops being to the left of the old line; as soon as his troops showed themselves, the enemy's guns opened upon them, doing considerable execution. The enemy's lines seemed to form a salient opposite Ayres where their new line joined on to the old one.[16]

Colonel Wainwright corroborates Roebling's account. He has Ayres' division, along with the batteries of Rittenhouse, Rogers, and Walcott, passing behind and to the left of Cutler and crossing the railroad, with the batteries going into position 900 yards in front of "the great salient of the enemy's works."[17]

The V Corps correspondence between Generals Ayres and Warren provides additional information regarding his division's location and activities:

> Ayres (11:15 a.m.): I have established my line to the left of General Cutler, across the railroad, on a crest in the open. I drove the enemy's skirmishers from it, and am now intrenching. Also shall establish batteries. The ground falls from the crest about 200 yards to a deep ravine. It rises from the other side gradually, about the same distance, to the first line of rebel works; still rising, you come to their second line. Their line runs beyond my left, which I have refused.

> Warren (1:10 p.m.): You must silence the battery in your front [at Rives' Salient], so as to keep them from firing down our lines to your right, when we advance. If I get an order to attack with the whole corps, I shall have you advance with the others. At present, I am waiting for the attack to come up from our right.

---

16 Roebling, "Report of the Operations of the V Corps," June 18, 1864.

17 *OR* 40, pt. 1, 481-82.

Warren (2:40 p.m.): General Burnside [IX Corps] and myself going to assault on our whole front at 3 p.m. You must move at that time against the works in your front. Any enfilading batteries on the left will soon cease as we advance. Have a brigade to cover your left.[18]

Unfortunately, Ayres did not receive his orders in time and he failed to advance in the mid-afternoon assault, as General Cutler would later lament:

Having formed my command on the left of the railroad in two lines, I moved forward, my right resting on the road, and drove in the enemy's pickets on his works in front of the town, General Ayres' (2nd) Division having in the meantime come in on my left. At 2:50 p.m., an order was received to advance on the enemy's works; at 3 o'clock an order saying the movement was general. I immediately put my command in position to advance and, at 3:20 p.m., moved forward, my 2nd Brigade (Colonel Hofmann) leading, supported by my 1st Brigade (Colonel Bragg). General Ayres, of the 2nd Division, did not receive the order in time to enable him to move simultaneously with me.[19]

Ayres assumed a defensive posture using the "heavy [previously Confederate] works running perpendicular to the line of battle, putting troops in those works for the night."[20]

Ayres' division, holding the left flank of Warren's V Corps, was situated on the old Confederate defensive perimeter between Batteries 22 and 24 on the evening of the June 18 assault. There were no V Corps troops either at the Jerusalem Plank Road or near the "Fort Hell" site.

Major General Ambrose Burnside's IX Corps also played a role in the drama, at the opposite end of the line farther to the north. Its position and activities, especially the tradeoff between tne V and IX Corps, offer further support about the location of Chamberlain's attack. This topic is explored in depth in the following chapter.

18 Ibid., pt. 2, 184.

19 Ibid., pt. 1, 473.

20 Ibid., pt. 2, 184.

CHAPTER 13

MORE EVIDENCE:
The Role of Burnside's IX Corps

I**T** is widely known that Major General Ambrose Burnside's IX Corps occupied the ground west of Taylor's Branch in front of Pegram's Salient during the latter part of June and July. The position would be used as a base from which Pennsylvania coal miners would dig a tunnel and pack the end with gunpowder. The explosion triggered heavy fighting on July 30 and left a gaping scar in the front lines that would soon be known as simply "the Crater." What is not as well understood is that General Griffin's 1st Division of the V Corps was largely responsible for initially securing the Federal foothold on the "Horseshoe" that made it possible for Union commanders even to conceive of the grand scheme that would eventually culminate in the July 30 disaster.

Seven regimental histories from the 1st Division—three from Chamberlain's 1st Brigade and four from Sweitzer's 2nd Brigade—confirm that those brigades charged and occupied the position from which Burnside's famous mine was later dug and exploded. There is no dispute that Burnside's IX Corps lines were exclusively north of the Baxter Road at that time.

For example, here are several accounts that address this point penned by members of Chamberlain's brigade:

> Horatio N. Warren, 142nd Pennsylvania: We were instructed to retire across the ravine as quietly as possible and build a line of works on the brow of the hill from which we charged. . . . From this position we were soon relieved by the IX Corps, from which command a regiment of miners dug under and mined the enemy's fort and works.

From this advanced position, they kept the pits we dug that day, after further strengthening them, full of men and kept them firing constantly for six weeks. The miners of the regiment at the same time were tunneling under their fort and works, which were, at the end of this time, blown up, burying a battery of artillery and quite a number of men. This was known as "Burnside's Mine." We moved to the left when relieved, extending our lines in that direction. Our next important work was building a fort, which was named "Fort Hell."[1]

Thomas Chamberlain, 150th Pennsylvania: Major Jones' command sprang nimbly through the hollow to the summit of the little hill, and seeing the long line of the 187th Pennsylvania following in admirable array, with the other supports close upon their heels, dashed swiftly into the second ravine and up its farther slope to the very base of the formidable earthwork which was subsequently blown up by Burnside's famous mine.[2]

Bates, *History of Pennsylvania Volunteers* (150th Pennsylvania): On the 18th, the V Corps became heavily engaged. At noon the brigade crossed the Suffolk Railroad, and took position to the right of the 4th Division, in a ravine, within three hundred yards of the enemy's strong works, which were subsequently blown up by the Mine.[3]

Survivors Association, *History of the 121st Pennsylvania*: In the morning of the 19th, the regiment was ordered out after being under severe fire for eighteen hours, forming behind the works, and remaining until the 20th, when it was relieved by troops of the Ninth Army Corps, and moved at dusk one mile to the rear.[4]

Here are others from Sweitzer's Brigade:

Major James A. Cunningham, 32nd Massachusetts: Toward night moved to the left, charged and took the crest of a hill, now occupied by the left of the IX Corps.[5]

---

1   Warren, *Two Reunions of the 142nd Regiment, Pa. Vols.,* 37.

2   Thomas Chamberlain, *History of the 150th Regiment, Pennsylvania Volunteers, Second Regiment, Bucktail Brigade,* 213.

3   Bates, *History of Pennsylvania Volunteers, vol. 4,* 654-5.

4   W. W. Strong, *History of the 121st Regiment Pennsylvania Volunteers by the Survivors' Association* (Philadelphia, 1906), 87.

5   *OR* 40, pt. 1, 460.

F. J. Parker, 32nd Massachusetts: While the engagement was not an entire success, it gave us the vantage ground of the crest of a hill, which we retained and whereon we established our line of entrenchments; and this was the position from which the Burnside mine was afterwards made and exploded.[6]

J. L. Parker and R. G. Carter, 22nd Massachusetts: The 1st Brigade, which had assaulted with us, had been previously repulsed. General Chamberlain being dangerously wounded, and falling back, left our flank exposed. After bringing off what dead and wounded we could, the line moved back and reformed, leaving the Twenty-second to dig rifle pits and hold the picket line. We were relieved under a brisk and galling fire towards morning. The crest, referred to afterwards, formed that part of the line of the IX Corps opposite Elliott's [Pegram's] Salient, where the mine was started.[7]

O. B. Knowles, 21st Pennsylvania Cavalry (dismounted): On the 18th of June, the day [Colonel Chamberlain was] so fearfully wounded, we made several desperate charges on the works in front of Petersburg. Immediately in front of my Regt. was the redoubt which our forces afterwards so unsuccessfully attempted to blow up ("Burnside's mine"). By actual measurement, we got within 55 yards of this work, but the fire was too fearful to advance further.[8]

Bates, *History of Pennsylvania Volunteers* (91st Pennsylvania): At dusk, the division moved to the left, and was ordered to charge the enemy occupying a hill, where the mine was subsequently sprung.[9]

According to Alice Trulock, Chamberlain's two lines of battle "stretched about two hundred yards each way from him, in all about a quarter of a mile in length."[10] Chamberlain's quarter-mile line advanced on Colonel Hofmann's right. If Hofmann was a quarter of a mile south of the site afterward selected for "Burnside's mine," then Chamberlain's right was at the mine site north of the Baxter Road—just as regimental historians from the 1st Brigade asserted.

6 Francis Jewett Parker, *The Story of the Thirty-second Regiment, Massachusetts Infantry: Whence it Came, Where it Went, What it Saw, and What it Did*, (Boston, 1880), 223.

7 Parker and Carter, *History of the Twenty-second Massachusetts Infantry*, 472-73.

8 Oliver Knowles to Joshua L. Chamberlain, December 15, 1865.

9 Bates, *History of Pennsylvania Volunteers*, vol. 3, 192.

10 Trulock, *In the Hands of Providence*, 208.

This is significant because all of the Chamberlain and Sweitzer regimental histories that mention the IX Corps and Burnside's mine place the assault *north* of the Baxter Road. If Chamberlain's brigade was relieved from a position on a crest that was later held by Burnside's corps (as multiple observers maintain), then at least part of its line of attack had to have been north of the Baxter Road. This completely discredits the theory that Chamberlain attacked the Rives' Salient along the Jerusalem Plank Road from the future site of "Fort Hell" nearly a mile to the left.[11]

In the clamor and confusion of battle, amidst the smoke of thunderous shelling, and reeling from a brutal wound, is it any wonder that Chamberlain's subsequent recollection might have been less than perfect? In fact, this seems to have been the case, as we shall see when we consider Chamberlain's reminiscence of one of his comrades and personal friends from the IX Corps who commanded a battery in support of the fateful June 18 charge at Petersburg.

11 Warren, "Two Reunions of the 142nd Regiment, Pa. Vols.," 37.

CHAPTER 14

MEMORIES CONTRADICTED:
Twitchell's 7th Maine Battery

As he compiled his information and wrote *The Passing of the Armies* during the last years of his life, Joshua Chamberlain's thoughts traveled back to the terrible day of his famous charge at Petersburg. He "remembered" catching a glimpse of Captain Adelbert Twitchell's 7th Maine battery positioned on the slopes above what he thought was Rives' Salient as he lapsed into a state of unconsciousness. This is how he wrote up his memory:

> Here passes steadily to the front as of yore the 7th Maine Battery, Twitchell, my late college friend, at the head: splendid recessional, for I saw it last in 1864 grimly bastioning the slopes above Rives' Salient, where darkness fell upon my eyes, and I thought to see no more.[1]

His recollection of this chance visual encounter with an old friend in a moment of extremity, if accurate, provides yet another strong piece of evidence that Chamberlain's 1st Brigade did not attack Rives' Salient from "Fort Hell."

Adelbert Twitchell was a college friend from Chamberlain's home state of Maine who went on to command the 7th Maine Light Artillery Battery. The unit was attached to Brigadier General Orlando B. Willcox's 3rd Division of Burnside's IX Corps. As noted earlier, the IX Corps was to the right of

---

1 Chamberlain, *The Passing of the Armies*, 338.

Warren's V Corps on June 18. Willcox's division was operating, in conjunction with Crawford's 3rd Division, V Corps, just north of the Taylor house on the right side of the Baxter Road.

Quartermaster-Sergeant Albert Twitchell penned *History of the 7th Maine Light Battery* (1892), documenting an engagement on June 18 in which the IX Corps drove the enemy across the Norfolk Railroad. In that action, Captain Adelbert Twitchell's battery took position on a crest commanding the enemy's line of works, just as Chamberlain accurately recalled:

> On the 18th, the Battery went into position beyond the woods, and was engaged at about 700 yards, with two lines of infantry in front. The enemy were here driven back by the IX Corps across the Norfolk Railroad; and the Battery, advancing, took position on the crest of a hill commanding the enemy's new line of works, and kept up a constant fire to prevent the strengthening of their works and to assist the Union troops in advancing.[2]

Captain Twitchell's battle report for June 18 is very specific as to the precise location of his guns. "My battery was ordered into position in rear of the line of the 2nd Division [IX Corps]," he wrote, "on the crest between the belt of pinewoods that extend out to the turnpike road, and the small clump of pines to the rear and right of the Taylor house."[3]

Twitchell's account poses a major problem for the "Fort Hell" attack scenario because, as noted, Burnside's IX Corps was never in the vicinity of "Fort Hell," the Jerusalem Plank Road, or Rives' Salient on June 18—and no writer or historian has ever to my knowledge argued otherwise. The IX Corps was north of the Baxter Road, to the right of the Taylor property, and so was Twitchell's battery.

Two days after the June 18 assault, the 7th Maine Light artillery moved even farther to the north, before returning to the vicinity of the Baxter Road and going into position near the brick wall of the Taylor ruins on June 23:

> Here [north of the road, to the right of the Taylor property] the battery remained until the night of June 20, when it moved to the right, with the 3rd Division, and took an

---

2 Albert Sobieski Twitchell, *History of the Seventh Maine Light Battery: Volunteers in the Great Rebellion* (Boston, 1892), 27-28. Captain Adelbert Twitchell and Quartermaster-Sergeant Albert Twitchell may have been brothers. They were born four years apart.

3 OR 40, pt. 1, 603.

"Twitchell's Battery Before Petersburg, June 25, 1864," by Andrew McCallum, an artist and war correspondent hired by Frank Leslie to provide material for his *Illustrated Magazine*. It was found in Orlando Willcox papers in private hands and photographed by author Garth Scott. The original was supposedly in the Orlando B. Wilcox Papers at U.S. Military History Institute at Carlisle, Pennsylvania, but the curators there are unable to locate it.

advanced position to the left of the Hare House, within 300 yards of the enemy, and opened fire on his works. Held this position, with frequent firing from both sides . . . until the night of June 23, when the 3rd Division returned to the left and the battery was placed in position near the Taylor house, about 50 yards in advance of the works known as Fort Morton, near Burnside's Mine.[4]

During the night of the 23rd the division moved to the left, and with four guns I relieved Mink's battery, of the V Corps, placing my guns in a redoubt to the right of the brick wall of the Taylor house. Tuesday, June 28, the left section was placed in position on the hill to the left of the turnpike road. The position is a commanding one, and has since been occupied by two batteries.[5]

Fifty years later, when Joshua Chamberlain wrote that his last visions were of Twitchell's battery and Rives' Salient, he had no knowledge that he was describing an impossible situation. Either his charge was from "Fort Hell," along the Jerusalem Plank Road as he seems to have believed, and the vision of

4   A. S. Twitchell, *History of the Seventh Maine Light Battery*, 27-28.

5   *OR* 40, pt. 1, 603.

Twitchell's battery was a figment of his clouded consciousness, or his attack was within eyesight of Twitchell and his guns, which means the attack was made nearly a mile away near the Baxter Road, and his memory concerning his position on the battlefield was simply flawed after the passage of so many years.

In all probability, Chamberlain recognized and remembered the colors of a familiar battery from his home state commanded by an old friend. On the other hand, it is easy to see how he might have been spatially disoriented in an unfamiliar setting, especially amidst the smoke and clouds of battle and the dimming of his aging consciousness.

Despite inconsistencies such as these, it is remarkable how accurate Chamberlain's recall was regarding the movements of his command and the appearance of the battlefield from his vantage point on the ground.

CHAPTER 15

UNDERSTANDING THE BATTLEFIELD:
The Terrain Never Lies

E ARLY in my study of the terrain at Petersburg, I made composite enlargements of tiled topographical historical maps, which I then spread out on the floor of my study. Tongue depressors represented infantry brigades, and dried butter beans represented artillery batteries. Moving the individual units in accordance with historical records helped me grasp the spatial-time issues and better understand what had transpired.

Knowing the terrain of a battlefield is crucial to understanding any engagement. Differences in elevation, the distance the assault must cover to reach the enemy lines, the presence or absence of ground cover and water obstacles, and natural or man-made defensive barriers, among others, play a role in determining movement, tactics, and the outcomes of combat.

Left Hanging in the Air

In "The Charge at Fort Hell," Chamberlain wrote that his brigade was "far advanced from the rest of the army," and that he had to place two good regiments on his exposed left flank to guard it.[1] In "Lines before Petersburg," Chamberlain lamented that his "left flank [is] in the air with no support

---

1 Chamberlain, "The Charge at Fort Hell," 5.

whatever." How could he have found himself in such an exposed situation if the 1st Brigade was securely in the center of the V Corps line, between Crawford's division and Sweitzer's brigade to its right, and the divisions of Cutler and Ayres to its left? The terrain provides the answer.[2]

Chamberlain's brigade made the farthest advance of any V Corps brigade during the mid-afternoon attack on June 18. Chamberlain estimated that the distance from the launching point of his 3:00 p.m. charge to the front of the enemy's works was about 300 yards. Cutler's 4th Division, to Chamberlain's left, was delayed in its progress because it had to rebuild burned bridges across the railroad to its front to facilitate the advance of the artillery batteries that accompanied the infantry. By the time Cutler was ready, Colonel J. William Hofmann, commanding his 2nd Brigade, estimated the enemy works to be about 700 yards distant. Ayres' division was farther to the left and rear, straddling the abandoned Confederate works running perpendicular to the line of battle (Batteries 22-24). Hofmann's artillery was 900 yards in front of "the great salient of the enemy's works."[3] Thus, the brigade and division lines were staggered in step-like fashion, leaving the left flanks exposed at multiple levels.

Chamberlain's line, anchored on its right flank at the Deep Cut of the Norfolk and Petersburg Railroad,[4] formed an acute angle with respect to the railroad because of the curvature of the track away from the Rebel works as it moved southeast. When he made his charge, his line was not advancing due west, but somewhat to the northwest. This is because the thrust of the assault was aimed more generally in that direction, and also because of the local terrain.

The ridges that temporarily sheltered the 1st Brigade from the Confederate barrage had a slightly oblique orientation with respect to the Rebel line. When the brigade made its downhill charge, it was along a slope of ground dropping off more to the northwest, than directly west. For this reason, the brigade's forward movement probably also had an accelerating rightward momentum as the men descended, first on a quick march, then at the double quick, and finally on the run, as described by Patrick De Lacy.[5]

---

2 Chamberlain, "Lines Before Petersburg, June 18, 1864."

3 Perhaps with the exception of Sweitzer's brigade, which advanced north of the Baxter Road; Chamberlain, "The Charge at Fort Hell," 6; *OR* 40, pt. 1, 473-476, 481-482; ibid., pt. 2, 184.

4 Chamberlain, "Lines Before Petersburg, June 18, 1864."

5 DeLacy, "Reminiscences to Chamberlain," 4.

Leading from the Right, Moving Toward the Right

When Chamberlain executed his "pardonable ruse" to get around the flank of the enemy, his goal was to get across the "Deep Cut" of the Norfolk and Petersburg Railroad north of the Baxter Road. He did this by moving first left and then right to get around the cut.[6] His goal was almost certainly to move back to the right and join up with the other assaulting brigade of his division under Sweitzer, which was attacking north of the Baxter Road.

Prior to the 3:00 p.m. attack, Patrick DeLacy's account places Chamberlain and his staff at the extreme right of the 1st Brigade:

> The 143rd Regiment Pennsylvania Vols. held your right on the front line, and I commanded the right company. When we halted and laid down, we were on the side of the ridge sloping to the rear. This ridge ran nearly parallel with the enemy's main line, and within four or five hundred yards of their main works.
>
> General, you and your staff sat down on the ground within about a yard from where I was lying on the ground within about a yard of my Company A, 143rd P. V. I believe you gave us the post of honor that day, right of brigade and front of line.[7]

DeLacy continued his narrative by describing conversations he overheard between his colonel and other staff officers, and he shared his canteen with the commander just a few minutes before the forward movement commenced.[8] DeLacy was describing the command post of the 1st brigade, such as it was.

The Pennsylvanian also wrote that Chamberlain led his men from the front, carrying the brigade flag himself. Chamberlain confirmed this in "The Charge at Fort Hell": "In five minutes time my flag bearer was shot dead. I took the flag from his dying hands, without a look at the poor fellow, and pressed on."[9]

---

6   See Chapter 5 for more details.

7   DeLacy, "Reminiscences to Chamberlain," 4.

8   Ibid., 4-5.

9   Ibid., 5-6; Chamberlain, "The Charge at Fort Hell," 10. If in fact Chamberlain advanced with the flag, it is fair to wonder about his motivation. He was the brigade commander, after all, not a color-sergeant. Chamberlain's proper position was behind the advancing lines so he could oversee his entire brigade. At the front of the charge, with a large banner in hand, his ability to effectively direct his command, or even to see much of it, would have been severely compromised, and it was dangerous to carry a flag into battle. Perhaps Chamberlain felt the moment was such that the objective could be achieved by nothing other than such inspiration.

It is not entirely clear whether the colonel led from the right front, as DeLacy's account suggests, or more from the center of a line that stretched for some 200 yards to either side of him, as Trulock supposes, with support from Horatio Warren's narrative.[10] Either way (and especially if the brigade moved on a diagonal line even slightly oriented toward the northwest), it is easy to see how Chamberlain could have migrated farther to the right during his advance. That movement could have easily placed his command in front of John Bigelow's battery position, which was also on the right flank of the brigade near the "Deep Cut." It was there that the commander fell, still carrying the flag[11] and in full view of the captain of the 9th Massachusetts battery, who then dispatched a contingent of artillerymen to carry Chamberlain off of the field.[12]

Standing on Spongy Ground

In his "Lines before Petersburg" communication, Chamberlain made particular reference to the "swampy, boggy" ground in his front, just before the charge.[13] Thirty-five years later, in "The Charge at Fort Hell," Chamberlain recalled being at the bottom of a slope "on the borders of a marsh or bog, which men could not well pass."[14]

Patrick DeLacy remembered the same difficult terrain, which he described as a muddy swamp:

> On the other side a small rivulet or stream ran down right along our front and washed out three or five feet deep and from four to six feet in width at the top with banks perpendicular. . . . The swamp and brush was hard to get through, as it was forty or fifty yards across at many places. It really was an obstacle like the sunken road at Waterloo

---

10 Trulock, *In the Hands of Providence,* 208; Warren, *Two Reunions of the 142nd Regiment, Pa. Vols.,"* 35.

11 Chamberlain, "The Charge at Fort Hell," 10-11: "I raised the flag, the Red Cross, high as I could and waving this in one hand and my saber with the other, towards the left, continued shouting and signaling, 'to the left: to the left.' In the hissing and roar and blinding flying earth, standing and so signaling, I felt a sharp hot flash that seemed to cut my backbone. . . . Perforce I dropped flag-staff and saber to the ground; holding them upright, however, without claiming much heroism for that, as I had need of both for my staff and stand."

12 Baker, *History of the 9th Massachusetts Battery,* 124.

13 Chamberlain, "Lines before Petersburg, June 18, 1864."

14 Chamberlain, "The Charge at Fort Hell," 10-11.

that you did not observe until we were mixed in it, and then we had the deep gully made by that small stream to cross. Many of the boys jumped across it and fell back into the mud and water and clambered up its steep sides and rushed on up into the field and nearly reached the enemy's breastworks.[15]

The significance of this forty- to fifty-yard wide area of swamp and brush at the bottom of the slope cannot be overlooked. The brigade had to traverse this marsh before reaching the four- to six-foot wide gully formed by the stream itself. Looking at a topographical map, one can readily see boggy low land close to the Confederate lines near the Baxter Road. There is no such marshy terrain south of Rives' Salient on a Jerusalem Plank Road approach, where the ground is more of a broad plateau on a divide between the Blackwater Creek and Taylor's Branch basins. Furthermore, the branches of Taylor's Creek northeast of Rives' Salient are headwaters, and thus likely to be associated with shallow ravines. The creek near the Baxter Road, however, is a confluence of multiple tributaries, producing higher flow, greater width and steeper banks, which match the descriptions penned by those who fought there.

It was on the border of this marshy bog at the bottom of the descent that Chamberlain made a half-face to the left and gave the command, "Incline to the left," in an effort to circumnavigate the swamp. It was at that moment that he felt a "hot sharp flash" in his back, and noted that a twelve-pound shell or case shot had exploded immediately behind him.[16]

The Mysterious Gap

Maps from the days immediately following the battle of June 18 show a discontinuity of the front line of Federal entrenchments north and south of the Baxter Road. There is an east-west dislocation of perhaps 100-150 yards between adjacent ends of the lines. The gap continues to show up on Union maps for several months, and yet it has never been adequately explained.

The fact that the Baxter Road and a confluence of multiple tributaries of Taylor's Branch pass directly through the center of this break in the line makes it difficult to escape the conclusion that the swampy terrain had something to

15 DeLacy, "Reminiscences to Chamberlain," 5-6.

16 Chamberlain, "The Charge at Fort Hell," 11. (On page 12, Chamberlain identifies the missile that had wounded him as a minié ball.)

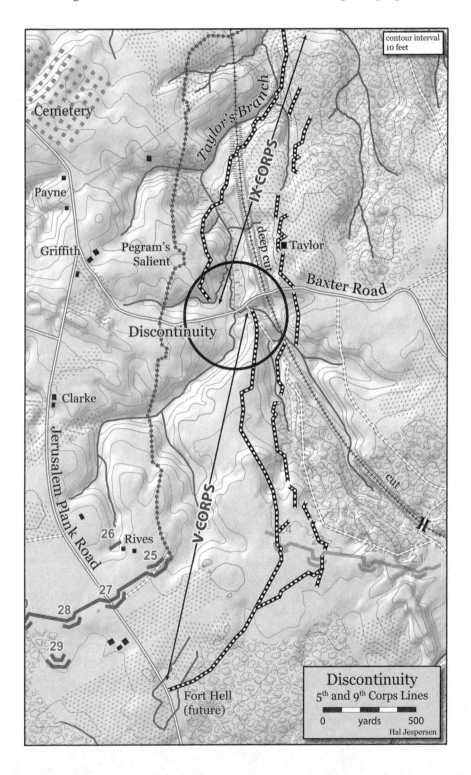

contour interval
10 feet

Cemetery

Payne

Griffith

Pegram's
Salient

Discontinuity

Clarke

Taylor's Branch

IX CORPS

deep cut

Taylor

Baxter Road

V CORPS

26
Rives
25

27

28

29

cut

Jerusalem Plank Road

Fort Hell
(future)

Discontinuity
5th and 9th Corps Lines

0   yards   500

Hal Jespersen

The facing-page map is based on Plate 64 (dated July 28, 1864) of the *Official Military Atlas of the Civil War*. How the lines are labeled does not seem to matter. On early maps such as this one, trenches north of the Baxter Road are associated with the IX Corps, while the lines to south are labeled "V Corps." As the V Corps continued its leftward migration, later maps (including a Michler "Map of the Environs of Petersburg, drawn from triangulations and surveys done between July 9 and September 25, 1864") show units of the 1st Brigade of Potter's Division, IX Corps, occupying the trenches extending south from the Baxter Road to Fort Sedgwick. Nevertheless, the gap persists—even within the line of a single corps.

---

do with the existence of the gap. First, it would have been a difficult place to fortify. The infantry had trouble just crossing the marshy bog, let alone trying to build on it. Secondly, it would have been a dangerous place to work because it was a salient and easily covered from multiple angles by Confederate sharpshooters and artillery. Finally, it would have been nearly impossible for an attacking enemy to traverse this terrain.

According to Horatio Warren of the 142nd Pennsylvania, his unit descended the crest from which Chamberlain launched his attack and passed through a ravine and up the bank on the opposite side. There, the men dug pits and remained until 3:00 a.m. the next morning, when the Pennsylvanians moved back across the same ravine to the original jump-off point for the attack. Once there, the men began fortifying the ridge. The Pennsylvanians, noted Warren, left behind pits filled with men who were later relieved by troops from Burnside's IX Corps including a regiment of miners who would go on to dig the mine to the Crater site.[17]

I believe the gap in the lines at the Baxter Road is where Warren's men crossed. The same spongy ground that impeded Chamberlain's charge now formed a natural protective barrier against a Confederate attack. If my assumption is correct, it provides additional evidence supporting a Baxter Road location for Chamberlain's attack.

Chamberlain's statement that he was bombarded by the big guns of Fort Mahone poses an additional potential problem, and opponents of the Baxter Road scenario have raised other criticisms as well. We now turn our attention to those issues.

---

17 Warren, *Two Reunions of the 142nd Regiment, Pa. Vols.*, 37.

CHAPTER 16

OBJECTIONS CONSIDERED:
Was it Fort Mahone?

In "The Charge at Fort Hell," Chamberlain described a large fort on his left that enfiladed the slope in his front with heavy guns, as did ten or twelve guns behind works in his front.[1] Advocates of the Rives' Salient scenario of Chamberlain's attack argue that Fort Mahone is the only possible candidate to represent the large fort on the left. Are there other potential explanations?

If Chamberlain's attack was from a point just south of the Baxter Road at a distance of 300-400 yards from the enemy's front, as he claimed, his brigade would have been within easy canister range from artillery positioned along the Confederate line. From the Baxter Road location, Rives' Salient would have been some 800-1,200 yards away, and Pegram's Salient to the right about 600-1,000 yards. These distances are well within range of 12-pounder Napoleons (1,600 yards) and 10-pounder Parrott Rifles (1,850 yards), as the sketch of Union artillery placements and targets from Plate 64 of the *Official Atlas of the American Civil War* (reproduced on the next page) clearly demonstrates.

The "Order of Battle for Confederate Forces, Department of North Carolina and Southern Virginia for June 10, 1864" lists six artillery batteries and their associated battalions attached to Bushrod Johnson's division: Bradford's Mississippi Battery (Coit); Cummings' Battery C, 13th North Carolina Battery

---

1 Chamberlain, "The Charge at Fort Hell," 6.

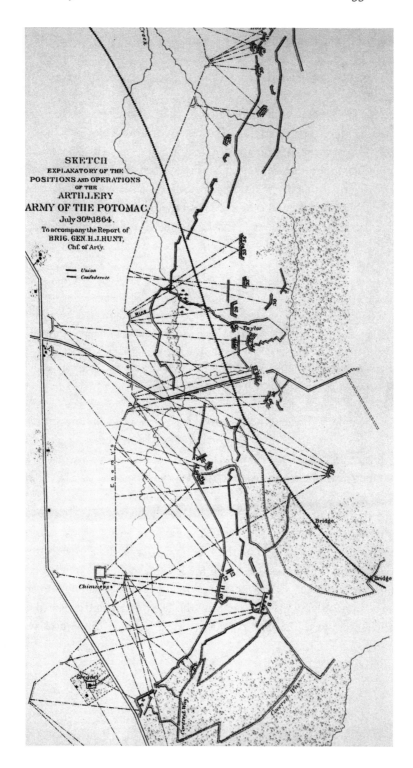

SKETCH
EXPLANATORY OF THE
POSITIONS AND OPERATIONS
OF THE
ARTILLERY
ARMY OF THE POTOMAC
July 30th 1864.
To accompany the Report of
BRIG. GEN. H.J.HUNT,
Chf. of Arty.

Union
Confederate

(Moseley); Miller's Battery E, 1st North Carolina (Wilmington Light) (Moseley); Pegram's Petersburg Virginia Light Artillery Battery (Coit); Wright's Halifax Virginia Light Artillery Battery (Coit); Slaten's Macon Georgia Battery (Moseley).[2]

Brigadier General William Pendleton, chief of artillery for the Army of Northern Virginia, reported that General Johnson deployed some of his artillery north of the Appomattox River on June 18, with the other guns positioned along the Harris Line and in its rear, from the river to near the Baxter Road. Artillery belonging the Longstreet's First Corps (Army of Northern Virginia) went into position on the Harris Line between the Baxter Road and the Rives house, as those batteries arrived during the day and night of June 18th. "Of this artillery," explained Pendleton,

> a portion of Coit's battalion—Bradford's three guns (20-pounder Parrotts), and Wright's battery—were, on the morning of June 18, placed in position on the north side of the Appomattox to sweep with an enfilade fire the left of General Beauregard's new line on the south of and resting on the river. The other guns were posted on that line and at commanding points in its rear to aid in the defense. They were nearly all effectively engaged on that day (18th) in repelling the attempts of the enemy on their front, reaching from the river to near the Baxter Road.

On the right of General Beauregard's forces, troops from Longstreet's First Corps of the Army of Northern Virginia took position as they arrived. On the night of June 18 Gibbs' battalion and a portion of Haskell's were placed on the line running from near the Baxter Road to the Rives house. They deployed under a hail of sharpshooter fire. Haskell's other guns were placed at commanding points along a second line in rear. The guns of A. P. Hill's Third Corps, also of the Army of Northern Virginia, were assigned positions on the line to the right of those held by the First Corps, with Richardson's battalion occupying the salient at the junction of the new line with the old works (Rives' Salient). The other batteries, including the Louisiana Washington Artillery Battalion, were ordered to cooperate with the Third Corps and arranged farther south and west in a line that extended to and covered the critical Weldon Railroad.[3]

2   *OR* 40, pt. 1, 891-93.

3   Ibid., 755-60.

In his 7:30 a.m. diary entry of June 18, Johnson specifically referred to Miller's battery of four guns on the right, and Pegram's four guns on the left of the Baxter Road. In the 4:00 p.m. engagement, Slaten's battery of two guns fired on the brigade assaulting Elliott's right to the south of the Baxter Road.[4] These three batteries account for ten of the guns assigned to Johnson.

As a result, Generals Beauregard and Johnson had ample Confederate firepower available near the Baxter Road to oppose an assault by Chamberlain on the Harris Line on June 18. Rives' Salient itself would have been to Chamberlain's left, and could easily have been mistaken for Fort Mahone in the later reconstruction of places and events. In fact, at 1:10 p.m. General Warren specifically instructed General Ayres (who was on the far left of the V Corps opposite Rives' Salient) to silence the battery on his front "to keep them from firing down our lines to [Ayres'] right."[5] This Rebel battery, which was on Chamberlain's left, almost certainly constitutes the large fort with heavy guns Chamberlain later mistook for Fort Mahone in "The Charge at Fort Hell."

At The Taylor House, "Three's a Crowd"

One objection that has been raised about relocating Chamberlain's (Griffin's division) attack near the Baxter Road on June 18 is that there was not sufficient space to accommodate all the units that claimed to have been there.[6] For example, the developer of a Joshua Chamberlain website quotes Captain Charles Porter of the 39th Massachusetts to support the argument that the presence of portions of Crawford's division on the Taylor property between the Baxter Road and a point opposite Elliott's (Pegram's) Salient meant Sweitzer's brigade had to have been south of the Baxter Road.[7] Therefore it is important to pay more attention to the Taylor property in general, and Crawford's presence there in particular.

William Byrd Taylor's 18th century Tidewater Virginia frame plantation manor house sat just north of the Baxter Road and east of the railroad cut. The Taylor property was directly across from Pegram's Salient, which would

---

4   Johnson, "Diary of Bushrod Johnson," 277-78.

5   OR 40, pt. 2, 184.

6   Susan Natale comment, November 24, 2015, on https://studycivilwar.wordpress.com/2015/10/09/joshuas-marker/.

7   Ibid., Susan Natale comment, December 3, 2015.

become the site of the Crater. Bushrod Johnson had used the Taylor house as his headquarters on June 17, but the quiet withdrawal of the Confederate army from its second to its final line of defense around Petersburg during the night necessitated its abandonment. In a diary entry for June 18, Captain Henry A. Chambers of the 49th North Carolina, Ransom's brigade, described acts of arson carried out by his regiment during the Confederate retreat. "Last night we evacuated our lines near Avery's farm and took up a shorter and better one near Petersburg," scribbled the Tar Heel. "We threw up works until the enemy appeared. We burned a house in our front."[8]

Henry Fitzgerald Charles of the 21st Pennsylvania Cavalry was advancing with Sweitzer's brigade just north of the Baxter Road on June 18. Charles described coming across the burning remnants of buildings during a charge down a little hill to take the "Deep Cut" of the railroad in front of his brigade:

> We started and took the cut, but while going down, some of us had to go thru where some buildings were burned down. There was still plenty of fire and hot ashes, and I got some fire in my shoes. My one foot was burned considerable, but I did not dare to stop to take the fire out, as they were feeding us plenty of grape and canister all around. We took the cut; it was about twenty feet deep, and the boys went down pell-mell, and quite a number got hurt by the fellow's bayonet behind him.[9]

A description attached to a surviving photograph of Cooper's Battery taken on the afternoon of June 18, 1864, draws attention to the ruins of the brick chimney at the Taylor house in the distance, lending further support to the notion that the buildings occupied by Bushrod Johnson less then twenty-four hours earlier, were destroyed by fire that very day.[10]

---

8   Bruce W. Bevan, David G. Orr and Brooke S. Blades, "The Discovery of the Taylor House at the Petersburg National Battlefield," in *Historical Archaeology* (1984), vol. 18, no. 2, 69; *OR* 40, pt. 2, 666-7; T. H. Pearce, ed., *Diary of Captain Henry A. Chambers* (Wendell, NC, 1983), 204.

9   Nietz, *The Civil War Diary of Henry Fitzgerald Charles,* 8.

10   H. W. Lanier, "Photographing the Civil War," 303-4. Today, "Taylor's Chimney" is one of the few surviving remnants of a Civil War-era dwelling on the eastern front at Petersburg. The ruin was first thought to be part of the house, but is now believed to be part of an outbuilding (probably the kitchen of the 1864 house). Several years after the war a new dwelling was erected at the former kitchen site, which survived until 1940. The main house, which was about 100 years old when it was burned by the Rebels in 1864, was 65 feet north of the current chimney remnants. Bevan, Orr and Blades, "The Discovery of the Taylor House at the Petersburg National Battlefield," 69, 70.

The Taylor property was a beehive of activity on June 18. Griffin's division of Warren's V Corps was to the right of the Baxter Road, as we have seen. General Willcox's division of Burnside's IX Corps was also there, as Willcox clearly stated in his official report:

> The division had a severe engagement, lasting nearly all day, moving up to, across, and beyond the deep cut of the Norfolk Railroad, in front of the Taylor house, driving the enemy into his new works, notwithstanding our very heavy loss, and finally establishing ourselves nearer to the enemy than any other portion of the army.[11]

In addition, General Samuel Crawford's division was with Burnside's men at the left of the IX Corps and on the right flank of the V Corps.[12]

Crawford's Division

Captain Charles H. Porter of the 39th Massachusetts served under Colonel Peter Lyle in the 1st Brigade of Crawford's division. Porter's speech to the Military Historical Society of Massachusetts, delivered on January 12, 1885, offers valuable information with respect to the deployment of Crawford's division:

> On the morning of the 18th, the Fifth Corps, on the extreme left, advanced and pushed the pickets of the enemy back over the Norfolk and Petersburg Railroad, and up the hill to the right and left of the Baxter Road, Crawford's (3rd) Division on the right, making close connection with the left of the IX Corps. Two brigades were in line, the 3rd on the right, the 2nd on the left; the 1st was in reserve. We assaulted the enemy's lines and fought our battle exactly on the ground where the mine was afterwards exploded, that is, where Elliott's Salient of the Confederate line was established. Our left reached the Baxter Road, and our right was well over to and beyond the site of this salient. This Baxter Road joins the Jerusalem Plank Road just beyond the crest of the hill, which it was Willcox's duty to take on the 30th of July, 1864. Although the assaults of the V Corps during the day of June 18 had failed, yet we were assembled again in three lines of battle, caps removed from the muskets, bayonets fixed, at 8:00 p.m., to rush over the lines if possible. We were formed in the ravine where the opening to the mine was afterwards begun. [This was on the north

---

11 *OR* 40, pt. 1, 571.

12 Ibid., pt. 2, 172.

side of the Horseshoe.] This assault was never made. At 11:00 p.m., the line was withdrawn and established on the hill opposite, where the fourteen-gun battery was afterwards built, which became known as Battery Morton. General Burnside's headquarters on the morning of the assault on the mine were established at this point.[13]

This deployment of the 3rd Division calls into question the multiple accounts that place Sweitzer's brigade of Griffin's division north of the Baxter Road. The area would have been very crowded, indeed.

Porter's account, however, is not the final word. Additional insight comes from correspondence found in the Official Records. As Crawford advanced toward the railroad cut, he observed the creek running through the deep ravine beyond it and became concerned that the cut and the creek would break his lines as they advanced. When Crawford asked General Warren whether he should proceed alone, The V Corps commander ordered Crawford to withdraw his command to the first good position behind the one he was then holding, and to maintain a connection with Burnside's IX Corps on Crawford's right and with Griffin's division on his left. The exact point of connection between the two V Corps divisions was to be worked out on the ground between Crawford and Griffin.[14]

Regimental reports muddy the waters for anyone looking for a tidy summation of Crawford's movements on June 18. The 16th Maine, 90th Pennsylvania, 107th Pennsylvania, 39th Massachusetts, and 13th Massachusetts all belonged to Colonel Peter Lyle's 1st Brigade, which Captain Porter claimed was in reserve. Accounts from these units provide a mixed picture, some suggesting withdrawal of the units to the east side of the cut, while others described advances to positions in the ravine west of the railroad and beyond.

For example, the history of the 16th Maine recounts the regiment's advance alongside the IX Corps, the taking of the railroad cut, and its subsequent withdrawal to the east side, where it busied itself with throwing up entrenchments:

13 Charles H. Porter, "The Petersburg Mine," in *Papers of the Military Historical Society of Massachusetts* (Boston, 1895), vol. 5, 221.

14 OR 40, pt. 2, 186.

In the assault that was made, the brigade advanced nearly a mile, forcing back the rebels, and gaining position on the Norfolk Railroad, within a mile and a half of the city. Withdrew from railroad cut, and formed in line of battle in the county road, along the base of the slope overlooking and near the railroad. Here the men worked diligently all night, throwing up intrenchments.[15]

In like manner, the 90th Pennsylvania advanced across an open space to reach the railroad cut. The brigade was massed for a charge, but subsequently abandoned the idea of attacking and fell back to entrench along the line of the railroad.[16] The same was true of the 107th Pennsylvania, whose skirmishers deployed across the tracks before withdrawing to a permanent entrenched line its men occupied until June 24.[17]

The 39th Massachusetts, on the other hand, after rushing into a railroad cut, moved across a ravine at dark to a point below the Confederate works, where the Bay State troops established a picket line near the future site of the Crater.[18] The account also mentioned the subsequent relocation of the regiment to a position near an old brick house opposite the Crater site, which was probably a reference to the chimney and brick wall of what was left of the Taylor dwelling.[19]

The 13th Massachusetts, also part of the Lyle's 1st brigade, did not turn back at the railroad cut. Instead, skirmishers fanned out off on the right flank where, protected by woods and a ravine, they passed through a gully and ascended a hill extending from the creek bank to the upper line of Rebel earth works, probably on the north face of the Horseshoe. Beginning on June 18, they deepened and extended that gully into a sunken route to provide safety of movement. The Bay State troops named their hill "Fort Crater." They expected to make a charge on the Rebel works to their front at 7:30 p.m. (an arrangement

15 A. R. Small, *The Sixteenth Maine Regiment in the War of the Rebellion* (Portland, ME, 1886), 191. The 16th Maine established its headquarters behind what was described as a "monster" oak tree whose trunk was about six feet in diameter. This tree can be seen on an 1865 photograph of the battlefield that has been digitally enhanced by Philip Shiman.

16 Bates, *History of Pennsylvania Volunteers,* vol. 3, 157.

17 Ibid., Bates, *History of Pennsylvania Volunteers,* vol. 3, 863.

18 Alfred S. Roe, *The Thirty-ninth Regiment, Massachusetts Volunteers* (Worcester, MA, 1914), 221-23.

19 Roe, *The Thirty-ninth Regiment, Massachusetts Volunteers,* 238.

similar to the one described in Captain Porter's account), but the plan was never realized.[20]

The 88th Pennsylvania, part of Colonel James Bates' 2nd Brigade of Crawford's division, crossed the railroad and participated in an attack by the entire corps about 5:00 p.m., getting within about sixty yards of the enemy line before falling back.[21]

Information concerning Colonel James Carle's 3rd Brigade of Crawford's division reaches us from the history of the 190th and 191st Pennsylvania regiments. According to Samuel Bates, these Pennsylvania troops fought hard on the left of the IX Corps on the evening of June 17, capturing an entire Rebel regiment. However, upon reaching the crest of the sandy ridge fronting the body of timber east of the Taylor plantation (which served as the Confederate battle line on June 17), Carle's command dropped to the ground and set to work building breastworks, which were held until the brigade was relieved.[22] There was no mention of any advance of significance on June 18.

All of this suggests that those elements of Crawford's division that did not withdraw shifted right and ended up in the ravine on the north face of the Horseshoe near the future site of the entrance to the mine tunnel. This would allow plenty of room on the south side of the Horseshoe, north of the Baxter Road, to accommodate Sweitzer's brigade.

By far the most interesting insight into the question of the whereabouts of Crawford's division comes to us in fascinating correspondence circulated among the commanding generals a few days later:

> Crawford to Griffin, on June 21: After receiving your reply to my note, I saw General Warren, who disclaims that any order to pass your troops through my lines was given to you on the 18th instant.

> Griffin to Crawford, on June 22: Respectfully referred to Major-General Warren, commanding V Corps, and if consistent with the interest of the service I should like to have this question of orders investigated at once, as I think I can establish the correctness of my statement.

20 Charles E. Davis, *Three Years in the Army, The Story of the Thirteenth Massachusetts Volunteers from July 16, 1861, to August 1, 1864* (Boston, 1894), 373.

21 Bates, *History of Pennsylvania Volunteers*, vol. 3, 73.

22 Ibid., vol. 5, 280. This claim is in line with General Crawford's official report of the action, as discussed earlier.

Warren, on June 23: I did not intend General Griffin to march his troops over General Crawford's. I thought General Griffin was to form on General Crawford's left. My orders, however, were so imperative to move forward that General Griffin may have had to do this without waiting to make different arrangements. The pressure under which I acted compelled me to urge rapidity of movement, but I did not suppose this thing would have happened. It was a very trying day to me, and I am willing to assume the whole or any fault rather than any feeling should exist between the two divisions. With so great difficulties as we have to contend with, annoying occurrences of this kind must be met with mutual forbearance.[23]

This exchange clearly shows that, while Crawford was withdrawing at least a part of his division from the railroad cut under Warren's orders, Griffin was advancing his troops through Crawford's lines, and stepping on some toes in the process.

It is noteworthy that General Crawford, in his official report covering the action of his division on June 17, made no mention of any engagement on the following day. Instead, his comments were limited to the lodging of a complaint over stolen trophies of battle during the evening combat of June 17. The reason is clear: not much of substance transpired within the 3rd Division on June 18.

Two of Sweitzer's regiments, the 91st Pennsylvania and the 22nd Massachusetts,[24] were relieved by units of Crawford's division during the early morning hours of June 19, suggesting those regiments of the 3rd division were relatively inactive over the previous twenty-four hours. In this context it is interesting to consider Samuel Bates' description of the action of the 91st Pennsylvania:

At daylight on the morning of the 18th, the [First] division moved down the first line of battle in rear of the Third Division [Crawford], when the order to charge across and capture the Suffolk and Petersburg Railroad was given. Advancing at double-quick the enemy was driven to his next line of works, and the line of the railroad, which had been previously captured and lost, was regained and held. A hot fire was kept up for over four hours. . . . At dusk, the division moved left, and was ordered to charge the enemy occupying a hill, where the mine was subsequently sprung.[25]

---

23 OR 40, pt. 2, 280.

24 OR 40, pt. 1, 461, 459.

25 Bates, *History of Pennsylvania* Volunteers, vol. 2, 192.

This correspondence helps us to better understand the day's events as they unfolded. Someone had already captured the railroad cut, and then given it up. This almost certainly describes the advance of Crawford's division and its subsequent withdrawal under orders from General Warren. Sweitzer's brigade was behind Crawford's division at the time the order to recapture the railroad was issued. The 91st Pennsylvania and other units from Griffin's division, acting on the imperative from General Warren to move forward rapidly, apparently marched through and beyond Crawford's lines to accomplish the task. This created the conflict between the generals that surfaced several days later in the correspondence.

In any event, three infantry divisions—Griffin, Crawford and Willcox— congregated near the Taylor house. Burnsides' IX Corps (Willcox) was to the north. Crawford's division was mainly east of the railroad cut, with several regiments perhaps advanced in the gully on the northeast slope of the Horseshoe at the site where Pennsylvania coal miners would later begin digging the entrance of the tunnel. Warren's V Corps line (Griffin, displacing Crawford) was across the railroad cut on the hill below the site of the Crater, with Sweitzer north of the Baxter Road and Chamberlain south of it.

Three army divisions is definitely quite a crowd. However, there was ample room at the Taylor house. What they say of real estate is certainly true of battlefields—it's all about location. The area around the Taylor plantation was an important place to be on June 18, 1864.

My journey of researching and discovery was nearing its end. It was now time to pull it all together.

CHAPTER 17

SUMMARY:
The June 18 Evidence Speaks for Itself

AT the end of the day on June 18, 1864, General Warren's four V Corps divisions were digging trenches on the eastern front of Petersburg. The price paid by the men for the privilege of occupying that ground was high: 389 killed, 1,899 wounded, and 38 missing.[1] Colonel Wainwright later wrote that the attack was "a fiasco of the worst kind," adding, "I trust it will be the last attempt at this most absurd way of attacking entrenchments by a general advance in line. It has been tried so often now and with such fearful losses that even the stupidest private knows that it cannot succeed."[2]

The divisions of Lysander Cutler and Romeyn Ayres held the left side of Warren's V Corps front, with Ayres' 2nd Division of three brigades on the far left and Cutler's 4th Division on his right. At that time, Ayres' three-brigade division formed the extreme left of the Army of the Potomac. Ayres was unsuccessful in his direct assault that day because of the long distance the men had to cover to reach the Confederate lines, and the flat and open nature of the terrain.[3] Ayres' left flank rested upon heavy works previously captured from the

---

1 W. F. Fox, *Regimental Losses in the American Civil War 1861-1865* (1889), as listed on www.civilwararchive.com/corps/5thcorps.htm.

2 Nevins, *A Diary of Battle*, 425.

3 Roebling, "Report of the Operations of the V Corps," June 18, 1864.

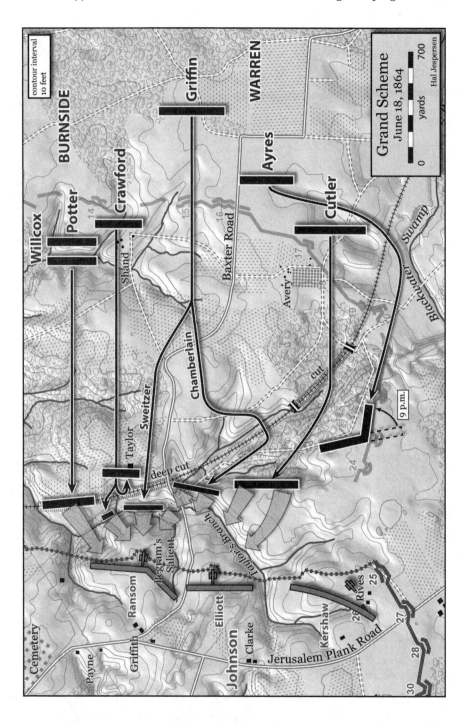

June 18, 1864, according to the sources: At 4:00 a.m., Cutler on the left and Crawford/Willcox on the right began advancing, driving Confederate skirmishers before them. Cutler was at the railroad by 7:30 a.m., but his progress was delayed by the task of rebuilding a bridge, which the enemy had destroyed. By 7:00-8:00 a.m., the other two V Corps divisions were also on the march. Ayres moved behind and to the left of Cutler, crossing the railroad. By 11:15 a.m. his division was straddling the old Confederate works on the left flank of the V Corps line. Griffin moved to fill the gap between Cutler and Crawford, with Sweitzer's brigade advancing primarily to the right of the Baxter Road, and Chamberlain moving toward the left to execute his "pardonable ruse" of surprising an annoying Confederate artillery outpost on a crest beyond the "Deep Cut" of the railroad. By noon, Crawford and Hartranft's brigade of Willcox's division, IX Corps, were in the railroad cut on the right; Sweitzer advanced beyond the cut to the ravine at the base of the Confederate works; Cutler and Chamberlain were moving toward the crests behind which they would seek temporary shelter. At 3:00 p.m., Cutler (Hofmann) and Griffin (Chamberlain) advanced from the center of the V Corps line toward the Taylor's Branch ravine on Sweitzer's left. The attack was quickly repulsed, and Chamberlain was severely wounded. At 6:00 p.m., Sweitzer, along with that part of Crawford's division that had moved beyond the railroad, together with elements of Willcox's and Potter's IX Corps divisions, made the final thrust over the Horseshoe, advancing toward, but failing to breach, the entrenched line in front of Pegram's Salient held by Ransom's brigade.

Confederates (Batteries 20-24) that ran perpendicular to the line of battle.[4] His troops were situated in front of, and about 900 yards from, Rives' Salient, which was described as the "great salient of the enemy's works."[5] The refused portion of Ayres' line faced south. There is no evidence of any other Union positions southwest of Ayres' division at this time.

Cutler's 4th Division of two brigades was on Ayres' right. Hofmann's 2nd Brigade had led the advance, with Bragg's 1st Brigade in support. A portion of both brigades stepped within about 75 yards of the enemy's works during the afternoon's assault before being driven back.[6] Lieutenant Gawthrop's map depicts the right side of Hofmann's brigade positioned just south of one of the tributaries of Taylor's Creek and within an eighth of a mile of the Baxter Road.[7] Bates' *History of Pennsylvania Volunteers* places the target of Hofmann's

4 *OR* 40, pt. 2, 184.

5 Ibid., pt. 1, 481-82.

6 Ibid., 473.

7 Carisio, *A Quaker Officer in the Civil War*, 67.

attack a quarter-mile south of the point later selected for the mine that resulted in the Crater.[8]

Charles Griffin's three-brigade 1st Division was on Cutler's right, straddling the Baxter Road. Chamberlain's 1st Brigade had advanced on Hofmann's right and to the immediate left of Colonel Sweitzer's 2nd Brigade.[9] Sweitzer was north of the Baxter Road, having taken ground on the "Horseshoe" in the immediate front of Pegram's Salient, the future site of the Crater. Bartlett's 3rd Brigade was held in reserve during the attack. Regiments from Chamberlain's and Sweitzer's brigades would later report being relieved by IX Corps troops whose lines were exclusively north of the Baxter Road.

Sam Crawford's 3rd Division started the day on the right of the V Corps line, advancing on the left of Orlando Willcox's IX Corps division, before being called back to a reserve position on the V Corps' right as Griffin advanced.[10] Some of Crawford's regiments were probably on the right of the "Horseshoe" below Pegram's Salient. Others were in reserve east of the railroad cut, waiting to relieve Sweitzer during the night.

In other words, the V Corps line fronted the Harris Line of Rebel works from Pegram's Salient on the right to a point opposite Rives' Salient on the left, where Ayres' refused line along the captured Confederate works bent back to better protect the left side of the Union line.

In the mid-afternoon on June 18, Warren reported at 3:15 p.m. that the center of his corps (not the extreme left in front of Rives' Salient) was attacking the enemy line under heavy fire.[11] This was the same time Chamberlain and Hofmann mounted their assaults. Lieutenant Colonel Lyman described watching the attack from a position near Warren's headquarters at the Avery farm as Chamberlain and Hofmann advanced and then fell back. It was during this advance that Colonel Chamberlain sustained his nearly mortal wound.[12] Bushrod Johnson, the commander of a Confederate division straddling the Baxter Road, described an attack of a Union brigade in two lines (which corresponded with Chamberlain's tactical formation) against General Elliott's

8   Bates, *History of Pennsylvania Volunteers*, vol. 2, 223.

9   *OR* 40, pt. 1, 455-56.

10 Ibid., pt. 2, 280.

11 Ibid., 180.

12 Lowe, *Meade's Army*, 213.

Rebel brigade south of the Baxter Road. According to Johnson, the advance occurred about 4:00 p.m.[13] Neither Warren nor Lyman at V Corps headquarters, nor Confederate commanders occupying positions farther to the south at Rives' Salient and Fort Mahone, mentioned any attacks of significance originating from the far left of the Union line on June 18.

It is now clear that the only basis for the scenario of an attack against Rives' Salient from "Fort Hell" is Chamberlain's recollections, as recorded in memoirs and reminiscences during the last two decades of his life, and the frequent repetition of those statements over the past century by various biographers and other writers.

Chamberlain was taken off the battlefield in traumatic shock after sustaining his nearly mortal wound to the pelvis. He suffered the convulsions and chills of septic shock for two months at the U.S. General Hospital in Annapolis, and did not return to duty for five months. As far as we can determine, he did not revisit the eastern front of the Petersburg battlefield for 18 years, and he did not write any specific recollections of the June 18 attack until 35 years after the event. He relied upon his memory and recollections in his "Reminiscences" speech of 1903.

There is a veritable mountain of historical evidence against the Rives' Salient—"Fort Hell" scenario—so much so that it cannot have occurred. For example:

1. Chamberlain's own statements that his right flank was situated on a deep railroad cut, and his attack launched from a point "not less than 300 yards" from the Rebel entrenchments;

2. Chamberlain's statement that there was an icehouse on his right front—a structure described in multiple other reports as being present on the Taylor property near the Baxter Road, but never in association with Rives' Salient.

3. Reports of a marsh or bog in the ravine on Chamberlain's front (40-50 yards wide, according to DeLacy), which forced him to give the fateful order, "Incline to the left" at the very moment he was being shot;

4. Chamberlain's statement that he could see Twitchell's IX Corps battery (at a point north of the Taylor ruins, north of Baxter Road) bastioning the slopes

---

13 Johnson, "Diary of Bushrod Johnson," 278.

above as he lapsed into unconsciousness, "where darkness fell upon my eyes, and I thought to see no more";

5. Chamberlain's description of Mink's battery firing from north of the Taylor house into an icehouse on his right front;

6. General Griffin's orders for Chamberlain to protect the 1st Division batteries of Phillips, Stewart and Richardson, positioned at the Baxter Road, and an order for Chamberlain to silence an advanced Confederate artillery outpost just across the deep cut of the railroad;

7. Colonel Tilton's report and the letter of General Knowles, which link the right of Chamberlain's brigade with the left of Sweitzer's, which was north of the Baxter Road;

8. General Warren and Lieutenant Colonel Lyman, whose reports confirm they went up on the open plain northwest of the Avery farm to watch Chamberlain's mid-afternoon attack at the center of the Union line;

9. The reports of Captain Bigelow, Colonel Hofmann, and Colonel Tilton, which place Chamberlain on Hofmann's right, and by Lieutenant Gawthrop's map and Samuel Bates' account, both of which have Hofmann's right near the Baxter Road;

10. Multiple reports describing the subsequent movement of Griffin's division, including Chamberlain's 1st Brigade, a mile to the left to the Jerusalem Plank Road on June 21;

11. Seven regimental histories from the 1st Division, V Corps, three from Chamberlain's 1st Brigade and four from Sweitzer's 2nd Brigade, which mention those units either charging and occupying the position from which Burnside's famous mine was dug and exploded, or being relieved by IX Corps troops;

12. The terrain and my restatement of Major Roebling's observations as "Roebling's Rule," which call into question the claim of Chamberlain and his biographers that his brigade, attacking isolated and alone against the permanent entrenchments of the Dimmock Line at Rives' Salient, made it within twenty feet of bayoneting the enemy inside their works. According to Roebling, Ayres' entire division was unable to make any advance of note on the left flank of the V Corps because the ground there was flat and unobstructed, and the distance from the railroad cut was quite far.

Furthermore, "the reason of Griffin and Crawford [advancing] so much closer lay in the fact of the rail road cut being much closer to the lines there, and the ground they had to advance over was steeper, so that the rebels fired over";

13. The report penned by Bushrod Johnson and the diary of the Confederate First Corps, both of which described an attack that could only have been launched by Chamberlain, occurring during the mid-afternoon against Elliott's brigade just south of the Baxter Road;

14. The silence of Generals Kershaw and Field regarding major engagements fought by their divisions on June 18.

My inquiry is not in any way intended to impugn the courage, heroism, intelligence, honesty, or integrity of the Lion of the Union. I simply believe Chamberlain was mistaken about a single point—his position on the battlefield. A simple mistake, perhaps, but a fundamental one with wide-ranging implications for our understanding of events on the left flank of the Union army on June 18. His confusion is understandable considering the ordeal he endured and length of time that passed before he put pen to paper. Memory is very unreliable. The recollection of a single observer on a specific point, especially when we there are official documents that contradict it in ways large and small, should never be accepted without question.

The annals of this event consistently tell a tale at odds with the theory of a charge against Rives' Salient from "Fort Hell." This evidence demands a fresh verdict.

CHAPTER 18

EVEN HEROES MAKE MISTAKES:
Smoke, Clouds, and Confusion

THANKFULLY I have never been in combat, but it is safe to conclude that in the midst of the smoke and clamor and death and maiming of battle, confusion and chaos reign supreme. The two primary concerns of every soldier in the heat of combat are to achieve the objective and stay alive while doing so. Trying to figure out your precise location on the battlefield and the identity of opposing infantry units, for example, is of secondary importance—much to the lament of future historians.

On June 18, 1864, as it does on each day, nightfall finally arrived. The din of combat fell away into fitful silence, and the men did their best to recover the dead within reach and aid the wounded. The coming of morning allowed the survivors to better survey the landscape to their front, exchange observations, and piece together what they had endured. By so doing, they established a context, a framework, for their shared experience.

In this respect, those who were wounded and taken off the field were at a disadvantage. Regardless of where a man fought, whether in a rear rank or leading the way at the front, a wound subjected him to severe physical and psychological trauma. Often, wounded men left the battlefield in a state of stupor, only to regain consciousness in another location, where healing and recuperation would occur in their own good time.

Time has a tremendous affect upon one's perspective, which cannot be fully or reliably formed in an instant, and certainly not in the midst of a bloody crisis. Perspective needs time to grow and develop, usually through serial observations, as an event or place is viewed from different aspects. As the platform of observation shifts over time, a fuller and more accurate picture usually emerges.

The events of history unfold sequentially. Context involves fitting things in their proper relationship in time and space. This requires knowing, or better yet, experiencing, what has transpired and what follows a particular event. It entails the observation of a specific occurrence in the setting of its surroundings. Being able to situate an event or a place in its proper context always deepens understanding.

Joshua Lawrence Chamberlain, a hero of Gettysburg and of the early fighting at Petersburg, was in the midst of smoke, clouds, and confusion on June 18, 1864. There, he was doing what brave officers do best—leading his men—until the moment he fell "amidst storm and disaster."[1] Because of his premature removal from the scene of conflict, Chamberlain was denied the opportunity to speak with his comrades and revisit the ground of crisis in the clear light of day. He was unable to reevaluate his initial perceptions, formed in smoke and chaos, against the standard of unclouded reality.

His status as a wounded warrior deprived him of the opportunity of making an early return to the site of his charge to sort out the "confused recollections of [his] personal experience."[2] He did not accompany his brigade to the rear when it was relieved. He did not move with his men to the left, as they subsequently occupied the ground where they would build "Fort Hell." He had no opportunity to experience the context of his action at Petersburg, and a period of thirty-nine years proved to be a distance too great to allow him to form an accurate perspective.

As a result, Chamberlain was one of the least qualified of the observers that day when it came to commenting on the question of where his attack took place. The fact that his accounts were compiled so long after the event makes them less reliable than those of nearly everyone else who wrote about the places and events of June 18. Those less celebrated actors in the drama, some of whom we have nearly forgotten, escaped the flying lead and iron to re-walk some of the ground, take in their surroundings, talk to others similarly situated, and reevaluate what they had passed through. They were able to record their impressions and observations over the days, weeks, months, and years that

---

1 Chamberlain, "Reminiscences of Petersburg and Appomattox, October, 1903, 161.

2 Ibid., 164.

immediately followed the engagement. The testimony of these observers is as substantial as it is nearly unanimous.

The record forces historians and students of the Civil War to confront the obvious question: If Joshua Chamberlain had succumbed to his wound and had not left any subsequent personal account of the charge of his brigade, would there be any question or controversy today concerning his whereabouts on June 18, 1864?

CHAPTER 19

FOR POSTERITY'S SAKE:
Setting the Record Straight

T HIS study set out to establish the whereabouts of a single brigade, in a single engagement, on a single day of the Civil War. The spadework conducted to find answers to these questions turned up several significant (and in some cases, unexpected) discoveries that help us better understand where Joshua Chamberlain's command fought, and place his effort within the broader context of events outside Petersburg on June 18, 1864.

Chamberlain's Fall

The central hypothesis of this study is that Chamberlain's 1st Brigade was not detached from the remainder of Griffin's 1st division. The historical evidence demonstrates this conclusively. Chamberlain's brigade did not attack Rives' Salient along the Jerusalem Plank Road from "Fort Hell" under an enfilading fire from Fort Mahone. In fact, the brigade's operations were limited to the vicinity of the Baxter Road, where it first attacked an advanced artillery post on the crest of an open slope across the Deep Cut of the Norfolk Railroad, and then assaulted north and south of the Baxter Road. Some of Chamberlain's regiments gained ground at the southern end of the "Horseshoe" in front of Pegram's Salient, the future site of the Crater.

Chamberlain probably suffered his severe wound just south of the Baxter Road at the edge of the swampy marsh alongside Taylor's Branch. By his own testimony, there was a deep railroad cut on his right flank. A line of infantry and

Morning mist over the Petersburg National Battlefield. *Author*

artillery was strongly entrenched on his front at a range of 300-400 yards, with projecting salients right (Pegram's) and left (whichever battery was occupying the "Otey" position at the time), sweeping his advance with a crossfire. A large fort (Rives' Salient) well to the left enfiladed the entire advance. A boggy swamp occupied the hollow between his brigade and its objective.

Chamberlain's famous downhill charge carried the men to the edges of this marsh, which hindered their progress. An experienced officer and capable tactician, he attempted to extract his men from the killing zone by ordering them to "Incline to the left." He personally raised the Maltese Cross high, motioned with his saber, and received the terrible wound that nearly killed him.

Taylor's Chimney

Taylor's Chimney is a prominent and distinctive landmark feature of the Petersburg National Battlefield. Unfortunately, the chimney has survived as an archaeological orphan, without much of a story to tell. The standard interpretation is a simple one: The house was burned as a result of the fighting sometime during the summer of 1864. *A History of Petersburg National Battlefield*, published more than three decades ago by the National Park Service, says about as much as it has been possible to say, up to this point:

> The house, together with the library of George Keith Taylor [a celebrated eighteenth century Virginia Federalist leader and jurist], was burned during the summer of 1864, but the exact date is not clear. After July 11, 1864, but not before, there are references to the house as the "ruin," or the "burnt house." On July 14, General Burnside, commanding the Ninth Union Army Corps, reported that the work on the battery at "the burnt house" was prosecuted every night. Then on July 26 he wrote, "Fourteen guns have been placed in the new battery near the burnt house." Burnside, it is certain, was referring to the Taylor house ruins.[1]

We now know, however, that the Taylor house served as division headquarters for Confederate Major General Bushrod Johnson on June 17, 1864. When Johnson's men retreated to their final defensive position at the foot of Cemetery Hill on the morning of June 18, they burned the Taylor dwellings, as recorded in Henry Chambers' diary. Henry Fitzgerald Charles and the 21st Pennsylvania Cavalry (dismounted) passed through the still-burning embers as his unit descended the slope into the Deep Cut of the railroad around noon on June 18. An image of the remains of the burnt dwelling is preserved on an historic photograph of Cooper's battery taken that very afternoon. In the days that followed, a standing brick wall of the Taylor house would provide shelter for various Union artillery batteries. A 14-gun battery near the burned house that would serve as General Burnside's headquarters during the Battle of the Crater would subsequently became Fort Morton.

Taylor's Chimney is a historical orphan no more. We now have a heritage rooted in facts surrounding the events of June 18, 1864, all of which were unearthed while digging for information about a single brigade on a single day in the war.

The Icehouse

Chamberlain reported an icehouse to the right-front of his brigade line as he was preparing for his final assault. The icehouse structure may have shielded

---

1 L. A. Wallace and M. R. Conway, "A History of Petersburg National Battlefield" (1983), 23-24.

Confederate skirmishers on their retreat across the ravines west of the railroad cut. Both armies coveted its contents in the heat of a Virginia summer day. The icehouse was the target of Union artillery fire from Mink's battery from positions both south and north of the Taylor ruins on June 18.

Historical maps and a modern LIDAR (Laser Light Detection and Ranging, or Light Radar) image, part of this investigation's research, suggest a possible location for this icehouse near the terminus of a farm road on a north-facing slope between two branches of Taylor's Creek, just south of the Baxter Road. National Park Service personnel, currently investigating the site, are cautiously optimistic that they may have identified the remains of this structure within the park's boundaries. A report from the 13th Massachusetts regiment of Crawford's division describes the construction, three days after June 18 assaults, of a sunken way leading down to an icehouse.[2] A zigzagging covered way south of the Baxter Road is visible on the modern LIDAR map of the park and happens to approach the structure of interest. This provides exciting possibilities for further archaeological exploration.

Griffin's Role in Securing the Horseshoe

Most historians acknowledge that IX Corps forces held the Federal lines north of the Baxter Road in the weeks following the initial assault on the interior defenses of Petersburg. General Burnside's men famously used this vantage as a platform from which to secretly bore a 510-foot tunnel to a point beneath the Confederate entrenchments, where a large amount of gunpowder was exploded on July 30, 1864, triggering the Battle of the Crater—one of the most notable events in the entire history of the Petersburg campaign.

What is not generally understood is that men from Warren's V Corps— mainly regiments from Griffin's division—were instrumental in securing the foothold at the "Horseshoe" on June 18. Any lingering doubt about this is removed by this July 3, 1864, entry in Major Washington Roebling's diary: "By this time the project of Gen. Burnside to dig a mine under the advance position which Gen. Griffin had taken possession of in the charge of the 18th began to attract some attention."[3]

---

2   C. E. Davis, *Three Years in the Army, The Story of the Thirteenth Massachusetts Volunteers from July 16, 1861, to August 1, 1864* (1894), 374-75.

3   W. A. Roebling, "Report of the Operations of the V Corps," July 3, 1864.

Sweitzer's 2nd Brigade (Griffin's division) was largely responsible for occupying the ground, probably with assistance from elements of Crawford's 3rd Division and Chamberlain's 1st Brigade. This difficult accomplishment would not have been possible if Chamberlain's brigade had been detached and sent nearly a mile to the south to assault Rives' Salient. Despite its failure to penetrate the interior lines of the Confederate defense of Petersburg, the final fixed-bayonet charge by Sweitzer's brigade to within 20 feet of the enemy works represents the farthest advance of any Federal infantry unit on June 18.

Under the Maltese Cross documents the history of the 155th Pennsylvania, part of Sweitzer's brigade on June 18. The narrative includes excerpts from the official reports filed by Generals Griffin and Warren that confirm some of the fallen Pennsylvanians were still lying within 20 feet of the Confederate earthworks on the morning of June 19.[4] The author credits Sweitzer's advance as the "high water mark" of the charge of General Meade's army:

> The advance of the V Corps on the 18th of June to within twenty feet of the enemy's works, where assaulted by General Sweitzer's Brigade, as officially stated, was the high-water mark of the charge of Grant's army in the siege of Petersburg. Immediately after the charge, on the following day, the regular siege of Petersburg was entered upon, the One Hundred and Fifty-fifth still holding its advanced position. The V Corps works, as laid out by General Warren, were commenced, and a line was constructed on the position gained by the advance of Sweitzer's Brigade in that memorable charge.[5]

Author Thomas Howe makes the same point in his Petersburg study *Wasted Valor*:

> Colonel Sweitzer pushed his men against the Confederate line north of the Baxter Road. The blue lines crossed Poor Creek and rushed to within twenty yards of the Rebel breastworks. Federal success seemed within reach. As the Federal line battled to the edge of the Confederate works, a Yankee soldier saw "some of the enemy . . . seizing their color-standards, preparing 'to get.'" Even though Sweitzer's men nearly

---

4   OR 40, pt. 2, 183.

5   155th Regimental Association, *Under the Maltese Cross, Antietam to Appomattox, The Loyal Uprising in Western Pennsylvania, 1861-1865, Campaign 155th Pennsylvania Regiment* (Pittsburgh, PA, 1910), 295-296.

gained the Confederate line, they failed to breach it. . . . Despite its failure, Griffin's division had reached the farthest forward point of any Federal charge that day.[6]

As noted earlier in this work, Brigadier General Oliver B. Knowles wrote a letter to Joshua Chamberlain shortly after the end of the war stating that the 21st Pennsylvania Cavalry (dismounted) had advanced to within 55 yards of Pegram's Salient. "Immediately in front of my regiment was the redoubt which our forces afterwards so unsuccessfully attempted to blow up ("Burnside's mine")," explained Knowles. "By actual measurement, we got within 55 yards of this work, but the fire was too fearful to advance farther."[7]

The casualties sustained in this charge by many of Griffin's regiments were heavier than the losses they sustained in any other engagement of the war. Most of the casualties suffered by the division reported for the two-week period dating June 15-30, 1864, occurred on June 18.

Little or none of this was widely recognized prior to the investigation that resulted in this study.

Griffin's Division Passed Through Crawford's Men

The notion that Crawford's 3rd Division might have been withdrawn after having secured the railroad cut north of the Taylor house, and that Griffin's 1st Division might have passed through Crawford's lines on his way to the "Horseshoe," is a new interpretation to students of the engagement of June 18. I believe it is correct, and that it deserves additional study.

The Inactivity of Kershaw and Field

Common wisdom has long held that the arrival of General Robert E. Lee's Army of Northern Virginia was the decisive factor that finally stemmed the tide of Federals sweeping toward the city of Petersburg on June 18. This interpretation understates the crucial role played by the men under General P. G. T. Beauregard's command.

The divisions of Joe Kershaw and Charles Field did indeed arrive in the theater of operations during the forenoon of June 18, but they were not heavily

---

6 Howe, *Wasted Valor*, 129.

7 Oliver B. Knowles to General Joshua L. Chamberlain, December 15, 1865.

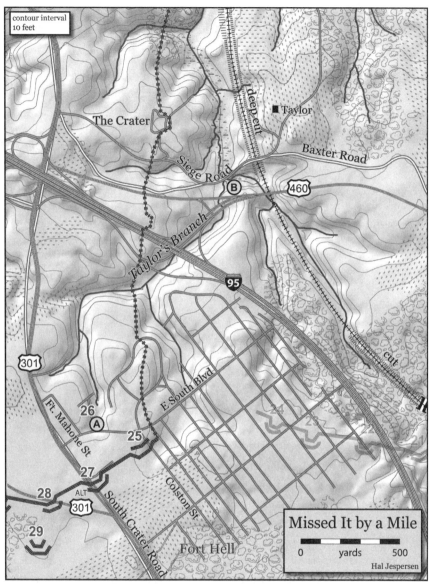

The Department of Historic Resources installed a marker at the intersection of East South Boulevard and Fort Mahone Street near South Crater Road (A) to commemorate Joshua L. Chamberlain's "On the Spot" promotion. It is also the location of his supposed "attack" on Rives' Salient from Fort Hell. We now know conclusively that Chamberlain did not make any attack in that location on June 18, 1864, and he was wounded about a mile away (B). The marker was not intended to denote the precise spot where his biographers place his wounding, as the site was chosen for its accessibility to motorists. As a result, the marker is *behind* the Confederate line of June 18, 1864. Its mistaken location perpetuated the myth that Chamberlain was operating isolated and alone.

engaged in the fight. Field's men initially deployed on an inactive front to the southwest near Battery 34, before moving left and north to back up and eventually relieve Bushrod Johnson's division during the night of June 18-19. Kershaw was behind and to the right of Johnson between the Jerusalem Plank Road and the cemetery, reinforcing and possibly comingling with Johnson's infantry during the course of the day. Much of the Army of Northern Virginia artillery went into line during the night following the major engagements. Union attacks (feeble by all Confederate accounts) were directed against Generals Elliott and Ransom (Johnson's division). Kershaw and Field did not report any major engagements on June 18. General Beauregard's forces were primarily responsible for stopping the Federal advance in the assaults that culminated in the nine-month "siege" of Petersburg. Beauregard deserves more credit than he has been accorded.

History as Presented for Public Consumption is Not Always True

If history is to be meaningful, it must be accurate.

In addition to proving where Chamberlain's brigade attacked that day long ago, my research has demonstrated yet again that established history on a particular event is not always true—regardless of how many writers repeat it. It is our responsibility as students of the war to always maintain a healthy dose of skepticism. It is essential that we not just accept explanations of historical events that have been handed down through the years, but critically reexamine the primary documents upon which narratives are based. Walking the terrain wherever possible, is also critically important.

A wide variety of firsthand documents unknown or passed over by previous historians, together with recent archaeological discoveries, have come to light in many areas of Civil War study. Technology like the Internet, GPS data, and aerial and satellite images make research easier and more precise. In order for history to be accurate and reliable, it must be scrutinized and routinely reevaluated. The more scrutiny that is brought to bear on any issue, the more precise will be our understanding of that event. Like tiny jigsaw puzzle pieces, even the smallest facts matter because we can never be sure which piece might hold the potential to unlock collateral secrets that change the way we view something of great import.

The Power of Cooperation

One final lesson from this undertaking is the power of cooperation. This book is the product of research by a physician, not a professional historian or author. Its conception was serendipitous. The project was completed in less than a year through the cooperative effort of a diverse group of individuals living in various parts of the country, most of whom were strangers to one another at the beginning of the journey. It is rather amazing that something like this is even possible.

We need more of this kind of cooperation and collaboration in medicine, history, politics, and business. Indeed, in all fields of human endeavor.

WALKING INTO HISTORY:
My Journey to Petersburg

IN April 2015, about the time I was wrapping up the writing of this book, I decided to follow the footsteps of Joshua Chamberlain on his "Reminiscences" tour. I started in reverse, first visiting Appomattox Court House and then moving on to Petersburg. Not coincidentally, it was also the 150th anniversary of General Lee's surrender of his Army of Northern Virginia to U.S. Grant. Much had changed since Chamberlain's visits to these hallowed places in 1882 and 1903.

My wife and I flew from Michigan to Virginia. Once in Richmond, we rendezvoused with my sister-in-law, Mary, who had traveled from Atlanta to be with us. We rented a car and drove the historic route from Amelia Court House and Jetersville, to Farmville, Virginia, where we spent the night. The next day, April 9, we drove along Route 460 under dark clouds that threatened rain to arrive at the Appomattox Courthouse National Historical Park.

Several thousand observers and reenactors had gathered to participate in the well-choreographed Appomattox Sesquicentennial program, with the historic Repasz Band providing period music. Virginia's Governor Terry McAuliffe and Senator Tim Kaine addressed the audience of approximately 2,500, all seated in folding chairs before a stage erected for the occasion. Edwin C. Bearss, the revered and retired former Chief Historian for the National Park Service, was awarded a framed print of the Mort Kunstler painting "Respect of an Army," which was specially commissioned in honor of the surrender anniversary. Dr. James Robertson, one of the country's preeminent Civil War historians, delivered the keynote address. Ten readers punctuated the proceedings with poignant poems and reminiscences. Instead of bullets and shell fragments, which are now part of the treasure of our national heritage and may not be removed from the hallowed ground, many of us took home commemorative U. S. Postal Service stamps, cancelled with a First Day of Issue postmark. The highlight of the first day of our tour was a two-hour reenactment of the surrender ceremony at the McLean House, which was followed by a bell that tolled for four minutes—one minute for each year of the Civil War.

The next day, April 10, I watched as my good friend Ted Chamberlain played the role of General Joshua Chamberlain, presiding (on both horseback and foot) over multiple reenactments of the somber "Stacking of Arms" ceremony along the Stage Road. It was there, 150 years earlier, that both armies faced one another with honor one final time. It was a moving and memorable moment.

The first phase of the visit at Appomattox was commemorative and ceremonial. The next portion was for an entirely different purpose.

Early on the morning of April 11, we drove 95 miles back to Petersburg where my motive, like that of Chamberlain more than a century before, was "to assure myself as to certain points" on that field. An expert team assembled to assist me in that objective: Julia Steele, Cultural Resource Manager at the Petersburg National Battlefield; Bryce Suderow, researcher and co-author of *The Petersburg Campaign*; David Lowe, National Park Service Cultural Resource historian, GIS specialist and editor of *Meade's Army: The Private Notebooks of Lt. Col. Theodore Lyman*; Dr. Philip Shiman, Department of Defense contract historian and specialist in new techniques for the study and use of contemporary photographs in historical research; and Philip's beautiful black border collie Leila. Armed with period maps and high-resolution magnified contemporary historical photographs, modern LIDAR images, and GPS equipment, we set out on a beautiful sunny morning for what promised to be an exciting day of exploration and discovery.

We began on Poe Lane, off Route 460, driving past the former site of General Warren's V Corps headquarters at the Avery house, which is now a vacant field, and down a gravel road to the Norfolk and Southern Railway. We walked the tracks north more than a mile, with David, Philip, and Leila making frequent excursions into the surrounding woods to study rifle pits, lunettes, other entrenchments (and to chase chattering squirrels). Some of the terrain had been altered, with large swaths of earth moved to build approaches for modern highways. Nevertheless, there was an obvious flat crossing south of Route 460,

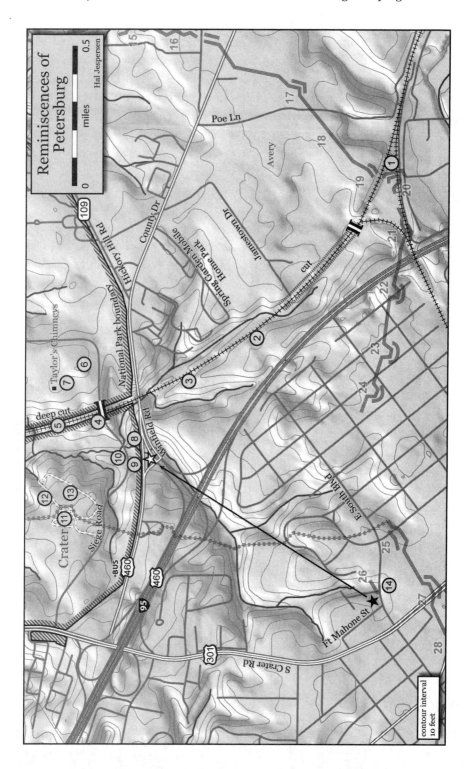

The numbers on the facing-page map represent the various vantage points for the photos that populate this Postscript. Each image also includes a brief explanatory caption that can be better understood by frequent reference to the map.

(Note that the black and white stars denote the original and new locations for the Chamberlain "on the spot" promotion marker.)

1. Norfolk Southern Railroad tracks near Poe Lane and the site of the Avery house.

2. Flat crossing near Spring Garden Mobile Home Park.

3. Approaching Route 460 and Siege Road Bridges from the south.

4. The Deep Cut of the Norfolk Southern Railway north of the Baxter/Siege Road Bridge.

5. In the "Deep Cut" in front of Taylor's chimney.

6. Vantage at Taylor ruins to view the Horseshoe and Pegram's Salient.

7. Taylor's chimney.

8. Swampy ground of Taylor's Branch near the Baxter Road.

9. Swampy ground south of Baxter Road.

10. Peninsula between the branches of Taylor's Creek.

11. Vantage on the Crater site to view Taylor's chimney.

12. Vantage on the Horseshoe to view The Deep Cut of the railroad and the Union picket line.

13. The "Horseshoe" looking southeast, with the Deep Cut to the left. The Union picket line, denoted by small stones, runs through the center of the image.

14. Black Star: The original placement of the Virginia Department of Historic Resources' Chamberlain Promoted "On the Spot" marker, E. South Blvd., near the Crater Road.

15. Line arrow to White Star: The site of the relocated Chamberlain marker near Winfield Road and Rt. 460.

Above: The "flat crossing," looking north. Chamberlain's brigade crossed the Norfolk Railroad into woods on the west side (moving right to left) just south of the Deep Cut, where the terrain was flat. Below: The current Siege Road follows the course of the old Baxter Road in this part of the park, crossing the railroad on a bridge near the lower end of the Deep Cut. The bridge carrying business route 460 runs just south of the park boundary, passing by the new site of the Chamberlain marker (which is located down the road a short distance to the left of this shot)." *Author*

and the "Deep Cut," which had played such an important role on June 18, 1864, was still clearly visible. The cut extended from just south of the Baxter Road (now the park's Siege Road) to a point north of Taylor's Chimney.

We enjoyed lunch in the brick warehouse district of Old Towne Petersburg, which doubled on occasion as a film set for movies such as "Lincoln," starring Daniel Day-Lewis, and "Ithaca," starring Meg Ryan and Tom Hanks. We studied the

Modern gravel fill has reduced the depth of the Deep Cut, but this view (looking north) gives a sense of the scope of the 20-40 foot drop-off that greeted Pvt. Henry Fitzgerald Charles and Sweitzer's brigade as they advanced from the Taylor ruins (on the right) toward the Horseshoe and Pegram's Salient (on the left). *Author*

This photo offers an excellent example of the steep slope where, according to Private Charles, "the boys went down pell-mell, and quite a number got hurt by the fellow's bayonet behind him." Inset: Taylor's chimney. The chimney (the tip of which is just visible in the main image) marks the approximate location of Bushrod Johnson's headquarters on June 17, 1864; the staging area for the advances of Sweitzer's brigade, Crawford's division, and Orlando Willcox's division on June 18; and the site of Twitchell's Union battery. *Author*

The Horseshoe and site of Pegram's Salient (the Crater), viewed from the site of the Taylor ruins. This is the view from the ranks of Sweitzer's brigade as his men prepared to descend the slope down to the railroad ravine and Taylor's branch to push Rebel skirmishers toward the Harris line and Pegram's Salient. Chamberlain's brigade advanced toward the Horseshoe from the taller trees visible on the left. *Author*

Swampy ground of Taylor's Branch near the Baxter Road. Chamberlain's men charged downhill here and encountered this obstacle—what one man described as similar to the sunken road at Waterloo. The soggy terrain prompted Chamberlain to order "Incline to the left," just before he was shot. *Author*

Swampy ground south of the Baxter Road. NPS historian and author David Lowe surveys the swampy ground traversed by Warren's V Corps troops on June 18, 1864. *Author*

The peninsula between the branches of Taylor's Creek (center right). This is near where "Sweitzer's and Chamberlain's blue clads stormed across the ridge separating the two branches of Poor Creek"—the action described in Ed Bearss' and Bryce Suderow's outstanding *The Petersburg Campaign: The Eastern Front Battles*. The quote inspired my investigation and led to this book. *Author*

The view of Taylor's chimney, about 700 yards away, as seen from the site of the Crater. This is what Confederate soldiers of Ransom's brigade saw when they looked east from Pegram's Salient. *Author*

A closer view of the Taylor Chimney as viewed from the Horseshoe. This was the vantage of Ransom's Rebels as Union infantry from V and IX Corps descended the slope in front of the Taylor ruins, jumped or slid into the railroad cut (denoted by the white lines), navigated across the ravine and creek bed, and crawled up the slope to the edge of the Horseshoe, which is immediately in front of the Harris line (foreground). *Author*

On the Horseshoe, looking southeast. The Union picket line is marked by white shells (center), and the Deep Cut is also visible (top left). Chamberlain's mid-afternoon charge crossed the terrain in the distance now obscured by tall trees (upper center and left). His 150th Pennsylvanians may have advanced as far as the southern end of the Horseshoe, just beyond the individuals pictured here, who are (left to right): Philip Shiman, David Lowe, Julia Steele, and Bryce Suderow. Leila (Phil's intrepid dog) is visible in the left-center. *Author*

architecturally unique clock tower on the roof of the 1838 Classic Revival style Petersburg Courthouse on Tabb Street and spotted a number of Civil War-era church steeples—all of which would have been familiar to Chamberlain.

After lunch, we drove to the site of the Virginia Department of Historic Resources' Joshua L. Chamberlain Promoted "On the Spot" marker. According to GIS positioning information, the marker was situated *behind* the Confederate lines of June 18.

Entering the Petersburg National Battlefield once again, this time by car (I had originally entered it this day on foot after walking about a mile along the Norfolk Southern Railroad track to a point north of Rt. 460), we traveled along the Eastern Front tour road and paused at Stop 3. This is sometimes affectionately known as "Fort Shiman," the popular Siege Encampment Exhibit that Philip Shiman helped develop decades ago. We walked the grassy fields at Taylor's Chimney and Fort Morton some 700-800 yards across the ravine from the site of the Crater. We crossed the Baxter Road Bridge and tramped through the woods and swamp to the south and west near Route 460.

The Chamberlain Promoted "On the Spot" marker at E. South Blvd. near Crater Road, the marker's original controversial location. (The marker has since been moved as a result of this investigation that led to the writing of this book.) *Author*

There, we came across a semicircular mound that may represent the ruins of the icehouse mentioned by Chamberlain in "The Charge at Fort Hell." Terrain conditions favorable for the launching point of the 1st Brigade's 3:00 p.m. charge appeared to be present in what is now a wooded area just south (and on the far side) of the Siege Road Bridge, west of the railroad.

We soaked in the remnants of the terrible devastation that is still visible at the site of the Crater and walked the Union picket line, which is delineated by white oyster shells marking the farthest advance of V Corps troops on June 18. By this time daylight was fading. I glanced east and enjoyed a golden glow settling over the clear expanse of the Horseshoe and Taylor property. There was no smoke, no flying lead or iron, no blood, and no death. Peace and tranquility reigned where once there had been conflict, chaos, and confusion. The field of former horror was now a scene of indescribable beauty. That picture, and scenes from the day we spent assuring ourselves of the points outlined in this book, will remain with me for as long as memory lasts.

A Monument to a Myth No More

THE placement of the Medal of Honor Recipients marker in Petersburg, Virginia, at the intersection of East South Boulevard and Fort Mahone Street near South Crater Road, perpetuated the notion of a heroic figure detached from his division, isolated from reinforcements and "taking care of himself." Already having survived a mile of open field combat, the hero assaults the strongest fortification (Battery 25 on the Dimmock Line), manned by the toughest veterans (Kershaw's and Field's divisions), all the while under raking oblique fire from fortified Rebel artillery. Miraculously, he advances within 25 feet of scaling parapets on a bayonet charge. Such is how epics and legends are made. Unfortunately, the marker's original location was a monument to a myth.

As this study demonstrates, the documents of history tell a different story. They speak of a noble citizen soldier—a distinguished hero of prior and subsequent battles—bravely leading his men on foot after his horse was shot out from beneath him in an earlier engagement. Although he did not confront troops from the Army of Northern Virginia, the Rebels he opposed were veterans fighting under Maj. Gen. Bushrod Johnson. They did not have the strong Dimmock Line for protection, but the gray infantry and their supporting artillery were firmly and resolutely dug in on the high ground. Chamberlain's charge against them at Petersburg was among the final futile frontal assaults of a Union line against an entrenched Confederate position in the Civil War.

With courage and determination, and while encouraging his tired and somewhat dispirited troops, Colonel Joshua Chamberlain stepped into the assault. Fearless, resolute, obedient to his calling, he advanced in the face of odds strongly stacked against his success. And as a veteran he would have known this. When he experienced the searing pain of hot lead piercing his pelvis, he continued to stand, urging his men forward until he could stand no more. He was borne from the field by his comrades with honor and respect.

The truth of what transpired is sufficient. The myth is superfluous.

The right flank of Joshua Chamberlain's brigade was anchored on the "Deep Cut" of the Norfolk Railroad, 300 yards from the Confederate entrenchments on the Harris Line. Sweitzer's brigade was to his right, north of the Baxter Road; Hofmann's brigade was to his left. Chamberlain fell in a ravine between the two lines. He was removed through Bigelow's battery, near the "Deep Cut" and probably less than 1/8th mile (220 yards) south of the Baxter Road. The site of his wounding and "Battlefield Promotion" is almost certainly within the confines of the current Petersburg National Battlefield Eastern Front site.

The information gleaned from this investigation was submitted to Dr. Jennifer Loux, Highway Marker Historian and Program Coordinator at the Virginia Department of Historic Resources, in August 2015. After considering the evidence presented, as well as supporting testimony provided by several historians and researchers including A. Wilson Greene, David Lowe, Jimmy Blankenship, and Bryce Suderow. The Director of the DHR, Jule V. Langan, announced her decision on September 17, 2015: The Joshua L. Chamberlain marker in Petersburg would be moved from E. South Boulevard to Bus. U. S. 460, also known as the Winfield Road, a highway location much closer to the site of Chamberlain's wounding on the battlefield.

Although the voices of many witnesses, past and present, were chanting in unison that Chamberlain's charge was not against Rives' Salient from the future site of "Fort Hell," the controversy refused to go gently into the night. As soon as the decision to move the Chamberlain marker was announced, a wail of protest arose.

In the euphoria of discovery, I (and others) lost sight of the fact that there are always at least two sides to every issue. The principle is part of the very fabric of human existence, whether the topic is grounded in philosophy, religion, science, politics—or military history. The human need to develop and advance independent alternate points of view is often stronger than the power of cooperation and collaboration. Now, others holding an alternative point of view were demanding the same prerogative for themselves.

Just as Colonel Charles Wainwright eventually realized the futility of trying to remove a firmly entrenched infantry line by frontal assault, so too did I discover the vanity of hoping to eradicate an established idea through the power of persuasion. It is something next to impossible to do. There will always be adherents and proponents of contrary positions. People will always be passionate about their ideas and their ideals, largely because they are emotionally invested in their conclusion. They can and usually will defend them at all costs.

I have done the best I can to present all the evidence I have uncovered. The matter is now out of my hands. My most sincere hope is that others will read this book carefully, weigh the evidence presented, walk the ground with the evidence in hand if at all possible, and reach their own conclusions.

Orders of Battle, June 18, 1864

Selected units that played a role in the June 18, 1864
events that are the subject of this study

Federal Forces at Petersburg, Virginia, June 18, 1864

Commander of all Union Armies:
Lieutenant General U. S. Grant

Army of the Potomac
Major General George G. Meade

V Army Corps: Major General G. K. Warren (869/17,078)

1st Division: Brigadier General C. Griffin

1st Brigade: Colonel J. L. Chamberlain; Colonel W. S. Tilton
121st Pennsylvania, 142nd Pennsylvania, 143rd Pennsylvania
149th Pennsylvania, 150th Pennsylvania, 187th Pennsylvania

2nd Brigade: Colonel J. B. Sweitzer
22nd Massachusetts, 32nd Massachusetts, 4th Michigan, 62nd Pennsylvania,
91st Pennsylvania, 155th Pennsylvania, 21st Pennsylvania Cavalry (dismounted)

3rd Brigade: Brigadier General J. J. Bartlett
20th Maine, 18th Massachusetts, 1st Michigan, 16th Michigan,
Brady's Michigan Sharpshooter Company, 44th New York,
83rd Pennsylvania, 118th Pennsylvania

2nd Division: Brigadier General R. B. Ayres

1st Brigade: Colonel E. M. Gregory

5th New York, 140th New York, 146th New York, 4th Infantry (US), 10th Infantry (US),
11th Infantry (US), 12th Infantry (US), 14th Infantry (US), 17th Infantry (US)

2nd Brigade (The Maryland Brigade): Colonel N. T. Dushane

1st Maryland, 4th Maryland, 7th Maryland,
8th Maryland, Purnell (Maryland) Legion

3rd Brigade: Colonel J. H. Kitching

6th New York Heavy Artillery, Maj. Jones
15th New York Heavy Artillery, Lieutenant Colonel Wiedrich

3rd Division: Brigadier General S. W. Crawford

1st Brigade: Colonel P. Lyle

16th Maine, 13th Massachusetts, 39th Massachusetts, 104th New York,
90th Pennsylvania, 107th Pennsylvania

2nd Brigade: Colonel J. L. Bates

12th Massachusetts, 94th New York, 97th New York,
11th Pennsylvania, 88th Pennsylvania

3rd Brigade: Colonel J. Carle

190th Pennsylvania, 191st Pennsylvania

4th Division: Brigadier General L. Cutler

1st Brigade: Colonel E. S. Bragg

7th Indiana, 19th Indiana, 24th Michigan, 6th Wisconsin, 7th Wisconsin,
1st New York Sharpshooter Battalion

2nd Brigade: Colonel J. W. Hofmann

3rd Delaware, 4th Delaware, 76th New York,
95th New York, 147th New York, 56th Pennsylvania, 157th Pennsylvania

Artillery Brigade: Colonel C. S. Wainwright

Massachusetts Light, 3rd Battery C): Lieutenant A. F. Walcott

Massachusetts Light, 5th Battery E: Captain C. A. Phillips
Massachusetts Light, 9th Battery: Captain J. Bigelow
1st New York Light, Battery B: Lieutenant R. E. Rogers
1st New York Light, Battery C: Captain A. Barnes
1st New York Light, Battery D: Lieutenant L. I. Richardson
1st New York Light, Battery H: Captain C. E. Mink
1st New York Light, Battery L: Lieutenant G. Breck
New York Light, 15th Battery: Captain P. Hart
1st Pennsylvania Light, Battery B: Captain J. H. Cooper
4th United States Artillery, Battery B: Lieutenant J. Stewart
5th United States Artillery, Battery D: Lieutenant B. F. Rittenhouse

IX Army Corps:
Major General A. E. Burnside (671/15,343)

1st Division: Brigadier General J. H. Ledlie

1st Brigade: Colonel J. P. Gould

56th Massachusetts, 57th Massachusetts, 59th Massachusetts,
179th New York,   100th Pennsylvania

2nd Brigade: Colonel E. W. Pierce

3rd Maryland, 21st Massachusetts, 29th Massachusetts,
179th New York, 100th Pennsylvania

3rd Brigade: Colonel E. G. Marshall; Colonel B. G. Barney

14th New York Heavy Artillery, 2nd Pennsylvania Provisional Heavy Artillery

Artillery:
Captain J. B. Eaton, Maine Light Artillery, 2nd Battery (B)
Massachusetts Light Artillery, 14th Battery, New York Light Artillery, 27th Battery

2nd Division: Brigadier General R. B. Potter

1st Brigade: Colonel J. I. Curtin; Lieutenant Colonel H. Pleasants

36th Massachusetts, 58th Massachusetts, 2nd New York Mounted Rifles,
45th Pennsylvania, 48th Pennsylvania, 7th Rhode Island

2nd Brigade: Colonel S. G. Griffin

31st Maine, 32nd Maine,   2nd Maryland, 6th New Hampshire, 9th New Hampshire,
11th New Hampshire, 17th Vermont

Artillery:
Massachusetts Light Artillery, 11th Battery,
New York Light Artillery, 19th Battery

3rd Division: Brigadier General Orlando B. Willcox

1st Brigade: Brigadier General J. F. Hartranft

8th Michigan, 27th Michigan, 109th New York, 13th Ohio Cavalry (dismounted),
51st Pennsylvania, 37th Wisconsin, 38th Wisconsin

2nd Brigade: Colonel B. Christ; Colonel W. Raulston

1st Michigan Sharpshooters, 2nd Michigan, 20th Michigan,
24th New York Cavalry (dismounted), 46th New York, 60th Ohio,
9th & 10th Ohio Sharpshooter Companies 50th Pennsylvania

Artillery:
Maine Light Artillery, 7th Battery (G): Captain A. B. Twitchell
New York Light Artillery, 34th Battery

Confederate Forces at Petersburg, Virginia, June 18, 1864

Department of North Carolina and Southern Virginia
General P. G. T. Beauregard

Johnson's Division: Major General Bushrod R. Johnson
Infantry: 351/3,996; Artillery: 29/559; Staff: 7/9

Ransom's Brigade: Colonel P. F. Faison

24th North Carolina, 25th North Carolina, 35th North Carolina,
49th North Carolina, 56th North Carolina

Elliott's Brigade: Brigadier General S. Elliott

17th South Carolina, 18th South Carolina, 22nd South Carolina, 23rd South Carolina,
26th South Carolina, Holcombe Legion

Johnson's Brigade: Colonel J. S. Fulton

17th Tennessee, 23rd Tennessee, 25th Tennessee, 44th Tennessee, 63rd Tennessee

Wise's Brigade: Colonel P. A. Page

26th Virginia, 34th Virginia, 46th Virginia, 59th Virginia

Gracie's Brigade: Brigadier General A. Gracie
41st Alabama, 43rd Alabama, 59th Alabama,
60th Alabama, 23rd Alabama Battalion

Artillery:
Moseley's Battalion: Major E. F. Moseley
Cummings' North Carolina Battery
Miller's North Carolina Battery
Slaten's Georgia Battery
Young's Virginia Battery

Artillery:
Coit's Battalion: Major J. C. Coit
Bradford's Mississippi Battery
Kelly's South Carolina Battery
Pegram's Virginia Battery
Wright's Virginia Battery

Hoke's Division: Major General R. F. Hoke

Clingman's Brigade: Brigadier General T. L. Clingman
8th North Carolina, 31st North Carolina, 51st North Carolina, 61st North Carolina

Hagood's Brigade: Brigadier General J. Hagood
Colquitt's Brigade: Brigadier General A. H. Colquitt
Martin's Brigade: Brigadier General J. G. Martin

Artillery:
Read's Battalion: Lieutenant Colonel J. P. W. Read
Blount's Virginia Battery, Macon's Virginia Battery,
Marshall's Virginia Battery, Sullivan's Virginia Battery

First Military District: Brigadier General H. A. Wise

Artillery: Boggs' Battalion: Major F. J. Boggs
Martin's Virginia Battery, Sturdivant's Virginia Battery

Army of Northern Virginia
General Robert E. Lee

First Corps: Lieutenant General R. H. Anderson

Kershaw's Division: Brigadier General J. B. Kershaw

Kershaw's Brigade: Colonel J. W. Henagan

2nd South Carolina, 3rd South Carolina, 7th South Carolina, 8th South Carolina, 15th South Carolina , 3rd South Carolina Infantry Battalion

Wofford's Brigade: Brigadier General W. T. Wofford

16th Georgia, 18th Georgia, 24th Georgia,   Cobb's Georgia Legion, Phillips Georgia Legion, 3rd Georgia Sharpshooter Battalion

Humphreys' Brigade: Brigadier General B. G. Humphreys

13th Mississippi, 17th Mississippi, 18th Mississippi, 21st Mississippi

Bryan's Brigade: Colonel M. P. Simms

10th Georgia, 50th Georgia, 51st Georgia, 53rd Georgia

Field's Division: Major General C. W. Field

Bratton's Brigade: Brigadier General J. Bratton

1st South Carolina,   2nd South Carolina Rifles, 5th South Carolina, 6th South Carolina, Palmetto Sharpshooters

Law's Brigade: Colonel W. F. Perry

4th Alabama, 15th Alabama, 44th Alabama, 47th Alabama, 48th Alabama

Anderson's Brigade: Brigadier General G. T. Anderson

7th Georgia, 8th Georgia, 9th Georgia, 11th Georgia, 59th Georgia

Gregg's Brigade: Brigadier General J. Gregg

3rd Arkansas, 1st Texas, 4th Texas, 5th Texas

Benning's Brigade: Colonel D. M. DuBose

2nd Georgia, 5th Georgia, 17th Georgia, 20th Georgia

Artillery: Major General William Pendleton
Brigadier General E. P. Alexander

Huger's Battalion: Lt. Colonel F. Huger
Haskell's Battalion: Major J. C. Haskell
Cabell's Battalion: Colonel H. C. Cabell

Chamberlain's Wound, its Treatment, and Civil War Medicine

As noted several times in this study, Colonel Chamberlain was leading his brigade on June 18, 1864, when he was shot through the right hip by a Minié ball, "which severed arteries, nicked his urinary bladder, fractured the left pelvic bones, and came out behind the left hip joint." The round also severed his urethra, produced excruciating pain, and in many cases would have resulted in death. Chamberlain, however, narrowly survived his injury, though it bothered him for the rest of his life. In 1914, an infection in his old wound probably contributed to his death.

Chamberlain wrote about his wound and its treatment. "The first thing done was to lay me upon a table improvised from a barn-window or door, and examine the wound," recalled the Maine officer. "I remember somebody taking a ramrod of a musket and running it through my body—it was too wide [long] for any surgeon's probe—to discover the bullet, which they did not at first observe sticking up with a puff of skin just behind my left hip joint."[1]

Wounded Civil War soldiers typically underwent such exploratory operations to remove lead projectiles (the .58 caliber Minié ball weighed in excess of an ounce) and other debris, such as pieces of clothing, dirt, and bone

---

1 For an extensive discussion of Chamberlain's medical condition, his various wounds, and his treatment, see Jack D. Welsh, M.D., *Medical Histories of Union Generals* (Kent State, 1996), 63-65; Chamberlain, "The Charge at Fort Hell," 14.

fragments that could lead to secondary infections. *The Medical and Surgical History of the War of the Rebellion* credits Surgeon-in-Chief W. R. DeWitt, Jr. with having performed the successful extraction of a "conoidal ball" from its position just beneath the skin of Chamberlain's left hip.[2]

Unfortunately, the removal of the slug does not undo the damage caused by its passage to its final resting place. In this case, there was a severing of Chamberlain's urethra, the final conduit for the egress of urine from the body. Disruption of that tract led to the pooling of urine in the soft tissues of the pelvis, rather than its complete elimination from the body. The essential surgical objective was to restore continuity of the drainage tract:

> Surgeons had three methods to accomplish this goal. [One] was to insert a catheter into the penis to gain access to the bladder. The current literature at the time detailed that immediate insertion of a catheter was necessary while also maintaining caution and "delicacy of manipulation." The catheter would be used to "realign the urethra, restore continuity" between bladder and urethra and "drain urine." Reports show that 40% of soldiers who were instantly catheterized recovered normal voiding. Understand that these catheters were extremely primitive. They were either metal or gum-elastic, which was "silken thread covered in a gum resin called copal." Obviously, these were not ideal instruments, yet they served an important purpose. While complications associated with catheterization, like creating false passages, did exist, the surgeons understood that the major cause of morbidity and death was due to sepsis from urinary infiltration into the surrounding soft tissue.[3]

According to a modern-day report of urological injuries in the Civil War by H. W. Herr, 79% of Civil War soldiers with urethral gunshot wounds actually survived, but only if catheterization was successful. Inability to divert the urine was invariably fatal.[4]

---

2 Joseph K. Barnes and others, *Medical and Surgical History of the War of the Rebellion, Surgical History,* in 2 volumes, 6 parts (Washington, DC, 1876), vol. 2, pt. 2, 363. As a surgeon, I find it interesting to observe how often bullets come to rest in similar locations—just beneath the tough, elastic outer envelope of the body, after having exhausted their energy in the destructive penetration of muscle, bone, and viscera.

3 Josh Knight, "Pelvis under Fire: Urological Injuries during the American Civil War," civilwarrx.blogspot.com/2014/11/pelvis-under-fire-urological-injuries.html.

4 Henry W. Herr and Jack W. McAninch, "Urological Injuries in the Civil War," *Journal of Urology* (April 2005), vol. 173, 1090-93.

A technical analysis abstracted from an article in the *Journal of Urology* provides insight into the complexity and devastating consequences of Chamberlain's injuries:

> While leading the Union charge to Petersburg, Virginia on June 18, 1864, Chamberlain was struck with a Minié ball anteriorly below the right greater trochanter [an eminence on the lateral part of the upper femur, or thighbone]. The ball coursed obliquely upward disrupting the bladder and urethra, and embedded behind the left acetabulum [the concave pelvic surface of the hip joint]. An unprecedented wound exploration in the field hospital was performed to extract the bullet and "reconnect severed urinary organs." Hope for recovery was nonexistent as urine was seen exiting the lower wound postoperatively. This genitourinary injury required four subsequent repairs during Chamberlain's lifetime and ultimately left him with a draining urethrocutaneous fistula at the penoscrotal junction [probably the result of erosions created by the use of indwelling metal urethral catheters]. . . . He was plagued during his life with recurrent cystitis and epididymo-orchitis, which in an era without antibiotics was especially miserable. Urosepsis is listed as the cause of death on his death certificate [fifty years later], and whether this was true is debatable. However, even if this wound did not cause his death, it surely contributed to it.[5]

Thirty-five years later, Chamberlain vividly recalled the despair and suffering that plagued him during the first weeks of his ordeal at Annapolis:

> For two months wrestling at the gates of death, in agonies inexpressible, though direfully enough betokened, convulsions, death-chills, lashings, despairing surgeons, waiting embalmers—"rejected addresses"—and all this under the eyes of the dear suffering wife, who had taken up her dwelling in the adjoining tent.[6]

The sorry fact for Chamberlain, and for many thousands of other Civil War veterans like him, was that they did not part ways with suffering at the door of the military hospital, nor did misery abate with the official cessation of hostilities at Appomattox. Far too often disability proved to be an enemy that refused to surrender and prolonged the struggle to the end of the soldier's life. Sarah Handley-Cousins poignantly captured the enduring consequences of

---

5   W. J. Harmon and C. K. McAllister, "The Lion of the Union: The Pelvic Wound of Joshua Lawrence Chamberlain," *Journal of Urology* (March 2000), vol. 163, issue 3, 713-16.

6   Chamberlain, "The Charge at Fort Hell," 17.

Chamberlain's "nearly mortal" wound in a 2013 New York Times opinion piece:

> The man . . . lived the majority of his life with pain, incontinence and infection. The wound quietly tortured Chamberlain for almost 50 years. Because of the damage to his urethra, Chamberlain often required the use of a catheter, which created a fistula at the base of his penis. The hole never healed. It leaked constantly and left him susceptible to chronic bladder and testicular infections that caused him, he said, "unspeakable agony." A surgery in 1883 attempted to close the fistula. Chamberlain barely survived, and his symptoms—including the fistula—soon returned. Over the next 30 years, infection plagued Chamberlain's self-described "weak spot," rendering him bedridden. . . . In 1893, after another health crisis, he applied for an increase in his pension, supported by affidavits from Army comrades—most notably the former general Fitz John Porter—who attested that Chamberlain was an "almost helpless invalid." . . . When he died in 1914, it was of an infection of the old wound.[7]

---

7   Sarah Handley-Cousins, "The Wounded Lion of the Union," *New York Times*, July 5, 2013.

Maps and Chamberlain's Story at Petersburg

AMERICAN Civil War literature is replete with detailed descriptions of the movements of men and armies. *The Official Records of the War of the Rebellion* (or simply, *OR*) constitutes the most extensive collection of primary sources. The *OR* includes selected firsthand accounts, orders, reports, maps, diagrams, and correspondence drawn from War and Navy department records of both the Confederate and Union governments. The records consist of 138,579 pages with 1,006 maps and diagrams assembled in 128 books organized as 70 volumes grouped in four series, published between 1881 and 1901.

In addition to the *OR*, researchers have access to many hundreds of regimental history books, thousands of pages of newspaper accounts, countless personal diary entries and letters from soldiers in the field, sketches and photographs. The Internet has made access to these materials significantly easier.

The plethora of written information notwithstanding, one of the central keys to unlocking the mystery of Joshua Chamberlain's whereabouts on June 18, 1864, was maps. Maps allow us to grasp concepts almost instantaneously that would otherwise require hundreds or thousands of words to convey. They show at a glance spatial relationships in terms of distance, direction, and size. One of the most important features of a battlefield map is topography—not just the roads, streams and buildings, but the elevations and contours of the land.

A portion of the J. F. Gilmer "Map of Approaches to Petersburg and their defenses, 1863." *Official Records Atlas, Plate 40.*

Historical maps vary greatly with regard to the types of information that they are trying to convey, and with respect to the degree of precision and accuracy with which they are drawn. Confederate engineers created the "Gilmer Map of the Approaches to Petersburg and Their Defenses" in 1863 to showcase the entrenchments of the Dimmock Line. This map depicts pre-siege homesteads, crops, roads and waterways, along with the fortifications, all rendered in color and with considerable detail. Elevation is shown by hatching.

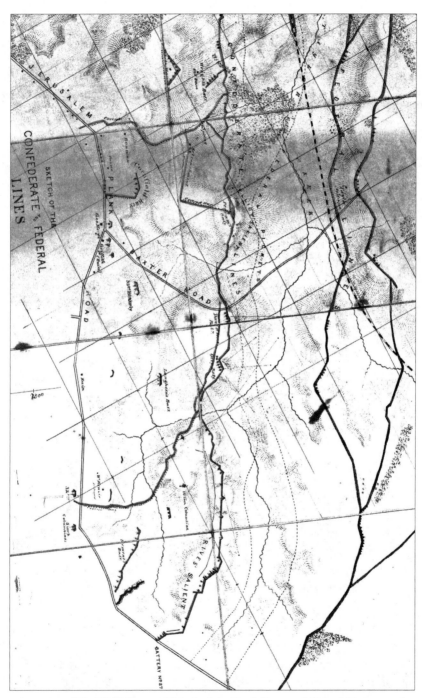

A portion of the W. H. Stevens "Sketch of the Confederate and Federal Lines around Petersburg." *Library of Congress Civil War Maps (2nd ed.), 610*

The Stevens "Sketch of the Confederate and Federal Lines around Petersburg" is another Confederate map, much more sparse in its rendering, depicting the opposing lines during the siege. The various Michler maps were drafted by Union engineers. They contain a good amount of information and are crisply executed, but there is no effort to depict elevations on many of them. Comparision of the maps, one with another, has proven to be frustrating, as the courses of rivers and roads are often strikingly divergent, in part due to the inevitable limitations of any mapmaker's vantage and perspective during wartime.

In researching Chamberlain's movements, it became obvious almost immediately that understanding the topography would be crucial to unraveling the story. As they say, "the terrain never lies." However, it was no easy task to synthesize existing historical maps into a credibly accurate representation of the ground on June 18, 1864.

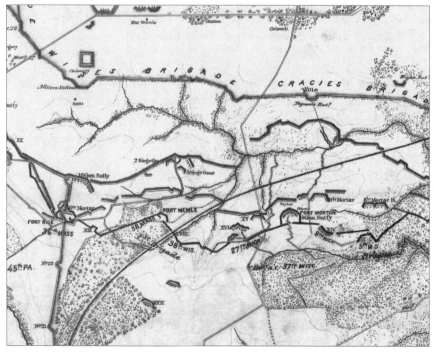

Portion of a Michler "Map of the Environs of Petersburg from the Appomattox River to the Weldon Rail Road Showing the Positions of the Entrenched Lines occupied by the Forces of the United States during the Siege." (Triangulations and surveys between July 9 and September 25, 1864.) *Records of the Office of the Chief of Engineers, RG77, drawer 150, National Archives, College Park, Maryland*

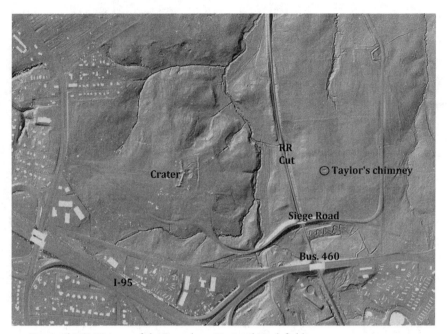

Cropped LIDAR map of the Petersburg National Battlefield. *Petersburg National Battlefield*

Topographic maps of the vicinity of Petersburg have been produced periodically beginning in 1892, but these maps are sometimes not much more consistent from decade to decade than the historical war maps, and they do not include the fortifications or the place names that served as landmarks for the battlefield of 1864.

LIDAR is a sophisticated remote sensing technology that measures distance by illuminating a target with a laser and analyzing the reflected light. When deployed from airborne workstations, in tandem with satellite GPS technology, it allows accurate and precise mapping of the earth's surface, without the confusion of forests and other vegetation that cover the ground in aerial photographs. A LIDAR map exists for the area of interest on the Petersburg National Battlefield. But, how do we know that current topography resembles the terrain as it was in1864?

One of the most precisely detailed of all the historical maps of the Petersburg Battlefield is the "Map of Defenses of Petersburg, Virginia, Showing the Positions of General Lee and his Staff during the Attack on Fort Stedman, March 25, 1865," also known as the "Manuscript Michler" or "Draft Michler" map. For our purposes, the map is incomplete, showing only the area to the north of the Baxter Road. However, this area is a crucial piece of the

"Map of Defenses of Petersburg, Virginia, Showing the Positions of General Lee and his
Staff during the Attack on Fort Stedman, March 25, 1865," also known as the
"Manuscript Michler." *Library of Congress*

puzzle of Chamberlain at Petersburg, as it includes the site of Pegram's
Salient/The Crater, the Deep Cut of the Norfolk and Petersburg Railroad, and
the Taylor farm—key landmarks in the story of Chamberlain's charge on June
18. Furthermore, it clearly depicts the prominent peninsula between the two
branches of Taylor's Creek north of the Baxter Road, a feature that is missing
on the Gilmer, Stevens, and Michler Atlas Plate 64 maps. In addition, this map
has detailed topographic contour markings at intervals of ten feet, and it shows
the elaborate network of Union and Confederate entrenchments that were
present near the end of the "siege."

The "Eureka!" moment came when I recognized that the contour of the
creek branches on the 1865 "manuscript Michler" map is essentially identical to
that of the ravines on the modern LIDAR map. I spent many hours serially
manipulating the sizes of the LIDAR and 1865 maps until they were
super-imposable. The correlation of terrain features was astounding! Except for
man-made modifications such as highways, buildings, and parking lots, the lay
of the land and the streams that run through it are essentially unchanged.
Furthermore, LIDAR shows remnants of many of the siege fortifications,
including the zigzag covered way south of the Baxter Road, the Crater, traces of

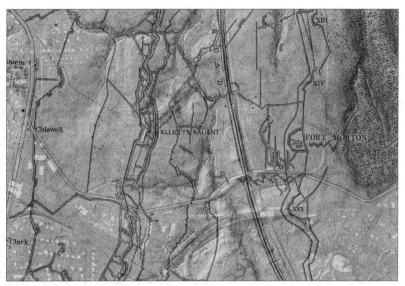

The 1865 Michler 8" to a mile series map overlaid on the LIDAR map with 33%
transparency. The overlay was done by Adam Baghetti, an intern working
under Julia Steele's supervision at the Petersburg National Battlefield.
This is a more complete version of the "Manuscript Michler," and
covers a larger area on the larger map. *National Archives*

old roads, parts of both Union and Confederate trench lines and remnants of
farm dwellings at the Taylor and Shand properties.

The topography has remained stable over the past 150 years, so it did not
take a giant leap of faith to accept the modern USGS "National Map," complete
with contour lines, as a reasonable representation of the terrain of 1864.

The next task was to find a good mapmaker. Initial queries came up short.
One cartographer lamented that it would take an engineer to fit the bill.
Fortunately, Theodore P. Savas, my publisher, knew of and has used the
excellent maps produced by Hal Jespersen. Hal eagerly accepted the challenge,
and he has proven eminently capable of executing any task assigned to him.

The first step was to make a base map of the entire area, incorporating the
topographic contours and streams. Next, roads, forests, fields and dwellings
were added; then the various lines of entrenchment. The final piece of the
process was to show the movements of the various corps, divisions, brigades,
and regiments, as described in the written reports.

The "hyper-accurate" maps were tedious to make, but Hal remained, to the
end, a patient and longsuffering "obedient servant." It is my hope that the fine
maps he has created will set a new standard of precision for Civil War histories.

Government Publications

United States War Department. *Atlas to Accompany the Official Records of the Union and Confederate Armies.* Washington: U. S. Government Printing Office, 1891-1895.

United States War Department. *The War of the Rebellion: A Compilation of the Official Records of the Union and Confederate Armies,* 128 Vols. Washington: U. S. Government Printing Office, 1880-1901.

Newspaper Articles

Anonymous. "Interesting Letter from Ransom's Brigade." *Raleigh Confederate,* June 23, 1864. www.beyondthecrater.com/resources/np/1864-np/jun-64-np/np-18640623-raleigh-confederate-ransoms-brig-2nd-petersburg/ (accessed May 3, 2015).

Anonymous. "Letter from Co. F, 21st Penna. Cavalry." *The Tribune* (Johnstown, Pennsylvania), July 1, 1864.

Anonymous. "Memorable Days." *The Plantation* (Atlanta), July 2, 1870: 374.

Bateman, L. C. "The Hero Of Gettysburg." *Lewiston Evening Journal, Illustrated Magazine Section,* September 1, 1900.

Bowen, A. A. "A Flag Episode of '64." *Confederate Veteran,* November 1893: 346.

Chamberlain, Joshua Lawrence. "Lines Before Petersburg, June 18, 1864." *Lewiston Evening Journal Illustrated Magazine Section,* September 1-6, 1900: 5.

Henries, H. C. "JLC at Annapolis." *The Bangor* (Maine) *Daily Whig and Courier,* June 28, 1864, www.joshualawrencechamberlain.com/atannapolis.php (accessed October 27, 2015).

Manuscripts

Chamberlain, Joshua Lawrence. "The Charge at Fort Hell." William Henry Noble Papers, Special Collections Library, Duke University, 1899. www.joshualawrencechamberlain.com/chargeatforthell.php (accessed January 14, 2015).

Davis, Robert Finshaw, Jr. "Diary of R. F. Davis, Company E, 7th Georgia Infantry." *MS #20, Confederate Miscellany 1b*. Special Collections, Robert W. Woodruff Library, Emory University, 1864.

DeLacy, Patrick. "P. DeLacy to Chamberlain." *Joshua Lawrence Chamaberlain Papers*, Box 3. Library of Congress, December 28, 1903: 782-3.

DeLacy, Patrick. "Patrick DeLacy Statement to Joshua Lawrence Chamberlain." *Joshua Lawrence Chamberlain Papers*, Box 4, folder: "Reminiscences to Chamberlain." Library of Congress, December 28, 1903: 1-21.

Humphreys, Benjamin G. "Sunflower Guards." *J. F. H. Claiborne Papers #151, Southern Historical Collection,* Manuscript Department, Wilson Library, University of North Carolina. Chapel Hill, North Carolina: 25, 26.

Johnson, Bushrod R. "UPR: Report of Major General Bushrod R. Johnson, C. S. Army, Commanding Johnson's Division, of Operations June 16-18, 1864," transcribed by Brett Schulte. www.beyondthecrater.com/resources/ors/vol-xl/unpublished-reports-vol-xl/upr-18640616-bushrod-r-johnson-june-16-18-1864/ (accessed 2014).

Knowles, O. B. "Letter to General Joshua Lawrence Chamberlain." *Joshua Lawrence Chamberlain Papers,* Box 4, folder: "Reminiscences to Chamberlain." Library of Congress, December 15, 1865.

Roebling, W. A. "Report of the Operations of the 5th Corps, A.P. in Genl. Grant's Campaign from Culpeper to Petersburg, as seen by W.A. Roebling, Maj. A.D.C. 1864." *Gouverneur K. Warren Collection*, Letterbooks Vol. 7, Box 24. Albany, New York: Roe Archives, New York State Library.

Rutherford, Willliam Drayton. "Diary of Col. William Drayton Rutherford," June 18, 1864. Source: Mac Wyckoff.

Warren, Horatio N. "Letter to Chamberlain, July 7, 1888." *Joshua Lawrence Chamberlain Papers*, Box 4, folder: "Reminiscences to Chamberlain." Library of Congress, 1888.

Maps

Gilmer, J. F., Stevens, W. H., Dimmock, C. H. "Map of the Approaches to Petersburg and Their Defenses, 1863." *War of the Rebellion Atlas Plate 40*. Washington, D.C.: Government Printing Office, 1891.

Hanson, Joseph M. "Events from June 15 through July 29." *Troop Movement Maps, Petersburg Campaign, Part of the Master Plan Petersburg National Battlefield*. United States Department of Interior, National Parks Service, 1942, Revised 1952.

Michler, Nathaniel. "Map of Defenses of Petersburg, Virginia, Showing the Positions of General Lee and his Staff during the Attack on Fort Stedman, March 25, 1865." *Library of Congress Civil War Maps (2nd ed.)*, 607.2.

Michler, Nathaniel. "Map of Petersburg and Five Forks." Library of Congress.

Michler, Nathaniel. "Sketch of the Entrenched Lines in the Immediate Front of Petersburg [1864-5] Surveyed under the direction of N. Michler, Major of Engineers, Bvt. Col. U. S. A." *Joshua Lawrence Chamberlain Papers*, Box 7 (ID No.:MSS15503). Library of Congress. Also in *Library of Congress Civil War Maps (2nd ed.)*, 609.

Stevens, Walter H. "Sketch of the Confederate and Federal Lines around Petersburg." *Library of Congress Civil War Maps (2nd ed.), 610*.

Published Primary Sources

Baker, Levi W. *History of the Ninth Mass. Battery*. South Framingham, Massachusetts: Lakeview Press: J. C. Clark Printing Co., 1888.

Bates, Samuel P. *History of Pennsylvania Volunteers, 1861-5* (5 Vol.). Harrisburg, Pennsylvania: B. Singerly, State Printer, 1870.

Beals, Thomas P. "In a Charge Near Fort Hell, Petersburg," in *War Papers Read Before the Commandery of the State of Maine, Military Order of the Loyal Legion of the United States, Vol. 2*, 105-115. Portland, Maine: Lefavor Tower Co., 1902.

Buell, Augustus C. *The Cannoneer: Recollections of Service in the Army of the Potomac*. Washington : The National Tribune, 1890.

Carter, Robert G. *Four Brothers in Blue, Or Sunshine and Shadows of the War of the Rebellion: A Story of the Great Civil war from Bull Run to Appomattox*. Austin: University of Texas Press, 1913; 1978.

Chamberlain, Joshua Lawrence. "Reminiscence of Petersburg and Appomattox: October, 1903." in *War Papers Read Before the Commandery of the State of Maine, Military Order of the Loyal Legion of the United States, Vol. 3*, 161-182. Portland, Maine: Lefavor-Tower Company, 1908.

Chamberlain, Joshua. *The Passing of the Armies; An Account of the Final Campaign of the Army of the Potomac, Based Upon Personal Reminiscences of the Fifth Army Corps*. New York: G. T. Putnam's Sons, 1915.

Chamberlain, Thomas. *History of the One Hundred and Fiftieth Regiment Pennsylvania Volunteers, Second regiment, Bucktail Brigade*. Philadelphia: F. McManus, Jr. & Co., Printers, 1905.

Clark, Walter. *Histories of the Several Regiments and Battalions from North Carolina, in the Great War 1861-'65, Vol. 3*. Goldsboro, NC: Nash Brothers, 1901.

Cook, Benjamin F. *History of the Twelfth Massachusetts Volunteers (Webster Regiment)*. Boston: Twelfth (Webster) Regiment Association, 1882.

Cowles, Luther E. *History of the Fifth Massachusetts Battery*. Boston: Luther E. Cowles, 1902.

Davis, Charles E. *Three Years in the Army, The Story of the Thirteenth Massachusetts Volunteers from July 16, 1861, to August 1, 1864*. Boston: Estes and Lauriat, 1894.

Dickert, D. Augustus. *History of Kershaw's Brigade.* Newberry, South Carolina: Elbert H. Aull Co., 1899.

Elliott, James Carson. *The Southern Soldier Boy: A Thousand Shots for the Confederacy.* Raleigh, North Carolina: Edwards & Broughton Printing Company, 1907.

Gibbs, James M. *History of the 187th Pennsylvania Volunteer Infantry.* Harrisburg, Pennsylvania: Central Printing and Publishing House, 1905.

Glenn, John F. "Brave Defence of the Cockade City, with the Sufferings in Prison of those Captured," in Brock, R. A., ed. *Southern Historical Society Papers*, Vol. 35. Richmond: Southern Historical Society, 1907.

Gould, Joseph. *The Story of the Forty-eighth, A Record of the Campaigns of the Forty-eighth Regiment Pennsylvania Veteran Volunteer Infantry During the Four Eventful Years of Its Service in the War for the Preservation of the Union.* Philadelphia: Alfred M. Slocum Company, 1908.

Grant, Ulysses S. *Personal Memoirs of U. S. Grant, Vol. 2.* Project Gutenberg (2004), 1885.

Hopkins, William Palmer. *The 7th Regiment Rhode Island Volunteers in the Civil War, 1862-1865.* Providence, Rhode Island: The Providence Press, 1903.

Horner, John B., ed. *The Letters of Major Robert Bell.* Gettysburg, Pennsylvania: Horner Enterprises, 2000.

Houghton, W. R. & Houghton, M. B. *Two Boys in the Civil War and After.* Montgomery, Alabama: Paragon Press, 1912.

Jarratt's Hotel. "A Guide to the Fortifications and Battlefields around Petersburg: with a splendid map from actual surveys made by the US Engineer Department." J. B. Ege, 1869

Johnson, Bushrod R. "Diary of Bushrod Johnson," in Hewett, Janet B., *Supplement to the Official Records of the Union and Confederate Armies*, Part 1, Reports, Volume 7. Wilmington, North Carolina: Broadfoot Publishing Company, 1994-2001.

Johnson, Robert U., Buell, Clarence. *Battles and Leaders of the Civil War,* Vol. 4. New York: The Century Company, 1884.

Jordan, William C. *Some Events and Incidents During the Civil war.* Montgomery, Alabama: Paragon Press, 1909.

Keiley, A. M. *In Vinculis; or, The Prisoner of War, being the experience of a Rebel in the Federal pens, interspersed with reminiscences of the late war, anecdotes of Southern generals, etc.* New York: Blelock & Co., 1866.

Lanier, Henry W. "Photographing the Civil War." *American Monthly Review of Reviews*, January-June ed. New York: Review of Reviews, 1911.

Lapham, William Berry. *My Recollections of the War of the Rebellion.* Augusta, Maine: Burleigh & Flynt Printers, 1892.

Leslie, Frank, and Louis Shepheard Moat. *Frank Leslie's Illustrated History of the Civil War.* New York: Mrs. Frank Leslie, 1895.

Lowe, David W., ed. *Meade's Army: The Private Notebooks of Lt. Col. Theodore Lyman.* Kent, Ohio: Kent State University Press, 2007.

Neitz, John. *The Civil War Diary of Henry Fitzgerald Charles, 1862-1865*. 1969; 2000. www.dm.net/~neitz/charles/ (accessed May 11, 2015).

Nevins, Allan. *A Diary of Battle: the Personal Journals of Colonel Charles S. Wainwright, 1864-1865*. New York: Harcourt, Brace & World, 1962.

Parker, Francis Jewett. *The Story of the Thirty-second Regiment, Massachusetts Infantry: Whence it Came, Where it Went, What it Saw, and What it Did*. Boston: C. W. Calkins & Co., 1880.

Parker, John L., Carter, Robert G. *History of the Twenty-second Massachusetts Infantry, the Second Company Sharpshooters, and the Third Light Battery, in the War of the Rebellion*. Boston: Regimental Association, Press of Rand Avery Company, 1887.

Parker, Thomas H. *History of the 51st Pennsylvania Volunteers and Veteran Volunteers*. Philadelphia: King & Baird, 1869.

Pearce, T. H. *Diary of Captain Henry A. Chambers*. Wendell, North Carolina: Broadfoot's Bookmark, 1983.

Porter, Charles H. "The Petersburg Mine," in *Papers of the Military Historical Society of Massachusetts, Vol. 5*. Boston: Military Historical Society of Massachusetts Cadet Armory, 1895.

Rives, Timothy. "Speech of Mr. Timothy Rives of Prince George and Surry in the Virginia State Convention on the 29th March, 1861: Report of the Committee on Federal Relations, being under consideration in committee of the whole." Richmond, Virginia: Charles H. Wayne, 1861.

Roe, Alfred S. *The Thirty-Ninth Regiment, Massachusetts Volunteers, 1862-1865*. Worchester, Massachusetts: Regimental Veteran Association, 1914.

Ropes, John C. "The Failure to Take Petersburg on June 16-18, 1864." In *Papers of the Military Historical Society of Massachusetts, Vol. 5*. Boston: Cadet Armory Ferdinand Street, 1906.

Small, A. R. *The Sixteenth Maine Regiment in the War of the Rebellion, 1861-1865*. Portland, Maine: B. Thurston & Co., 1886.

Strong, William W. *History of the 121st Regiment Pennsylvania Volunteers by the Survivors' Association*. Philadelphia: Catholic Standard and Times, 1905.

Twitchell, Albert Sobieski. *History of the Seventh Maine Light Battery, Volunteers in the Great Rebellion*. Boston: E. B. Stillings & Co., 1892.

United States Army Maine Infantry Regiment. *Reunions of the Twentieth Maine Regiment at Portland*. Waldoboro, Maine: Samuel L. Miller Press, 1881.

United States Army Pennsylvania Infantry Regiment. *Under the Maltese Cross, Antietam to Appomattox, The Loyal Uprising in Western Pennsylvania 1861-1865, Campaigns of the 155th Pennsylvania Regiment*. Pittsburgh, Pennsylvania: 155th Regimental Association, 1910.

Warren, Horatio N. *Two Reunions of the 142nd Regiment, Pa. Vols*. Buffalo, New York: The Courier Company, 1890.

Secondary Sources

Anonymous. "Diary of a Civil War Soldier Recalls Siege of Petersburg." *The Progress-Index* (Petersburg, Virginia), September 26, 2015.

Austin, J. Luke. *General John Bratton: Sumter to Appomattox, In Letters to His Wife.* Sewanee, Tennessee: Proctor's Hall Press, 2003.

Barnes, J. K. *Medical and Surgical History of the War of the Rebellion, Surgical History,* Part 2, Vol. 2. Washington: Government Printing Office, 1876.

Bearss, Edwin C., and Suderow, Bryce A. *The Petersburg Campaign: The Eastern Front Battles, June-August 1864,* Vol. 1. El Dorado Hills, California: Savas Beatie, 2012.

Bertera, Martin N., Crawford, Kim. *The 4th Michigan Infantry in the Civil War.* East Lansing, Michigan: Michigan State University Press, 2010.

Bevan, B.W., Orr, D.G., Blades, B.S. "The Discovery of the Taylor House at the Petersburg National Battlefield." *Historical Archaelolgy* , Vol. 18, no. 2 (1984): 64-74.

Carisio, Justin. *A Quaker Officer in the Civil War: Henry Gawthorp of the 4th Delaware.* Charleston, South Carolina: History Press, 2013.

Chick, Sean Michael. *The Battle of Petersburg, June 15-18, 1864.* Lincoln, Nebraska: Potomac Books, 2015.

Gillispie, Elizabeth A. "An Examination of an Ice House at Old Town Plantation." *Georgia Southern University Electronic Theses and Dissertations.* Electronic Theses & Dissertations. Paper 624. Spring 2012

Goulka, Jeremiah E. *The Grand Old Man of Maine: Selected Letters of Joshua Lawrence Chamberlain, 1865-1914.* Chapel Hill, North Carolina: University of North Carolina Press, 2004.

Handley-Cousins, Sarah. "The Wounded Lion of the Union." *The New York Times,* July 5, 2013.

Harmon, W. J., McAllister, C. K. "The Lion of the Union: the pelvic wound of Joshua Lawrence Chamberlain." *Journal of Urology,* Vol.163, no.3 (March, 2000): 713-16.

Herr, H. W., and J. W. McAninch. "Urethral Injuries in the Civil War." *Journal of Urology*, Vol. 173, no. 4 (April, 2005): 1090-93.

Hess, Earl. *In the Trenches at Petersburg: Field Fortifications and Confederate Defeat.* Chapel Hill, North Carolina: University of North Carolina Press, 2004.

Howe, Thomas J. *Wasted Valor: The Petersburg Campaign, June 15-18, 1864.* Lynchburg, Virginia: H. E. Howard, 1988.

"Joshua L. Chamberlain Promoted 'On the Spot'". 2014. Www.hmdb.org/marker.asp? marker=79063 (accessed January 19, 2015).

Knight, Josh. "Pelvis under Fire: Urological Injuries during the Civil War." November 2014. civilwarrx.blogspot.com/2014/11/pelvis-under-fire-urological-injuries.html (accessed November 10, 2015).

Longacre, Edward G. *Joshua Chamberlain: The Soldier and the Man.* Conshohocken, Pennsylvania: Combined Publishing, 1999.

Matthews, Richard E. *The 149th Pennsylvania Volunteer Infantry Unit in the Civil War.* Jefferson, North Carolina: McFarland & Company, Inc., Publishers, 1994.

Nesbitt, Mark. *Through Blood & Fire: Selected Civil War Papers of Major General Joshua Chamberlain.* Mechanicsburg, Pennsylvania: Stackpole Books, 1996.

Person, G. J. "Crossing the James River, June 1864." *Engineer: The Professional Bulletin of Army Engineers*, September-December 2009: 58.

Robertson, William Glenn. *Backdoor to Richmond: The Bermuda Hundred Campaign*. Baton Rouge, Louisiana: Louisiana State University Press, 1987

Robertson, William Glenn. *The First Battle of Petersburg: The Attack and Defense of the Cockade City, June 9, 1864*. El Dorado Hills, California: Savas Beatie, 2015

Scott, Robert Garth. *Forgotten Valor: The Memoirs, Journals, & Civil War Letters of Orlando B. Willcox*. Kent, Ohio: Kent State University Press, 1999.

Smith, Diane Monroe. *Chamberlain at Petersburg: The Charge at Fort Hell June 18, 1864*. Gettysburg, Pennsylvania: Thomas Publications, 2004.

Trulock, Alice Rains. *In the Hands of Providence: Joshua L. Chamberlain & The American Civil War*. Chapel Hill, North Carolina: University of North Carolina Press, 1992.

Vautier, John. *History of the 88th Pennsylvania Volunteers in the War for the Union, 1861-1865*. Butternut Press, 1986.

Wallace, Lee A., and Conway, Martin R. *A History of Petersburg National Battlefield*. Washington: History Division, National Park Service, Department of the Interior, 1983.

Wallace, Willard Mosher. *Soul of the Lion: A Biography of General Joshua Lawrence Chamberlain*. New York: Thomas Nelson, 1960.

Index

Acknowledgments

Rarely, if ever, can it be said that anything important was accomplished by a single person working in isolation. We are creatures designed to live in community, cooperating to achieve things of significance. Our need for interdependence is never more evident than when we venture into unfamiliar territory. Such was certainly the case with the writing of this book.

The manner in which it was conceived and developed, leads me to believe that *Joshua Lawrence Chamberlain and the Petersburg Campaign* is a book that was somehow meant to be. However, the simple fact is that it would not exist, were it not for contributions, large and small, from many individuals, most of whom only became known to me through the process of investigating and writing this study.

Bryce Suderow, quintessential researcher and networker, was a mentor in the truest sense of the word, suggesting countless resources and avenues of investigation, and guiding and encouraging me throughout the process.

Julia Steele, historical archaeologist and Cultural Resource Manager at the Petersburg National Battlefield, provided troves of historical maps, sketches, and photographs, along with tireless support. I value highly our new-found friendship.

I must also thank my good friend and Civil War Round Table colleague Dr. Ted Chamberlain, a founding member of the World Chamberlain Genealogical Society. Ted and Joshua share a seventh great grandfather, William Chamberlain, making Joshua and Ted fifth cousins three times removed. Ted introduced me to the Chamberlain biographical corpus, read early iterations of the manuscript, and made valuable suggestions early in the writing process. He also brings Joshua Chamberlain to life in the 21st century as a member of the Confederation of Union Generals.

Dr. Philip Shiman, fortifications specialist, spent a day in the Library of Congress digging up material I was unable to access. He and NPS historian/GIS specialist David Lowe graciously shared their knowledge and expertise, helping me to confirm important points on the battlefield, and in the manuscript.

Hal Jespersen, one of the finest cartographers working today, understood my vision and brought the text to life with clear and precise maps. Without his work it would be nearly impossible to follow the often complex discussion within these pages.

Brett Schulte provided a wonderful research tool in his Siege of Petersburg Online website, and energized my effort with his offers to promote and disseminate the findings on the Internet. His deep interest in all things Petersburg is a great benefit to students of the Civil War.

A. Wilson Greene—historian, writer, and director of Pamplin Park—read an early draft of the manuscript while on a riverboat trip down the Mississippi, and provided helpful suggestions that made the study better. He also affirmed and validated the work, for which I am very grateful.

My publisher, Theodore P. Savas, believed in the manuscript enough to undertake its publication. After enrolling me for many months, tuition-free, in his School of Patience, he personally threw himself into the project with an unexpected vigor and focus, bringing everything to a rapid and satisfying fruition. In the process, he taught me much about how to live life on a grand scale! I wish also to thank everyone at Savas Beatie for their support throughout this book's development, and in the marketing effort that will follow.

Through it all, my loving and devoted wife Ellen graciously bore my preoccupation, embraced a newfound passion for the Civil War, proofread the text better than any professional copy editor, and proved, once again, that I made a very wise choice when I asked her to marry me nearly thirty-eight years ago.

To each one mentioned here, and to the many others who also had roles to play, I express my profound appreciation, not only for your individual contributions to this work, but for your personal encouragement, support and friendship. Our shared experience has been a major highlight of my life.